Carol Vorderman's
better homes

Carol Vorderman's
better homes

Patricia Monahan

Better Homes is a Granada Television production

Executive Producer: Zoë Watson

Series Producer: Nigel Mercer

Producers: Harry Bell, Tris Burns

Production Manager: Tracy Manser

Researchers: Dan Henshaw, Jayne Howells, Peter Mann

Cameraman: Howard Somers

Sound: Ian Hills, Phil Smith

Editors: Jon Pinsky, Owen Turner

Production Secretary: Claire Newberry

Runners: Richard Lynn, Lesley Perkins, Brian Wheelock

acknowledgements

THE AUTHOR WOULD LIKE TO THANK EVERYONE
ON THE BETTER HOMES TEAM FOR PROVIDING INFORMATION,
DESIGN PLANS AND ARTWORKS, GENERAL ADVICE
AND ASSISTANCE WITH ALACRITY AND GOOD HUMOUR.
SPECIAL THANKS ALSO TO KERRIN EDWARDS, JULIAN FLANDERS,
TRACY JEUNE, PETER MANN, KAREN McNALLY, NICKY PARIS,
NATHALIE ROUSSETY, CRAIG STEVENS, MAY CORFIELD
AND SUE WICKENDEN

photographs

ALL PHOTOGRAPHS © GRANADA MEDIA GROUP,
EXCEPT PAGE 37 ST. JOHN POPE AND 97
(TOP AND BOTTOM RIGHT) CORBIS/EDDIE RYLE-HODGES

design and editorial

DESIGN/SECTION, FROME

first published in 1999 by

GRANADA MEDIA

an imprint of

ANDRE DEUTSCH LTD

76 DEAN STREET

LONDON W1V 5HA

www.vci.co.uk

in association with

GRANADA MEDIA GROUP

copyright © Granada Media Group 1999

ISBN 0 233 99749 0

printed and bound in the UK by

BUTLER & TANNER LIMITED, FROME AND LONDON

contents

**Do you want to make your property a 'better home'?
Then, you've picked the right book. Within these pages are tips,
designs and practical information which will allow you
to do just that.**

better homes
introduction

Carol Vorderman

by | **CAROL VORDERMAN**

I have to admit that the making of *Better Homes* has taken us all by surprise. We've tackled massive makeovers, been up against impossible deadlines and always tried to do the very best for the families we help.

You know how the programme works. Two lucky families tell us briefly what they would want to make a 'better home'. Something along the lines of, 'We want to add an extra bedroom to the house. Ideally we'd like a loft conversion.' We put one of our designers on the case and that wish is converted into the most stunning transformation of their home the family will ever see. In addition, the family whose makeover puts most value on their house, wins £5000. In the first series alone, we added conservatories, created beautiful kitchens and put a complete top floor onto a bungalow. You name it, the *Better Homes* team has done it.

Making each programme takes less than five days. We start filming on Monday. The designers are allowed into the house by the afternoon. They have to be finished by Friday morning: a total of about 90 hours to complete the job. It's not long, but it is long enough.

So why have we put this book together? Well, in response to tens of thousands of letters from you, we felt we wanted to bring together the main elements of the programme.

Firstly, the fundamental idea behind *Better Homes* is to show how you can improve the value of your property. Our *Better Homes* estate agent Michael O'Flaherty has put together his top tips which include his favourite advice, 'Add rooms, add value' and 'Add bedrooms, add real value'. But while you're busy thinking of ideas there is one thing you must always bear in mind. Don't run away with the idea that if you spend £15,000 on a kitchen, your property price is going to go up by the same amount. Although you may be lucky and be selling a property in a rising market, this

hardly ever happens. When you're thinking about major improvements to your own home, be careful with the money and make alterations to improve the quality of how you live.

The most important part of any home makeover is working out what to do and why. One of our designers, Orianna Fielding Banks, has put together a chapter to help you do just that. She'll ask you questions which will get to the heart of your problem. Do you really want to knock two rooms together, or just give a sense of space? There's advice on how to plan the work, how to use colour and light, and if you're on a low budget – how to play tricks on the eye with pots of paint.

Because *Better Homes* is a television programme, we concentrate on the most eye-catching projects. If someone asked us for double glazing rather than a new kitchen, then we wouldn't be interested. That doesn't mean, however, that the less glamorous side of

makeovers is ignored. We'll often add new boilers, radiators and windows because heating and light add to the quality of living immeasurably.

Our DIY expert Dave Wellman – or 'Welly' as we all know him – has an entire chapter covering this side of home makeovers. He's included a maintenance checklist and plenty of ideas of how so-called 'mundane' matters can improve the value of your home. How to choose the right builders, how to deal with planning permission, getting the best quotes and learning to 'know your house'. Welly covers the lot.

In a *Better Homes* programme, we have less than half an hour to show you what's been done. In this book, we've the space to show you the projects in more detail. We've split the *Better Homes* makeovers into different areas of the house, and for each one we show you exactly what was done to the rooms (or gardens) in glorious detail.

We want to give you the power to make the best improvements to your home.

We all have our favourite projects. One of mine is from the second series, when designer George Bond took charge of a 3-bedroom semi-detached house in Durham. He took a plain back room and converted it into a classical dining room: not only that he built a stunning orangery as an extension – all in 90 hours. It was so beautiful that before

The second series of *Better Homes* features some stunning makeovers. These two dining rooms in Durham are amongst the most spectacular. (Above) Orianna Fielding Banks created a marvellous room for eating complete with an office space that can be hidden by a roller blind during formal meals. While (Right) George Bond took a plain back room and converted it into a modern but classical dining room – an amazing transformation in just 90 hours.

the family came home I kept walking into the room just to stand in it. Somehow with the proportions he'd used he had managed to generate an aura which left you physically breathless. The man is a genius.

Another clever idea was when Welly converted a couple of rooms above a garage in Newbury into a one-bedroom flat complete with kitchen, balcony and bathroom. He changed its proportions totally when he ripped out the low ceiling and raised it as high as the roof, adding an electrically operated roof window to give even more light. Brilliant.

Designer Toby Buckland did wonders working in a very long garden in Manchester in the middle of the winter. It rained all week and the garden looked just like a hippo's mud bath, but it was worth it in the end. In spite of all the problems, Toby added the greater amount to the value of his property.

Even though it didn't win the prize, Stephanie Dunning's kitchen makeover in

Halifax probably made the biggest single difference to someone's quality of living. Aine is a single mum living in a small, old terraced house with her two young children. She was thinking of moving because the house depressed her. Stephanie gave her a country kitchen with a work island in the middle, an area to eat in, and a space where they could spend happy hours together. Aine's life changed completely. She started an Open University course and wouldn't move home for the world.

I love making *Better Homes* and through all of the long, cold days and nights, we've had a great team working their hearts out. I do want to publicly thank the man to whom this programme really belongs, our series producer and smiling, lovely person Nigel Mercer. During the first series, Nigel worked seven days a week through a very cold winter. He was a great leader and an inspiration. Nigel – you're the tops – from all of us.

meet the *better homes* team

better homes

Toby Buckland

Toby Buckland is botanic garden trained and has worked in gardening for fifteen years. He strongly believes that gardens should be used for having fun as well as for looking at. He puts this ethos into practice in the gardens he designs and builds for *Better Homes*. Toby is now a full-time freelance gardener, gardening broadcaster and writer. Photograph by Howard Rice

John Cregg

John Cregg has run his own design company for fifteen years. He has worked on a whole range of diverse projects, from the England team's changing room at Twickenham to a rest room for the staff on a North Sea oil rig. Despite their diversity, John thinks all interior design projects have four things in common: needs, lighting, colour and shape, though the first two are the most important. Satisfy the basic needs and you're half-way there. Light it well and the job can be complete.

Stephanie Dunning

Stephanie Dunning's career path towards interior design was preceded only by training to be a physiotherapist at St Thomas' Hospital in London. She cut her teeth in the world of interiors in London's Battersea and Fulham in the 1980s, and now runs a thriving business designing and project managing from her studios in London and Wiltshire with her husband and business partner Peter Everard. Their philosophy is to create a finished design which suits the client. Photograph by Barrett & Co

Kitty Edwards-Jones

Kitty Edwards-Jones is a freelance interior designer. She is as happy designing contemporary interiors as she is classical ones, but her real passion is Art Deco 1930s style. Her design work has included everything from a simple room scheme to a gold award-winning giant 'human tassel' designed for the IDDA Fantasy Fashion Gala and featured on Granada TV's *This Morning*, and *The Clothes Show Live*.

Orianna Fielding Banks

Orianna Fielding Banks is at the cutting edge of contemporary furniture and interior design. Based in London's fashionable Shoreditch, her showroom – Pure – exhibits her collection of large-scale contemporary furniture, lighting, screens and rugs. She has appeared on several television shows, including: *GMTV*, *Style World*, *Fantasy Rooms* and *This Morning*, as well as *Better Homes*. Photography by Michael Banks

Ginni Gillam

Ginni Gillam has been a garden designer for ten years. Her current projects include a country garden restoration in Wiltshire and a new garden in London which incorporates water features and a movie screen! Her dream project would be to restore a group of timber-framed glass greenhouses and fill them with her favourite plants. Photograph by Sue Sharples

Zoë Gingell

Zoë Gingell graduated from Chelsea School of Art. She went on to design sets for the theatre, working in TV and film as a scenic artist and designing murals for private houses. On *Better Homes*, she enjoys the experience of working with 'real scenery'. Inspired by interior design, Zoë finds satisfaction in directly improving someone's living environment. She is currently working for Think 1 Design in London, as well as on private commissions. Photography by Christabel Gingell

Eugenie Van Harinxma

Suzie Horton

Genevieve Hurley

Kieran Kelly

Chris Maton

Michael O'Flaherty

Dave Wellman

Eugenie Van Harinxma studied at the Inchbald School of Design in London. She started her own design business in 1992 and has not looked back. Now based in Chelsea, she has worked on both building and design projects in New York, Monte Carlo and Florence as well as in her home town, London, in the past few months. Her design philosophy is simple, 'always listen to the client' – a piece of advice that has served her well.

Suzie Horton is based in Manchester and enjoys a continued relationship with Rawfish Design Consultants specialising in both commercial interiors and graphics. She also works with 'House', a furniture and interiors design company in Didsbury. Her design philosophy is 'try not to follow trends … choose colours, materials and shapes that you feel most comfortable with and allow your own personality to shine through; then your design will become instantly unique'. Photograph by Paul Moffat

Genevieve Hurley graduated from the College of Marketing and Design in Dublin. She then set up her own interior design practice where she worked on many high-profile domestic and commercial interior projects. Now based in London, she has appeared on *This Morning* as well as *Better Homes*. While keen to continue her television work, she divides her time between working as a design consultant and travelling to China for her Dublin-based company Indochine. Photograph by Kathryn Heslin

Kieran Kelly's special interest is in making replica sixteenth- to eighteenth-century Irish Furniture. But his extensive knowledge of structural design has been important in the success of the 'design build' projects on *Better Homes*. However, his expertise is not limited to exteriors and many of his interior designs have been used in the BBC's *Real Rooms* series. Photograph by Richard Morris

Chris Maton began his working life as a bricklayer, eventually starting his own construction company. A stint at the Cambridge Botanic Gardens gave him an extensive plant knowledge. Today he combines these two skills designing and building innovative gardens. He is also a lecturer at Writtle University in Essex. Photograph by Chris Maton

Michael O'Flaherty has been involved in property matters for over thirty years. He now works in Maidenhead, Berkshire, for Roger Platt Estate Agents. As well as housing, Michael is passionate about music, sport and the arts, and lives out his fantasies of playing cricket for England and guitar for Bruce Springsteen's E Street Band through his son Calum and his daughter Mollie.
Photograph by Brian Foster-Smith

Dave Wellman's two major interests, performing and building, are combined in his work on *Better Homes*. He learned building skills in order to fund his activities in amateur theatre. A stint working on ITV's *This Morning* led indirectly to his involvement on *Better Homes*, and he loves it. He hopes to continue working with Carol, Adrian, Neil and the team until Hollywood snaps him up – 'but then optimism was always one of my strong points!', he says. Photograph by Granada Media Group

introduction

part one

choosing a colour scheme that works

add *fun* to your house

clever design solutions

add rooms, add value

theory

get to **know** your house

get the **wow** factor

finding a builder and *getting a good quote*

In *Better Homes* two families compete to see whose home improvement adds most value to their property. Of course this is a lot of fun, but unless you are a property developer 'adding value' is rarely the reason you make substantial changes to your home.

changing lifestyles need better homes
adding value

by MICHAEL O'FLAHERTY

There are four main reasons why you might decide to embark on a programme of home improvements: to add space; to change the use of a space; to update and improve particular rooms; to improve and maintain the fabric of the house.

The first three may be a response to a specific need, or simply a desire to improve the quality of your life. The last is probably the most important, but usually the least exciting.

Adding space
Adding space is probably the most common reason for embarking on major work on a home – it was certainly the case in the first two series of *Better Homes*. These changes are usually forced on you by circumstances: perhaps there is a baby on the way, the children are growing up and need their own bedrooms, you or your partner have decided to work from home and need a workspace; or you need accommodation for a parent, or an *au pair*.

The first option to consider is moving, but moving costs money. Apart from the agent's fees, there's stamp duty, solicitor's fees, and the cost of engaging a removal firm. Unless you are moving into a brand new, fully kitted-out home, there are likely to be costs at the other end too – curtains, carpet or kitchen equipment may need replacing, and even small items like rubbish bins and doormats go missing or don't suit, and they all cost money. There are other reasons for staying – you may be very happy with your home, your neighbours and your area, the children will have made friends and you have slotted into the community. And if you have already lavished time, care and money on your home, and your garden is just coming into its own, can you really bear to leave it all behind? Another important consideration is the cost of property – the differential between what you have got and what you'll have to pay to get what you need may mean that moving simply isn't an option.

The best solution is often to extend or to convert another space such as a loft, a basement or a garage. Adding rooms is certainly the best way to add value to your house – hence the programme's catchphrase 'add rooms, add value'.

Building an extension
In my opinion, the very best way of adding rooms is to build a two-storey extension. This will give you whatever you need on the ground floor – a new or larger kitchen, perhaps, or an extra cloakroom – and a bedroom or bedrooms, and possibly a bathroom, on the first floor. Adding a good size bedroom immediately takes a house into another price bracket, and will add real value – 'adding bedrooms adds real value'. An extra bathroom is also a definite bonus.

Obviously a two-storey extension will cost more than a single storey extension, but you will increase the size, convenience and purchaser appeal of your home. As an example, in the area where I am practising one would anticipate a four-bedroom semi would sell for some 15 per cent more than a three-bedroom semi. Therefore the benefits of adding that fourth bedroom are plain to see.

If you do go for the two-storey extension option, make sure that the architectural style of the extension and the materials from which it is constructed match those of the original building. The best extensions look as though they have always been there. Take your proportions and window, door and roof styles from the main house. It is also worth taking a walk around the area to see what other people have done – it will give you an idea of what the planning authority is likely to accept. My advice is to avoid flat roofs like the plague; they look unattractive, don't fit in with our architectural styles and have a maximum life of about 10 years. If you're going to the bother and expense of building an extension, you might as well put a proper gable roof on it.

The decision to build out will be affected by a combination of factors including the price of the house, what similar local properties offer, how determined you are to stay in that house, and for how long, and what you will want to do when you eventually sell. Obviously you have to balance the costs against what you will achieve because you must be sure that you aren't over spending.

The only time you should avoid building on, rather than building up or converting, is if it will drastically reduce the size of your garden, or you have to sacrifice parking space. People who buy houses in a particular price bracket expect the amenities that go with a house of that size in that

Ray and Pam's bathroom (see page 118)
Claire and Colin's kitchen (see page 76)

At Swinton we saw a superbly improved bathroom which complemented a rolling programme of DIY and added £2,500 to the value of Ray and Pam's house.

In Claire and Colin's house a luxurious kitchen/breakfast room made excellent use of a relatively narrow room and added £4,000 to the value of the property. As I've said before, 'If you are going to improve one room, make it the kitchen'.

location. The specifications of your house should be broadly in line with those expectations. So while a small cheap 'starter' house would sell with a small garden and no off-street parking, a four-bedroom house in a good area that lacked a good garden and parking might hang around on the agents' books; you'll have to wait and may have to accept a reduced price. These days people expect to have parking space and, over a certain price bracket, you will definitely reduce the attraction of your property if you can't provide off-street parking for at least two vehicles.

adding value

Sally and Graham's front garden (see page 54)

David and Janet's summer-house (page 150)

On our visit to Doncaster a tremendous garden makeover created a fine first impression for a house that already had three important factors – location, accommodation and presentation – and added £5,000 to the property's value.

But the winners were David and Janet. The store/garage on their older cottage was transformed into a delightful conservatory/ morning room, increasing the value of their house by £6,000, so 'Add rooms, add value'.

Loft conversions

The other way of increasing the size of your home is to extend into the loft. This is a very popular solution and it can make a great deal of sense. However, not all properties lend themselves to this treatment. Again, start by having a look around the neighbourhood to see how loft extensions have been tackled – this will give you a clue to what is possible, and what is likely to be permitted. There are some definite dos and don'ts when converting a loft space. The main problem is getting enough height – if you haven't got enough

head height it won't count as a 'proper' room when you come to sell. However, it may be the only viable solution and may solve your problems cost-effectively, but don't be disappointed if the extension doesn't add as much value as you thought. In cases like this, the time you intend to remain in your home becomes an important part of the equation – if you intend to move within the year it is definitely worth saving your cash and putting up with cramped conditions for a little longer.

The loft in Smethwick (page 104) is an example of this sort of conversion. The designer, John Cregg, did a beautiful job and managed to create a proper staircase which is always a plus. However, the ceiling height was restricted so that I couldn't stand up unless I walked down the middle, and when the twins were interviewed their heads were sticking out of the skylight. But the soccer-mad boys – Thomas and David – had no problems, and the new bedroom/play space eased the serious overcrowding in the rest of the house. So for the Bradys this was definitely the right solution – but it is always going to be a children's room.

If you go for the loft conversion option, do try and find the head height, put in a proper staircase – not a spiral staircase – but don't let the staircase take space from an existing bedroom. As with extensions, the loft conversion should be in keeping with the period, proportions and architectural style of the building. Match roof-lines, windows and building and roofing materials. Have an informal chat with the local planning officer at a very early stage. The extension will be less intrusive if the extension windows are kept to the back of the building. In my work I see some truly horrid loft extensions. The scale of some completely overwhelms the original building, making it look top heavy, and others have no visual relationship with the house proper. Fortunately, planning departments are

more enlightened now and owners are more aware of how these things should be done. *Better Homes* certainly illustrates the value of spending time, effort and money on the design stage of such a project. All our loft extensions settled into the original building very neatly, so that in years to come it really will be difficult to see the joins – and that is how it should be.

Remember that there are a great many practical, planning and engineering considerations to be dealt with before you decide to extend into the loft – Dave Wellman

Steve and Clare's loft bedroom (see page 104)

Ashley and Julie's kitchen (see page 80)

In Smethwick we saw a most colourful loft conversion, albeit hampered by restricted headroom and access. The children loved their room and it added £4,000 to the value of Steve and Clare's home.

However, we saw greater value added to Ashley and Julie's home where a kitchen, cloakroom and utility room completed an already delightful home. The £6,000 lift in value illustrated the financial benefits of lifestyle selling.

addresses some of these on p.35 – so you must always seek professional advice. The rafters need to be reinforced before you put in a wood floor, and you need to talk to your planning and building regulations departments before you install roof lights or dormer windows. In some areas these are only permitted on the back of the house, but in others, particularly conservation areas, they are not allowed at all. If the attic is to be used as a bedroom it must also conform to stringent fire regulations.

Other conversions

Many older properties have basements or cellars which can sometimes be converted to other uses. Basements are usually already habitable spaces with ceilings, plastered walls and basic services, and are easily adapted to a new purpose. Remember that a change of use will have to be notified to the planning authorities. Cellars are an altogether tougher proposition, as they generally need quite a bit of work to make them habitable. They are often damp, poorly ventilated and devoid of natural light. You may also need to excavate the floor to give you the necessary head height, in which case the walls will require underpinning – all very costly and disruptive procedures. Nevertheless, converting a cellar may turn out to be your best and most cost-effective way of find the space you need.

John Cregg and Eugenie Van Harinxma did a superb cellar conversion in Halifax (page 144). After extensive damp treatment the room was transformed into a multi-pupose family room, with a fold-down bed for guests. Tracy and Nigel have three children and only one reception room and three small bedrooms. The kids couldn't use them as study/bedrooms and they needed extra space. They turned their cellar into another reception with a fold-down bed. The only problem was the access – it was down a very narrow staircase and as you

walked into it you had to squeeze past the boiler. That said, it solved the family's space problem and utilised an otherwise wasted

Aine Marie's kitchen (see page 68)
Nigel and Tracy's cellar (see page 144)

It was a close call in Halifax where the complete modernisation of a kitchen transformed the lifestyle of Aine Marie and her children, and put £3,000 onto the value of the house.

However, the addition of one flexible room in the former basement/coal cellar of Nigel and Tracey's home added £3,500, thus illustrating one of the favourite maxims of the series: 'Add rooms...' I think you know the rest!

space. My only reservation about creating a family room – what North Americans call a 'rumpus room' – on the ground floor or in the basement is that your social life on the ground floor may be disrupted by children to-ing and fro-ing, so try and ensure that access to these spaces is not through the main reception rooms.

Garage conversions are increasingly popular and there are several in the second series of *Better Homes*. I used to dislike them

because you finish up with a garage-sized room 16 x 8ft (5 x 2.4m) which is ideal for … keeping a car in. Often, people just block in the garage door opening, and put in a door and window with no reference to the architecture of the main dwelling. In the worst examples, the driveway comes to a sudden stop in front of the conversion and there is no effort to conceal the original function and layout. But, I must say, seeing some of the projects in the show has changed my mind. With a lot of thought and a good designer it is quite possible to create something that works well and looks good. The projects in the series have tied in with the house superbly. In one case the converted garage becomes part of a new double-fronted façade, in another a pitched roof mirrors that of the main building, while in a third the garage façade was extended upwards so that the window line links quite nicely. Internally they were given different treatments, varying the floor levels and layout so that you get away from the original 16ft x 8ft (5 x 2.4m) rectangle, and knocking through into the main house to create a linked space. In one case the designers have opened up the back wall of the garage to put in double doors which opened onto the patio and barbecue area.

These conversions illustrate the value of involving a professional designer, rather than a builder. A builder is always going to assume you want the cheapest solution, and will inevitably suggest a solution which is easy for him.

Updating and improving your home

From time to time, you may decide that a particular room no longer suits your needs. Simply redecorating won't do, you need to have a major rethink about how the space should be used. There are two ways of looking at these home improvement schemes. The first is the 'lifestyle' consideration – how will it

adding value

Alison and Andrew's garden (see page 164)
Denise and Barry's living room (see page 88)

Toby Buckland's dual-purpose garden in Northenden certainly added the 'wow factor' to Alison and Andrew's traditional semi-detached house and showed how the creation of really useful and usable space outside can add real value to a home – in this case £5,000.

Next door Denise and Barry's small living room was beautifully restyled, and was opened up by adding a small conservatory extension – transforming their life-style and putting £3,500 on the value of their house.

improve the quality of your life? The second is: will it add value to the house? The first is really the most important and only you can decide how important it is to have a new kitchen or bathroom. However, your budget and the time you intend to stay in the house must come into the equation. There are some rules of thumb regarding adding value – but it is rarely worth embarking on a scheme simply to add value. Developers and builders who refurbish properties as a business buy cheap and work to very tight margins – their financial calculations are very different to those made by someone

who intends to live in the property. If you are intending to sell, the only works that are really worth doing are general maintenance, fixing eyesores, tidying away clutter and completing half-finished jobs.

If you are contemplating an early sale it certainly won't be worth putting in a new kitchen, for example, unless yours is truly ghastly. Although a kitchen adds value, it won't necessarily add the full cost of a fabulous designer kitchen. However, a good kitchen is something that can sway potential purchasers – it tends to be top of their must-have list, after location, price and a garage. So if you are going to stay in the house for a few years, and you want to improve just one room – make it the kitchen. The amount you spend must also relate to the value of the property, if you put a £15,000 kitchen in a £40,000 terrace you are never going to get your money back. But if you love cooking and you are going to stay there for the next 15 years, then it may be well worth the outlay. But remember that kitchens can date awfully quickly. Before you rush out and invest in a new set of kitchen units, see if you can update the existing ones. There is no point in replacing a perfectly good kitchen simply because it looks dated. Replacing tiles and work surfaces, and adding new doors and door furniture can transform the appearance of a kitchen very economically. If you do decide to go for new, don't think you have to go for designer names – there are some excellent budget and medium price products around from the big name chain stores. Do spend money on installing the kitchen – shoddy workmanship will put purchasers off and may affect the selling price.

Bathrooms are another area of the house that can suffer from wear and tear. This is also an area where technology has improved and consumer expectations have increased. If your bathroom looks tired you'll find that it

doesn't cost a huge amount to bring it up to scratch – nothing like the amount you could spend on a kitchen, for example. Choose a plain white suite that won't date, and I would always recommend installing a power shower. See if you can fit in a second bathroom, or even a shower room, and a downstairs cloakroom. If you add another bathroom don't lose a bedroom – you could be putting the

Alison's garden (see page 172)
Kathy and Martin's kitchen (see page 62)

Arnold in Nottingham was perhaps my favourite programme because it was fun and emphasised a serious point – by all means add the 'fun factor' to your house but remember, when you come to sell, it may not appeal to everyone. A jacuzzi surrounded by palm trees transformed Alison's tiny garden, and provided entertainment for her sons, their friends and the grown-ups too – and added £3,000 in value.

But who will ever forget Orianna Fielding Banks' twenty first-century kitchen – perhaps the room of the series? And it put £5,000 on Kathy and Martin's house. So once again, 'If you are going to improve one room, make it the kitchen'.

Sue and Phil's veranda (see page 160)
Bob and Anne's log cabin (see page 176)

In Liskeard we saw the addition of two recreational facilities: a log cabin and an American-style deck. The deck completely transformed Sue and Phil's bungalow – particularly the kitchen/breakfast room which was suddenly opened out into the garden – and added a winning £5,500 to the potential selling price.

The log cabin in the grounds of a charming yet small, detached cottage, provided much needed extra room for Bob and Anne, and their family – and added £5,000 in value. But whatever the accommodation, here was a property that would always sell because of the estate agents' favourite cliché: location, location, location.

value of your house at risk. Idiosyncratic features like saunas, jacuzzis, 'his and hers' basins, and gold taps may appeal to some purchasers but repel others.

Improving the garden

One of the fascinating things about the series is the extent to which a well-designed and well-presented garden can add value to a house. I don't think people had been aware of that before. Basically, as long at the house is OK, the biggest plot in the road will always sell for the most money, and large gardens always sell well. But a well thought out and well-tended garden is a real selling point. A combination of a few good summers, a taste of outdoor living on foreign holidays and influences from America have woken us up to the potential of the garden as an outdoor living space. In the garden in Northenden (page 164) Toby Buckland created two external rooms, one for the family to use for relaxing and entertaining, and another for the children. He put the children's part nearest the house so that Alison, who is a childminder, could keep an eye on her charges.

The garden at Liskeard (page 160) was a real eye-opener. Kieran Kelly and Ginni Gillam used American-style decking to link the house with the garden, giving the previously rather closed-in bungalow an entirely different aspect. So not only was the garden transformed, but the house was as well, and a garden which had hitherto been more or less redundant suddenly became an important part of the home and family life.

The three Ss

If your home is in a really poor state of repair you should start by spending your money on the things that you don't see. Make sure the 'envelope' is sound – the roof, the walls, the windows. Check all the timbers for woodworm, and treat them if necessary. Get damp patches treated. Then look at the electrics, the plumbing and the heating. When you've done all that work and spent all that money, there'll be nothing visible to show for it, but your house will be sound and you'll reap the benefits when you come to sell. These are the sort of things that surveyors look for. There are always damp and timber problems in

older properties, and roofs always need looking at, especially flat roofs. Even homes built in the 1970s don't always meet modern building regulations and surveyors will often insist that you need more roof support. Electrical regulations are also getting tougher,

Andrew and Lisa's loft (see page 124)
Paul and Joyce's conservatory (see page 48)

Another visit to Cornwall saw the addition of two bedrooms and a shower room in Andrew and Lisa's loft conversion in Falmouth. You might have expected it to achieve more than a £7,500 uplift in value, but they had reached the ceiling for a semi-detached property in this area.

In passing, honourable mention must be made of Stephanie Dunning and John Greg's conservatory/porch which increased the value of Paul and Joyce's home by £7,000 and gave them the perfect retirement home.

so even in a property which is 10 years old the structural survey report may say 'doesn't meet current Electricity Board Regulations'. Make your house solid, sound and saleable – the

Alison and Geoff's bedroom (see page 108)
Jackie and Joe's kitchen/living room (see page 94)

Despite the noise of the main Chester Road, the improvements made to the kitchen and living room of Jackie and Joe's 'parlour' house in the charming Merseyside village of Port Sunlight added a substantial £3,500 in value.

Furthermore, the superb redecoration of Alison and Geoff's bedroom added £2,000 and showed that value can be added by pristine presentation, despite a tad of over-personalisation.

three Ss. There is no point in getting involved in other improvements and decorative schemes until you've got the basics right.

Use your estate agent

May I make a plea from the heart here – please use your estate agent. I always find it strange that we don't get invited in when people are contemplating major work on their home. Agents all offer free valuations, so get them in and talk it through. They will tell you what will add value and they will also point out features that are really going to be a problem when you are selling your house. I'm delighted when

people ring me up and say, 'Oh, we are thinking of having an extension, would you come round and just give us an idea on value.'

The flexible home

Sometimes it's not 'extra' space you need, but 'different' space. Lifestyles have changed and peoples' requirements and expectations have changed, so they need to change the house to meet those new requirements. Most houses weren't designed for our style of living. More people are working from home and even people who have taken early retirement may decide to do a little consultancy to keep their hand in. The home office doesn't necessarily need to be allocated a separate room, it can be accommodated in another space – see for example the bedroom in Port Sunlight where Genevieve Hurley slotted in a neat office space.

Up to the 1960s, the standard house had two reception rooms, kitchen, three bedrooms and bathroom. Then the open-plan living room became fashionable. The sound of sledge hammers pounding into interior walls reverberated around the country, and sales of RSJs rocketed. Typical 1960s and 1970s housing has one through reception room on the ground floor. Often the hallway walls went as well to give that oh-so-modern open-plan living space.

In the 1990s everyone wants to have a living room, a dining room and a separate, but large, kitchen. A second reception room can be an ideal place for the kids to do their homework or entertain friends, it can house computer equipment, or be an office space. Basically, a second room offers more choices than an open-plan arrangement. So whatever you do, don't knock down walls to create a through lounge. If you want a larger living area you could take an idea from the Georgians and put in a pair of partition doors which will act as room dividers. These can be opened up to create a through space or closed to create two separate rooms.

The conservatory firms have made an absolute fortune by offering people a relatively cheap way to add living space at ground level.

Fashions come and go every few years, but some things never lose their appeal: original fireplaces and surrounds, sash windows, decorative plasterwork and panelled doors are always popular. And today's eclectic styles allow you to mix the old with the new very successfully.

Jeannette and Terry's granny flat (page 130)
Sarah and Spencer's loft (see page 136)

And finally, there is always a shortage of property with self-contained 'granny' or 'au pair' accommodation. Statistics show that approximately 7 per cent of UK households have one or other parent living with them. The addition of such accommodation in Jeannette and Terry's detached home in Newbury saw the greatest increase in value of the whole series: £9,000!

It was a close-run thing, however. Sarah and Spencer's superb loft conversion showed that if you need extra accommodation and moving is not an option, go upwards if you can. And remember, 'Add bedrooms, add real value' – in this case, £8,000!

Improvements that will increase the value of your home:

- Add an extra bedroom
- Adding a garage
- Modernising the kitchen
- Adding flexible ground floor accommodation.
- Adding self-contained space, for example a granny flat or *au pair* accommodation
- Updating the bathroom
- Adding an *en suite* bathroom
- Improving the garden to create an 'outside room'
- Installing double glazing
- Redecorating, or completing an outstanding project
- Adding recreational features such as a summer house, loggia, sun deck or swimming pool – but beware, pools are costly to maintain, you may not reclaim the full cost when you sell, and if it takes up too much of the garden it may actually deter some buyers

Avoid the following 'improvements':

- Extensions that occupy the entire garden
- Stone cladding
- Removing period features, such as fireplaces and ornate coving
- Anything out of keeping with the nature of the property, for example uPVC double glazed windows in a period property
- Over-personalising your home

To improve the kerb appeal of your home:

- Tidy the garden, front and back and add some colourful shrubs – if you don't like gardening just make sure that the grass is cut and the hedges trimmed
- Repair any broken gates, walls or fences
- Give your front door and windows a lick of paint
- Make sure your door number is clearly visible
- Wash net curtains

Preparing to sell:

- Spring clean your house from top to bottom
- Clear away clutter. If your house is really stuffed with things, it may be worth packing some away – it will make the house look bigger

- Clear out cupboards – people will open them!
- When it comes to furniture, less is more – less furniture will create an illusion of space and looks modern. If you have a lot of furniture consider putting some in the loft or into storage
- A coat of paint will make a room look fresh and bright – choose a pale neutral shade or white
- Touch up or repaint any chipped or worn paintwork
- Get rid of mould in kitchens and bathrooms
- Open windows before a viewing so that the house smells fresh and airy
- Make sure that the entrance is well lit
- If it is dark turn lights on throughout the house before viewers arrive. It will make the house seem bright and welcoming

Tricks that sell:

- Fresh flowers add a splash of colour and give a house a cherished 'homey' feel
- Copy tricks from builders' show homes. Laying a table, for example, will add interest to the room
- Turn off distractions like the radio or TV when people come to view
- Show your best rooms first. Let prospective buyers enter rooms first – it makes them look bigger
- Hold conversations in the larger and better rooms
- Have doors standing open, it will allow light to filter through the house and makes small rooms look bigger
- Don't forget to mention all the good, saleable features of your house to your prospective buyers, such as double glazing, good security, a combi boiler, convenient transport, shopping, or good schools
- Buyers will ask why you are selling – have your answer ready
- Don't include carpets, curtains or cookers. They can be used for subsequent negotiations
- Keep children (and their toys) and boisterous dogs under control while prospective buyers are viewing – both in the house and in the garden.
- Hide the cat litter tray
- Tidy away personal stuff like make-up, and anything that could be embarrassing
- Have your solicitor's details to hand

The scented home

Of the five senses, smell is the most evocative and has a profound effect on the way we respond to places and situations. Filling your home with the aroma of freshly ground coffee and home baking have become a bit of a selling cliché but, nevertheless, scents, pleasant or unpleasant will affect potential buyers at a subliminal level. Make sure all soft furnishing are clean and aired – smells linger in fabric. Open windows to give the house a good airing. If you have animals use proprietary products to wash fouled areas. Cigarette smoke lingers and can make a home smell fuggy. Air fresheners are a bit iffy – the perfumes can be overwhelming and aren't to everyone's taste. They also suggest that you've got something to cover up. Some of the old-fashioned room fresheners are more natural and less intrusive. Here are some tips:

- A dish of vinegar left out overnight will absorb smoke and cooking smells from the atmosphere.
- If you're cooking cabbage or cauliflower put few drops of lemon juice in the water to prevent the smell pervading the house
- If you're painting a room cut an onion in half and leave it cut side up while you work, then throw it away. It will reduce the paint smells.
- Bathroom smells can be dispelled by lighting a match for a few seconds
- Freshen a musty cupboard with a dish of bath salts
- Use lemon peel, or drops of vanilla essence on cotton wool balls to freshen drawers
- Fresh herbs like rosemary placed under the grill will give the kitchen a warm herby smell
- If you have an open fire, burn orange and lemon peel
- Pot pourri and dried lavender will create subtle scents throughout the house
- Aromatherapy oils affect people's moods. Put drops of your favourite oil on a piece of cotton wool and leave it in a warm place. Lavender is fresh, clean and relaxing, clary sage has a warm, nutty scent and makes people feel relaxed and comfortable, and lemon grass has a wonderful lemony smell
- Place a lemon-scented geranium in a pot in the hallway or on a windowsill – rub the leaves as you pass to release the perfume

Don't rush headlong into a major home renovation scheme. If you spend time assessing your needs and planning the project, you will produce a scheme which is effective, efficient, economical and aesthetically pleasing.

Design
planning a makeover
inspiration

by **ORIANNA FIELDING BANKS**

Your home is a complex 'machine for living': a place to eat, sleep, work and relax, a focus for the family and somewhere to express your personality and tastes. However, it is inevitable that as your needs, circumstances and tastes evolve, you will need to make changes to your surroundings. People often make these changes in a fairly unplanned way, reacting to situations as they arise, but this approach rarely produces the best results. Start by identifying major problems (such as lack of space), look at your requirements, list your likes and dislikes, and use this information as the basis for your scheme. A well-designed scheme will not only stand the test of time, but it will also add to your enjoyment of your home and increase its value and saleability.

The projects described in this book are all fairly ambitious. All involve different levels of structural work, and a lot of specialist skills such as joinery, electrics, plumbing and plastering. These unseen works play as important a role in the final scheme as the decorations and furnishings. In every project the owner set us a challenging problem and we came up with a design solution. Although the end results are very different and each transformation has its own 'look', they were all arrived at by going through the same design process.

Identifying the problems

It is important to be as precise as possible in identifying what the problem actually is. If, for example, your children have got to the age where they need more space to themselves, but you decide that the house simply needs decorating, you will spend time, effort and money on that and still find that practical problems remain. Once you start looking for problems you will probably find a whole host of them. Start by making a list – lists are really very useful things – and then

identify the most important items on it. This process can produce some surprising results. You might find that the thing that is really bothering you is easily and cheaply solved, you might even decide that the only sensible solution is to move!

Making a floor plan

Once you have decided on your main requirements and a broad strategy, you can make a floor plan. You will need some 5mm gridded paper, some plain paper, a tape measure, ruler, pencils, and scissors. On the plain paper make a sketch of the floor plan, including all the recesses, chimney breasts, door and window openings. (If you have an original set of house plans you can base your plans on those.) Measure all the walls and openings and note these measurements on the sketch. Make your measurements in millimetres. Sketch the doors, indicating the way they open and the arc

of the swing. Measure and mark fitted items like radiators, cupboards, and bookshelves. Transfer this information to the gridded paper, using a scale of one 5mm square to 10cm. So if a door opening is 800mm it will take up 8 squares on the squared paper. Now measure any free-standing elements that will be going into the room, and draw them up to the same scale on another sheet of paper. Identify each object and indicate which is the front. Cut out these shapes and move them about on the floor plan to test different arrangements.

Making a wall plan

You can also draw up wall plans or elevations. These are especially useful for planning the best way to organise equipment and storage units in a kitchen. An easy way to create wall plans is to take photographs of the space you are planning to change, trace off the main elements, then take photocopies of the tracing. You can then use these photocopies to explore different designs and colourways.

Finding inspiration

Professional designers have up-to-the-minute knowledge of the latest products, materials and design trends. But these days it is much easier for the non-professional to keep up with the latest developments in interior design. There are many magazines which deal with home design: some specialise in areas like kitchens or bathrooms and are quite technical, or obviously intended for the trade; others look at design trends more generally and have a broad target market. Most 'lifestyle' publications have features on makeovers and occasionally take a detailed look at beautiful and interesting homes, and newspapers often have interiors and shopping columns. In addition to *Better Homes*, television has a large variety of makeover, DIY and garden programmes. Browse through magazines and

catalogues and keep tear sheets of colours, styles and products that catch your eye. This is a great way of collecting design ideas and will help you to formulate your look.

It is also a good idea to make a list of the things you'd really like: a place to put the computer or a collection of old glass bottles, somewhere to be quiet, a favourite colour. Keep the list handy as a reminder – and every time anyone thinks of an idea, jot it down. It can be hard to know what you like – it is often much easier to decide what you don't like. Make a list of things you really don't like or want – the 'don't want' list can be just as revealing and helpful as the 'must have' list.

Finding the solution

Success in any major design or redecorating project depends on thorough planning. You need to consider the practical elements – the structure, the design, and the style of decoration – and tailor those to meet your available budget. This is not easy and it is at this point that 'the professionals' are called in.

The problem-solving process is the most thrilling part of design, and somehow when you've got it right you know it. The very best design solutions solve the problem, look good and often have added benefits. Working with a designer can help you achieve all this. Potential clients sometimes worry about costs spiralling out of control, and find the thought of hiring a professional designer or architect rather daunting. They are also concerned that the designer will ignore their wishes. A designer's role is to listen to the client, find out their wants and needs, their likes and dislikes, so that together they can find a solution that suits the individual. A good designer is really an enabler who helps the client to realise their dreams.

So how do you go about finding a designer? There are lots of designers out there, and their training, experience and specialist areas vary. The best way of finding someone is by word of mouth. Failing that you can contact organisations such as the Royal Institute of British Architects (RIBA) to find an architect, or the Interior Decorators and Designers Association to find an interior designer, and you can look in the Yellow Pages or in advertisements in specialist magazines. The sort of help you want will depend on the nature of the project. So if you are building a large extension, you might decide to approach an architect or interior designer. However, not all architects will handle domestic work. Some suppliers – of kitchen units, for example – provide a design and installation service, and this may be the answer for you.

Normally the designer will come to the site to discuss your ideas, and the service they offer. Find out what the initial consultation will cost – often the first consultation is free or refunded against the project total. Start by setting a budget and a brief and find out what the payment basis will be. The sort of input you want will depend on the nature and scale of the job. You might want a few ideas for a kitchen or garden, or you might want the designer to come up with plans for a large extension. In the latter case, they can do some or all of the following: provide drawings, deal with the planning office, get in quotations from builders and suppliers, manage the project and source fittings, paints, wallpapers and furnishings. The nature of the contract, the payment and payment terms should be set out clearly in writing at the beginning of the project. The contract should include details such as the number of revisions to the plans that are costed for, and the charge for additional work. The designer will generally charge a percentage of the gross project value total: normally between 8 and 15 per cent.

The first meeting is important because you need to know that you can communicate with the designer, and that they have an understanding of your needs, and are generally on your wavelength. The next stage is usually a set of rough visuals and plans setting down the ideas you have discussed.

So what do you get for your money? A professional designer will help you express your ideas and translate them into a well designed, highly finished scheme. They will steer you through the pitfalls of planning and building regulations. They will step back and take an overview, anticipate problems, and share their in-depth knowledge of products and materials. A good designer will prevent you from making expensive mistakes, and in the long run they really will save you money – or rather, ensure that you get maximum value for money. And don't worry if you are working to a tight budget – a good designer will regard this as a challenge, and limited funds often produce the most creative solutions.

Preparing a mood board

It can be difficult to decide on a style and to visualise the look you want to create. Start by thinking about the colours, patterns and styles that you like. Look in your wardrobe and around your house. If you've got a piece of fabric or a vase that you like put it in the room to be decorated and see if it sets any bells

Design dos and don'ts

- Think of the way the room is used, and how it interacts with other spaces
- Identify the problem/s
- Make a 'must-have' list
- Identify the best features in the room
- Allow time to plan the project
- Consider the overall character of the house – does everything go together?
- Think about noise – don't put living areas above childrens' bedrooms, for example
- Save money by using clever decorating techniques
- Set a budget

- Think about basics like the electricity supply and the heating system
- Do spend money on things that will suffer a lot of wear and tear: the boiler, carpets in heavy traffic areas, the sofa
- Save money by giving existing furniture a makeover
- Consider lighting requirements early on
- Ask an estate agent to value your home as it stands, and with the intended improvement
- Collect reference material: catalogues, colour charts, samples
- Visit shops and specialist exhibitions like The Ideal Homes Exhibition
- Be clear about the brief

- Visit neighbours' homes to see how they have dealt with similar problems
- Consider the age and style of your home, especially if it is listed, or in a conservation area or National Park
- Talk to a designer
- Spend money on one single gorgeous object – it will give you pleasure and lift the whole scheme
- Work out a schedule that will fit in with your life and family needs – school holidays, for example
- Be flexible and prepared to listen to novel suggestions
- Prepare yourself for the disruption that home improvements involve

Design dos and don'ts

DON'T:

- Launch into a series of one-off improvements
- Solve one problem when you could solve several
- Get distracted by decorating when there are major problems
- Cut corners on important items like the electrics and the heating system
- Start a project you don't have the time or money to complete
- Spend so much money that you take the property over the 'ceiling' price for the area
- Go for eccentric designs if you intend to move soon
- Be a follower of fashion – wacky designs date quickly
- Forget about comfort
- Forget about about practical things like storage
- Think that design is about applying paint

ringing. What you are looking for is a hook on which you can hang the rest of the decorative scheme.

A designer will produce a collage of ideas on colour, pattern and style to help you visualise the impact of the scheme when it is finally put together. These are called sample boards or mood boards and may include paint and fabric swatches, pictures of entire rooms and details such as light fittings. The sample board is a very useful tool in the designer's armoury and a simple way of testing out ideas. You can make your own very easily. Collect inspirational pictures, samples of wallpaper, wallpaper borders, fabric and floor coverings. For plain walls, paint a piece of card in the required colour and stick that to the board. Fix these to a piece of card or polyboard in approximately the right proportions. Display the board in the room so that you can see it frequently and check the effect in different lighting conditions.

Lighting

Lighting is one of the most important aspects of the home, but is sometimes seen as purely functional and is therefore neglected or completely overlooked. Modern lighting systems allow us to create mood and atmosphere. Just think of the way that lighting is used in the theatre and you will see that is quite possible to transform entirely the appearance of a space with

lighting. It is important to consider lighting at an early stage in the planning of a major extension or refurbishment, because the wiring has to be installed at the beginning of a project.

It is useful to consider the different categories of lighting. Background lighting provides general illumination and allows you to find your way around a room. It is usually provided by central pendants, recessed ceiling lights or wall lights. Atmospheric lighting is used to create mood and visual interest. This is achieved by using dimmer switches, concealed lighting, up-lighters, carefully placed side lights and floor lights. Task lighting is designed to allow you to carry out specific activities: standard lights for reading, desk lights for working, and spotlights and strip lights on kitchen work surfaces. Display lighting – picture lights, for example – allow you to highlight favourite objects.

The different parts of your house will need different lighting. A bright porch light is welcoming, makes opening the door at night easier, allows you to check your visitors and deters burglars. The hall should also be bright and welcoming. Bright task lighting is essential over kitchen work surfaces. Down-lighters or spots should be placed directly above and slightly to the front of the work surface. Fluorescent or incandescent tubes can be concealed behind pelmets under wall-mounted cupboards. In a combination kitchen and

dining area, use separate lighting systems for each area.

The living room requires a clever combination of lighting to zone areas of background, mood and task lighting. It is the area that will set the tone and look for the rest of the house. Architectural features such as alcoves, cornicing and architraves can be highlighted with clever use of spot or up-lighting.

For bathrooms, choose enclosed fittings that will not be affected by the damp atmosphere. Place mirror lights at eye level for the best light by which to shave and apply make-up.

In bedrooms, aim for soft background lighting. You will also need lights to read by. The switches should be easily accessible when you are lying in bed. You can also have the bedside lights on a two-way switch so that you can also turn them on from the door.

Always get a professional to check the electrical loading – you must be sure that you have sufficient power to supply the additional lights and powerpoints in your scheme. Plan switches according to the way you use your house, ensuring that lights can be switched from the bottom and the top of the stairs. Install several circuits in every room to give you maximum control of your lighting.

Lighting forms an intrinsic part of any successful interior design scheme and requires as much time, thought and planning as choosing a colour, fabric or floor covering.

design and inspiration

Colour is a powerful and exciting tool which can be used to create a mood, suggest an historical period, evoke a sense of place, or change the apparent proportions of a room. It is often the cheapest, simplest and most effective way of transforming your home.

colour for the decorator

A lucky few are blessed with an instinctive feeling for colour. They unerringly find just the right fabrics, papers and paints to create an elegant living room, or a bright but comfortable family kitchen. The rest of us struggle with sample pots and swatches, and still manage to get it wrong. If you master a few basic principles, and take some tips from the professionals, you will find it much easier to achieve the effects you want. You will also be able to assess a scheme, identify the problems and put them right simply and quickly, and often at very little cost.

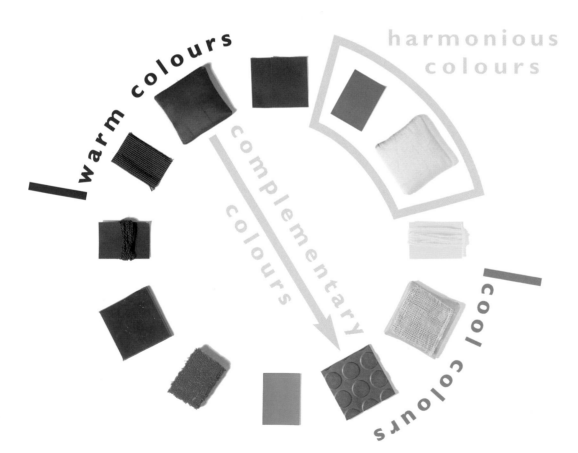

The 12-colour wheel

The colour wheel is a simple visual device to help you understand and remember some basic colour relationships. Our wheel shows the three primary colours: red, yellow and blue. These colours are unique in the decorator's palette because they cannot be mixed from other colours. Between the primaries you will find the secondaries: orange, green and violet. These are mixed from the adjacent primaries. Between each primary and secondary pair you will find a range of intermediate colours like bluish-green and yellowy-green; reddish-orange and reddish-violet – these are the tertiaries, and they are especially pleasing and very useful to the decorator.

red **primary**	red-orange **tertiary**
blue **primary**	yellow-orange **tertiary**
yellow **primary**	blue-green **tertiary**
	yellow-green **tertiary**
orange **secondary**	blue-violet **tertiary**
green **secondary**	red-violet **tertiary**
violet **secondary**	

The language of colour

A basic knowledge of the language of colour will help you to understand the way colour works. It will also allow you to discuss the effects you are trying to achieve with your family, and with specialists like designers and paint suppliers.

Accent colour

A small area of colour which contrasts with the predominant colour range: a touch of a bright colour in an otherwise neutral scheme, for example, or splashes of 'complementary' red in expanses of green. The accent colour adds zest, creates variety and pace and can also be used to highlight an attractive or important feature.

Advancing colours

When a warm or dark colour is applied to the walls of a room, they appear to come forward, making the room seem smaller. You can use this quality to make a barn-like space seem smaller and cosier, or to visually lower a ceiling that seems too high for the space. See also 'Receding colours'.

Broken colour

The interspersing of one colour with another, so that when they are viewed from a distance they appear to be a single colour. Decorative paint effects such as sponging, stippling and ragging are examples of broken colour. They are used because they add texture and depth to a flat surface. Small patterns and multi-coloured weaves are also examples of broken colour because the details of colour and pattern become blurred with distance, resulting in a generalised colour and tone. This is why it is important to view wallpaper and fabric samples from a distance as well as close up.

You can also 'break' a colour by adding a small amount of its complementary to neutralise it.

Colour temperature

Some colours look warm and others look cool, and there is a general consensus about which are which. The colour circle can be divided into two halves. In one half we find the warm colours – yellows, reds and oranges. On the other side are the cool colours – blues, violets and greens. Colour temperature is experienced in a very definite and strong way. In one experiment people in a blue room set the thermostat four degrees higher than others in a red room. The temperature of a colour affects the extent to which a colour appears to advance or recede. See 'Advancing colours' and 'Receding colours'.

Complementaries

The complementary pairs are the colours which appear opposite each other on the colour wheel. Every primary is complemented by a secondary: red by green; yellow by violet; blue by orange. When two complementary colours are placed alongside each other, both look brighter and more intense. If red and green are side by side the red looks redder and the green looks greener than if they were on their own. When complementaries are mixed together just the opposite happens – they neutralise each other. If your paint is too bright you can 'knock it back' by adding a tiny touch of its complementary.

Cool colours

Cool colours, like blue and green, tend to be calming and tranquil. In experiments cool colours such as blue have been shown to make muscles relax, respiration and heart rate slow down, and blood pressure drop. Cool colours are an obvious choice for rooms in which you want to relax or sleep. Note that within the cool colours there are variations in colour temperature – so some blues are cooler than others. A greeny, aqua blue is cooler and crisper than a purply blue, while lemon yellow will appear relatively cool when placed alongside a warm golden yellow. Very subtle nuances can have an enormous effect on the overall impact of a colour scheme. So if one yellow looks wrong, or makes you feel as though the walls are closing in on you, try another.

Cool colours appear to recede in space – see 'Receding colours'.

Dye

A substance which dissolves in liquids and imparts its colour to materials by staining or being absorbed.

Earth colours

These naturally occurring inorganic pigments are produced from clays, rocks and earths which have been coloured by metallic oxides. Among the earliest pigments used by mankind, they were used in the cave paintings at Altamira near Santander in northern Spain created 15,000 years ago, and in the cave paintings at Lascaux near Montignac in the Dordogne in France. The earths include a glorious range of muted yellows, reds and browns, and a few greenish shades. All the natural earths are 'impure' colours – they contain traces of organic matter, clay and other impurities which create the subtle differences between the pigments from different regions and give them their 'knocked back' appearance.

Harmonious colours

These are colours that seem to go together. The colours that fall between two primaries on the colour wheel will 'go together' harmoniously because they have their parent primaries in common, although in different quantities. Other harmonious ranges include the neutrals, earth colours, warm colours, cool colours, and pastels. However, if colours in a room are too harmonious the result can be boring, so consider introducing an 'Accent colour' or colours.

Hue

A hue is a specific colour, defined in terms of its redness or blueness, but not its lightness or darkness. It is the aspect of a colour which dictates its location on the colour wheel.

Intensity (or Saturation)

This describes the purity or brightness of a colour. The colours around the outside of the colour wheel are at maximum intensity and cannot be made stronger. They are 'pure' colours. You reduce the intensity or saturation of a colour by 'knocking it back' with another colour – a colour 'broken' in this way retains its hue.

Knocked back

A colour that has been rendered less intense by adding another colour – see also 'Intensity'. The neutrals and earth colours are examples of knocked back colours.

Limited palette

A restricted range or 'palette' of colours – it is simpler to work with than an extended or unlimited palette.

Neutrals

One of the most important ranges of colours are the neutrals or coloured greys. Unlike the primaries, secondaries and tertiaries, these are not pure colours. They are colours which have been greyed, muted, dulled, knocked back or dirtied but they still have an identifiable hue. This category of colours provides an almost unlimited range of subtle shades beloved by decorators, from cool pearly greys, through soft duck egg blues and eau de nil, to the warm tones of sand and the natural earths. You can neutralise a colour by adding black, grey, or a touch of its complementary. The neutrals provide a useful foil for brighter colours, and a primarily neutral palette is usually enlivened with touches of an accent colour.

Palette

The surface on which artists mix their colours and hence a selection or range of colours.

Pigment

A coloured material which does not dissolve in a liquid, but is finely ground, bound with a binder and is applied to a surface in the form of paint. Artist's pigments are also applied as pastels and other drawing materials.

Primaries

The primaries are red, yellow and blue. These are important to artists because they cannot be mixed on the palette from other colours and, in theory, every other colour can be mixed from them.

Pure colours

The primaries, secondaries and tertiaries are all described as 'pure' because they are derived from two primary colours.

Receding colours

If cool or pale colours are applied to a wall, the wall will appear to sit back in space. The same wall painted in a warm or dark colour will appear to advance. You can exploit these qualities in your decorative schemes to adjust the apparent size and dimensions of a room. Paint a small room a deep, terracotta red and it will feel small and cosy. Paint the same room an intense blue and it will feel more spacious. Paint it a pale, cool aquamarine and it will feel bigger still.

Saturation (see 'Intensity')

Secondaries

The secondaries are derived from the primaries: red and yellow produce orange; yellow and blue give green; red and blue give violet.

Tertiaries

A tertiary colour is created by mixing a secondary colour with an adjacent primary in equal quantities. On the colour wheel there is a tertiary between each primary and secondary – they are useful colours like bluish-green and yellowy-green; reddish-orange and reddish-violet. When these are neutralised you find some of the most beautiful and subtle colours in the decorator's palette.

Tint

Add white to a hue to create a tint. e.g. pastels.

Tone

Tone, or value, is the lightness or darkness of a colour. White and black represent the two extremes of the tonal scale. When you darken a hue it is called a shade – a hue that has been lightened is called a tint. Every hue on the colour wheel has a tonal value – so blue is darker in tone than yellow, which is naturally light in tone. Tone is an important and sometimes overlooked aspect of any decorative scheme. Great variations in tone can look very busy, but you can make apparently disparate colours like blue and yellow sit together easily by choosing shades that have a similar tonal value. Pastels are all tints of hues and tend to have an intrinsic tonal harmony. If you find it difficult to assess the tones in a room, you'll find that half-closing your eyes makes it easier to find the contrasts and similarities.

Warm colours

The hot colours like red and red-orange are energetic and insistent. It has been shown in experiments that colours can have very dramatic effects on mood, efficiency and general wellbeing. If you focus on a bright light which is shone on a warm colour such as red, a chain reaction occurs. Muscular tension increases, you tend to lean towards the light and vivid colour. Respiration and heart rate speed up and blood pressure rises. Finally there is an increase in brain activity which is strong enough to be electrically recorded. Warm colours appear to take up more space than cool colours. If two boxes are painted red and green respectively, people judge the red one to be heavier. Warm colours also appear to advance – see 'Advancing colours'.

Planning a colour scheme

Colour can have a profound impact on the appearance of your home and on the way you feel, so it is worth spending time investigating the possibilities and deciding what colours you really like. You will find the process revealing, rewarding and very enjoyable.

Start by finding a colour theme that inspires or excites you, and develop a palette of colours based on that theme. The character and appearance of a colour is affected by the nature of its surface, so think in terms of textures as well as colours. A flat, matt paint makes a colour look dense and intense because the surface absorbs the light – a gloss paint surface reflects the light giving the colour a lighter and more lively quality. Broken paint effects and small patterns create vibrant optical effects and give the wall luminosity and depth. Some of the most interesting and sophisticated effects are created by playing off textures and surfaces. This is an especially effective way of

Above and top right: examples of working mood boards created by Orianna Fielding Banks' company Pure Design.

introducing variety into a monochrome scheme. You could, for example, apply gloss colour through a stencil onto a matt surface in the same colour to create a subtle self-coloured pattern. A shiny, gloss-painted floor can be used to reflect light back onto the walls.

Light and colour

Natural light has a colour and you should consider the orientation of the room and the nature of the light when you are choosing a colour scheme. North-facing windows give a cool, bluish light throughout the day. Because the light is so even, artists favour this aspect for their studios. In cool or north-facing rooms use a warm palette based on orange, red and russet shades to compensate for the bluish light. South-facing rooms receive a warm, orange light throughout the day. Balance this with a pale palette with blue and lilac undertones. East-facing rooms receive a warm light in the morning, while west-facing rooms have a warm light in the afternoon. Choose a colour scheme which looks good in different light conditions and relates to the way you use the room. So if your bedroom faces east and you like to feel tranquil in the early morning you might favour a cool palette of colours. But if you are an early riser and like to feel energised first thing, you might go for a warmer palette.

The nature of the artificial lighting used will also affect the feel of the room and the way that colours appear. Halogen lighting, which is increasingly popular, closely mimics the bright, uplifting qualities of natural daylight. Traditional tungsten light bulbs have a very warm yellow quality which will neutralise some delicate lilacs. Fluorescent tubes are available in two versions: ordinary tubes have a cold blue quality, while broad spectrum fluorescent tubes are designed to simulate daylight. By designing and controlling the lighting values, it is possible to reflect or respond to seasonal changes. Changing the colour of a bulb can subtly transform an interior. By using a soft-toned, honey-coloured bulb in a table lamp you can cheer up a cold, north-facing room. Or you can cool a warm environment by placing a turquoise film (gel) over a fluorescent strip – creating a dramatic change without redecorating.

Choosing a palette of colours

Almost anything can trigger an idea for a colour scheme; it might be a photograph in a magazine, a favourite flower, coloured fabrics that appeal strongly to you, the colours used in an historic house, a friend's house, somewhere you visited on holiday. Sometimes you are searching for a feeling and mood rather than a specific colour range. Perhaps you have been to Italy and have returned with your mind's eye full of sun-baked stucco and plaster in faded earth tones – terracotta bleached to the palest pink, and façades skimmed with golden ochres. These textures and colours have a powerful resonance and, with a bit of thought, you can compile a palette which captures the essence of the experience.

White-on-white schemes

White is still one of the most popular colour choices, but today white isn't simply white – the choice of whites is quite bewildering. You can choose from pure white, dusty white, pebble white, pearl white, bleached white, or snow white. By mixing a selection of different whites, you can create an environment which is light-filled and calm, with barely discernible modulations of tone. This would provide a wonderful backdrop for colourful accessories, or you could develop the white-on-white theme with furniture covered in white fabrics in different textures – slubby tweeds, damasks, brocades and various weaves.

Monochrome colour schemes

Some of the simplest colour schemes are based around a single colour. You can create variety by using the colour in a range of light and dark tones, with a pale version for the ceiling, a darker tone on the walls and with architectural details such as architraves and cornices picked out in another shade. You might find the inspiration for your mono-chrome scheme in an existing furnishing, ornament or even a painting or print. When you have decided on the theme colour you can start to collect paint swatches, and wallpaper and fabric samples and make yourself a sample board (see opposite). These days it is possible to find paint in every colour under the sun – some suppliers will even mix a paint to match an existing colour. You can turn up with a piece of paper or fabric, even a piece of china, and they will match it for you.

back versions of the colours. On the warm side, this gives you a cluster of sunny colours that fall between red and yellow – many are colours from nature like peach, orange, tangerine, and nasturtium. The knocked back versions are earth shades like terracotta, umber and yellow ochre. On the cool side, there are some lovely colours between blue and red – flower colours like lilac, lavender, heather and violet, and fruit colours like plum, grape and damson. Between yellow and blue you will find the jewel colours like jade, emerald and aquamarine. The knocked back versions of this range gives you some designer favourites like celadon – a greyish green glaze used on Chinese pottery – eau-de-Nil, the colour of the Nile, so beloved in the 1920s, and pistachio. As with the monochrome schemes, if you choose to use related harmonies, you may need to introduce an accent colour to give the room a lift.

Monochrome schemes are easy to use and easy to live with, but you may have to introduce a contrast colour to avoid visual monotony. You can introduce an accent colour with accessories such as rugs, flowers, pictures or ornaments. Traditionally, crisp white or soft cream has been used on woodwork to frame and emphasise the predominant colour scheme, but you could ring the changes with a splash of a contrast colour, lime green with lilac, or sizzling orange with a warm blue, for example.

Related harmonies

The secondary and tertiary colours that occur between two primaries on the colour wheel make a good basis for a colour scheme. These ranges of colours have a natural affinity because they all contain a little of the parent primaries. You can extend these palettes with light and dark tones, and slightly knocked

The pastel palette is pretty, fresh and delicate – it offers the colours of sugared almonds and springtime flowers.

Earth, spice and autumnal colours

From the spice palette we get a gorgeous selection of russets, toasted browns and golden ochres, with flashes of bright burnt orange. These colours are old colours, earth colours which can be dug out of the ground and have decorated homes throughout the world since the dawn of time. The terracotta shades conjure up the warmth of a Mediterranean shore, while orange teamed with black, lime green and blue evokes the crisp geometry of Deco.

From the natural world we get a glorious palette of earth reds and browns, the colours of autumn leaves and spices like nutmeg, ginger and cinnamon.

Pebble colours and textures

The pebbles you'd find on shingle beach provide a harmonious range of cool and warm greys, and lovely knobbly textures. Capture this

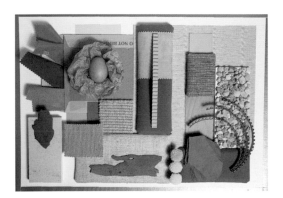

Pebbles provide the inspiration for this palette of neutrals enlivened with weaves and slubby textures.

mood with delicate knocked back greys and almost whites overlaid with pearly translucent glazes. With such an understated palette, the quality of the surface becomes important so look for texture in textiles and other materials.

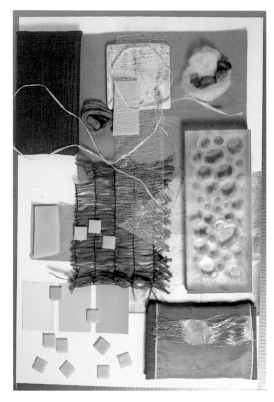

From deep aquamarine to cool blue-greys the colours of sea and sky are never out of fashion.

Jewel and berry colours

These are opulent colours which take their names from semi-precious stones like amethyst, emerald and ruby. They can have the clarity of stained glass or the faded charm of ancient tapestries. They'll make a statement in a hallway, look grand in a dining room and serious in a study. Look for luxurious fabrics like velvets and silks, the intricate patterns of oriental rugs, and tassels, braids and other trimmings. For a contemporary twist wash layers of a jewel-bright colour onto walls and team this with neutrals enlivened with dry-brushed metallics.

design and inspiration

Sea and sky schemes

The blues and aquamarines of sea and sky provide a tranquil but airy palette which would work well in almost any room. These are the blues and greens of the Greek islands, the south of France and the Caribbean. Used at their maximum intensity, they have a natural exuberance, but in their more restrained incarnations they are elegant and cool. Team them with blond woods in a contemporary kitchen, with metallics in a modernist living room or with crisp white detailing in a gracious drawing room.

The metallics

Although gold, silver, bronze and pewter have always had a place in the decorative arts, these colours have been given a contemporary twist in recent years. Metallic paints, polishes and leafs are now widely available and easy to use. Their reflective surfaces are a brilliant way of bringing light into a room – use metallic paint on a wall opposite a window to reflect light back into a room, and a metallic ceiling can look stunning in a room which is decorated with pale colours. They can also be used to highlight architectural features – apply the metallic colour using a drybrush technique, or rub the colour back to create a broken or aged effect.

Prepare colour swatches

When you have decided on your colour scheme try it out on a colour board. If you are satisfied with that then you can start to source fabrics, wallpapers and paints. If you've employed the services of a designer he or she may do that for you. Your samples should be as large as possible – it is very difficult to judge the impact of a colour or pattern from a tiny sample. If you are using paint, buy some sample pots and apply paint to strips of lining paper, or sheets of cardboard, and then prop or pin them in the room, together with the wallpaper and fabric samples. Leave them where you will catch sight of them out of the corner of your eye as you move through or past the room. It is important to see them at different times of day, in natural light and under artificial light. Move the samples around so that you see them in the sunniest spot, as well as in the darkest corner. The difference between the same colour seen in natural and artificial light can be so startling that you find yourself checking to see that it is actually the same. In the examples shown on this page we have taken our inspiration from a variety of sources.

The history of colour

We have an unlimited choice of colours, but this was not always the case. Nature provides few good purple dyes or pigments. In ancient times the most costly colour was Tyrian purple, which was used to dye the cloaks of Roman emperors and magistrates – it took over 12,000 shellfish (*Murex brandaris* or *Murex trunculis*) to produce less than 1 gram of the dye. In 1856 William Henry Perkin discovered Perkin's violet, a synthetic dye derived from coal tar. Soon, other purples were invented and were used so extensively in fashion, decoration and painting that the 1860s became known as the 'mauve decade'.

In the past, being a painter and decorator was a hazardous business because so many of the materials were poisonous. A beautiful blue-green artificial pigment called emerald green or Paris green was invented in 1814. An arsenic derivative, it was so poisonous that it was also sold as a rat poison. It has been said that the Paris green in his wallpaper was responsible for the death of the exiled Napoleon.

Berry reds and fuchia pinks and crimsons provide a gorgeous palette that demands sumptuous silks, brocades and velvets.

Do your homework before you embark on a home improvement scheme. Be clear about what you want to achieve, and realistic about likely time-scales and budgets. Good preparation will allow you to deal confidently with contractors, and with planning and other authorities.

getting the work done
practicalities

by DAVE WELLMAN

My most important bit of advice to any home owner is – get to know your house. After all, it is probably the most expensive thing you will ever buy, but you'd be surprised how little some people know about something which has cost them many thousands of pounds.

You can glean a lot of information about a house before you make a purchase – from the vendors, the sale's particulars and from your surveyor's report. As soon as you move in, spend time familiarising yourself with the house and its construction. You will need this information when there are the inevitable household crises, such as appliances springing a leak or circuits fusing. And if you know which walls are load-bearing, where the hot and cold water pipes and drains run, and the location of the principal electrical circuits, it will be much easier to make sensible decisions about future improvements. For example, if you understand your heating and plumbing systems you will be in a good position to think constructively about the location of a new bathroom, and will be able to brief a designer or contractor.

Start by locating the stopcock so that you can turn off the water to stem a flood or change a washer. Next, find the electricity consumer unit and study it. It will have a mains switch which allows you to turn off the power in an emergency, or if you are carrying out electrical repairs or installations. In some units the on/off mains switch is replaced by a residual current device (RCD). The consumer unit also carries fuses to protect the circuits in the different parts of your house. In modern consumer units these have small automatic switches called miniature circuit breakers (MCBs); old fuse boards have rewirable fuse carriers.

Each consumer unit also has an earth terminal. If the fuse carriers are not labelled to show which circuit the fuse protects, you should identify and label them – there are different ones for lighting and socket circuits. The electricity meter will be located alongside the consumer unit.

Find the gas meter and see where the main gas pipes run. Study your central heating system and establish what type it is. This will be useful information if you decide to extend the central heating – out to a garage or up to a loft extension, for example. The type, size and location of the boiler and the various tanks will dictate what you can do.

Assembling this basic information about your home is very important. Houses should have logbooks so that you have a record of what is where, and what changes and additions have been made in the past. Keep a file of manuals, surveys, guarantees and any other information that you might need to refer to later. As a builder, I love it when I walk into a house where the owners know where things are, and can lay their hands on all the relevant documents.

It is also a good idea to know the run of your soil drainage and storm drainage pipework – this becomes important if you are considering adding any form of extension to your house, and could affect budgets.

Rules and regulations

For many people, extending their home is a sensible alternative to buying a larger property, and may also be a way of adding value to their home (page 14). This may be necessitated by an expanding family, the need to provide accommodation for an *au pair* or parent, changes in lifestyle or, increasingly, the practice of working from home. There are, however, restrictions on what you can do to your home and it is important that you are aware of these if you are to avoid disappointment or falling foul of the law. Planning laws are designed to prevent intrusions upon privacy by adjoining properties, and to maintain the visual integrity of the property, the street or the location. Building regulations ensure that alternations don't compromise the safety of the structure, or the health or safety of the inhabitants or their neighbours. Listed building regulations ensure that properties of historic or architectural interest retain their special qualities.

Talk to the planning department

It is a good idea to contact the planning department at a very early stage, even before you commission any drawings or plans. I've always found planning officers very helpful and well informed. They can give you a broad indication of what is going to be acceptable and what isn't, and this can save you a lot of wasted time, and possibly money. Tell them briefly what you want to do. If it is an extension, give them the approximate dimensions, how many storeys and how close it will be to your neighbour's boundaries. Give them an idea of the style – pitched roof or flat,

for example – the building materials and the use; is it to be a playroom or a bedroom? In most cases they will tell you straight away whether planning permission is required and whether it is the sort of structure they are likely to favour. They will often indicate what adjustments will be required to make it acceptable. If you do need planning permission they will send you an application form.

Planning permission

Planning permission is usually required for any alteration that affects the use, the size and siting of a house or building, or any change that will affect your neighbours. It may also be necessary for changes that affect the appearance of a building and the way it blends with its surroundings.

Whether or not planning permission is required for an extension depends on factors such as the percentage by which the extension will increase the size of the original buildings, the height of the extension and the percentage of the plot that it will cover. Generally, councils expect alterations or extensions to reflect the scale and character of the original buildings – they want to ensure that the changes enhance, rather than detract from, the appearance of the property and, of course, this is also precisely what you want. They will be concerned with the size, shape, and bulk of the structure, and the roof pitch and will generally require the use of matching materials and appropriate doors, windows and other architectural features. An extension must not reduce your neighbour's privacy, block their daylight or seriously interfere with their outlook. Single-storey extensions up to three metres (9.8ft) in length are normally acceptable for semi-detached and terraced houses. For terraced housing a single-storey rear extension may be built on the boundary, otherwise a one-metre (3.2ft) setback is normally required. Two or

Practicalities

more storeys are not normally permitted on the boundary. On a semi-detached or detached property a distance of one metre is usually left between the extension and the boundary so that the extension can be maintained without going onto the neighbouring property. More than one metre may be required for a two-storey extension to prevent it being too overpowering. An extension should not be too large for the garden nor too high and out of scale with adjacent buildings.

With roof extensions the considerations are the overall increase in volume and the way the extension relates to the height and planes of the existing roof. Dormer windows should normally sit below the existing roof ridge.

It is always best to check at an early stage to establish whether planning permission is required for any development. Occasionally, planning permission is given retrospectively, but it is not worth the risk and you may be required to demolish or correct work for which permission is refused. It is also a good idea to discuss your plans with your neighbours, then you can anticipate objections and avoid misunderstandings which may cause delays.

It normally takes at least five weeks for planning permission to be granted and may take longer, so it is important to get this in hand well before you intend work to start. A public notice will be posted outside your house to inform your neighbours of your plans and inviting them to register their objections.

Listed buildings

When a building is 'listed' it means that it is included on a list of buildings that are considered to be of sufficient historic or archi-tectural interest to merit special protection. This list is drawn up by the Department of National Heritage on the advice of English Heritage.

Listed buildings are divided into three categories: grade I, II* and II. Grades I and II*

represent about 6 per cent of all listed buildings and are of national importance. Grade II are buildings of local importance but still warrant preservation – they account for about 91 per cent of all listed buildings. All buildings built before 1700 which survive in anything like their original conditions, and most buildings built between 1700 and 1840 will be included, although there is a selection process. Generally buildings from the period 1840-1914 are listed when they demonstrate important advances in building technology, or if they are by significant architects. Later buildings of special quality have recently been added to the list. There are some 500,000 listed buildings nationally, representing something like 4 per cent of the building stock.

Listing covers the whole building and listed building consent is required for any alteration which affects its character or setting. Repairs carried out in matching materials do not usually require consent, but it is always best to contact the planning department before commencing work. The council has powers to prosecute where work is carried out on a listed building without consent. Owners who neglect a listed building may be served with a repairs notice forcing them to carry out work necessary to ensure the preservation of the building.

It is worth noting that some works on listed buildings are zero rated. For detailed information about which construction services are free from VAT you should consult VAT Notice 708 'Construction of buildings', available from your local VAT Advice Centre, which will be found under Customs and Excise in the telephone directory. You must apply to the local planning authority for listed building consent before the work is commenced if you intend to claim the relief. You obtain the relief by employing a VAT registered builder who will then be able to zero rate the relevant services and materials. You cannot claim it by refund or on work you do yourself. Only approved alterations are zero rated and must be carried out to the fabric of the building, the walls, roofs, internal surfaces, floors, stairs, landings, doors and windows. Repair and maintenance is not zero rated. Before you start work, contact the local VAT Advice Centre with the following information: confirmation that your home is listed; full details of the works to

be done; indication of which works are repairs and maintenance; and why the works are being carried out.

Conservation areas

These are areas which the local authority considers merit preservation. They may or may not contain listed buildings. Generally, it is illegal to demolish buildings in such areas or to change the external appearance of a building, or alter original features without consent from the planning department. So, for example, if a terrace has a roofline which is largely intact, you are unlikely to get permission for a loft extension. Where alterations are approved the council will generally insist on the use of traditional materials and features.

Building regulations

Any structural alterations will require building regulations approval, even if you do not need planning permission. Building regulations are designed to ensure that your home is properly constructed, and that alterations don't compromise the structural safety of the building. So if you put a door in a structural wall, remove a chimney breast or build into the loft, you will probably require building regulations approval. The department also becomes involved if there are safety or health issues, so access, means of escape and safety in case of fire in a loft conversion will be their concern. Matters relating to public health are also an issue, so they will become involved if your plans affect drains. Your builder or

practicalities

architect will be able to advise you on the areas that require building regulations approval.

You or your architect or builder will have to supply full plans showing all constructional details, or to complete a form called a building notice. Scale drawings have to accompany a building notice. Apply for approval well in advance so that you can discuss your plans with the building control officer. They will tell you if you need to contact any other departments regarding sanitation, fire escapes and so on. You must give at least 48 hours notice before starting work, so that the building control officer can arrange a site inspection if necessary. You should give 24 hours notice before covering foundations or laying drains, and you must advise the officer when the work has been finished.

Finding contractors and builders

The type of professional help you need for a

home improvement scheme will depend on the scale and nature of the job, and also on whether you have the skills or the time to contribute to the job yourself. Today most people are far too busy to undertake anything other than the most basic home improvements. You can save money by doing it yourself, but if the work has to fit around your job, your home may be disrupted for weeks on end. If the job is fairly small – updating a bathroom, for example – you may decide to bring in individual craftsmen as you need them; a plumber, an electrician and a tiler perhaps. You'll probably find that the plumber will be able to recommend people he or she normally works with, and this is probably the ideal situation. For larger jobs, such as a loft extension, you will probably need to hire the services of a builder who will employ craftsmen such as plasterers, carpenters, plumbers and electricians. They may sometimes subcontract some of this work. If you employ an architect or designer they will be able to give recommendations, and as they've probably worked with the firm before, they will be able to tell you about their good points and their weaknesses.

The best way to find a builder or any craftsman is always personal recommendation. As soon as you move into a new area start to build up a contact list. At some time you are going to need an electrician, a plumber and a heating engineer, plus someone to do decorating and maintenance. Do this before the need arises so that you are prepared for emergencies. Ask the people you buy your house from if they can recommend anyone. If you see work going on in a house near you, stop and talk to the homeowner, and to the builder. Before you employ anyone to undertake anything major, ask to see examples of their work. Do you like what you see? Is the plastering good? Are the clients happy with the result?

Find out whether the builders were pleasant and considerate, or noisy and obstructive – if people are working in your home it is important that you can get on with them. Did they go over schedule or over budget?

If that route fails, then you can try the Yellow Pages and local advertisements. You can also contact building institutions such as the Federation of Master Builders and the Building Employers Confederation, who will have lists of firms operating in your area, and also offer warranty schemes that guarantee materials and workmanship. The Guild of Master Craftsmen also has lists of different types of contractor.

If you ring firms cold you will have to use your intuition and judgment to assess their competence and reliability. Are they easy to get in touch with? Did they return your call and turn up promptly for a meeting? What sort of vehicle were they driving, and did it display the name of the firm and its phone number prominently? Did they respond enthusiastically and creatively to your ideas? Did they seem to know what they were talking about, and were they informative about planning and building regulations and possible restrictions? Were they willing to put you in touch with previous clients? Be mistrustful of builders who are evasive about their previous activities, or don't seem to have a permanent base. Finally, did you like them?

Finding the right builder involves a certain amount of luck, but if you do your homework you can minimise the element of chance.

For some jobs such as loft extensions, kitchen and bathroom refurbishment and the erection of conservatories, you can call upon the services of specialist companies that offer a complete package. The advantages are that they should know their business because they are specialists; the disadvantages are that they may come from outside the area which makes it difficult to check up on them, or to chase them up afterwards if anything goes wrong. Also, this can be an expensive route. However, if you choose a reputable firm it may be the right answer for you.

Getting quotes and budgeting

You should normally ask three contractors to quote for the job. Do this well in advance of when you expect work to start – most good contractors are busy and need plenty of notice. If it is a relatively straightforward job, a site visit should be enough to give them the information they need. However, it is a good

Practicalities

idea to list the elements of the job as you see it, so that all the contractors quote on the same basis. For more complex jobs your architect or designer will provide drawings and specifications. Allow about a month for the quotes to come in, and then go through them carefully to ensure that you are comparing like with like. See how many people they have costed for, and how many days they have allowed for the job. And remember, the cheapest quote isn't always the best value. The contractor may be using cheaper materials or may have underestimated the job.

The quotation document should also list the contractor's terms and conditions, and it is worth going through these carefully. They will cover payments terms, how variations to the specification will be agreed, details of guarantees, indemnity schemes and insurance. The quotation should also indicate how long the prices are valid for.

For a big job you will need a formal contract – if you are employing an architect they will draw this up for you. On smaller jobs the quotation may comprise the contract document. One thing you must clarify with the contractor is who is going to be responsible for getting all the relevant permissions and approvals for work done.

Most contractors will ask for stage payments for large jobs, with an upfront sum to cover materials. If they are established, they should have credit with suppliers and be able to cover the cost of materials until you pay for them. I always insist on money for materials up front, or the client can buy the materials themselves. That way they feel involved and they know that I'm not making anything on the materials.

It is important to budget realistically, and if you are working on an old building you should allow something like 20-25 per cent for contingencies. I'm afraid there are always

some unforeseen surprises in old buildings. I have a restaurant in Hastings and when I did the original refurbishment on the kitchen there, I took away some hardboard that covered up a doorway. I was delighted because I wanted a doorway. Then I discovered that the doorway had no lintel, just a piece of timber. A 12-inch (30.5cm) solid wall supporting two storeys and a roof was resting on half a brick – it was really scary. Whoever had done the job had just chopped out an opening in the wall – how they didn't kill themselves I don't know. I had to build a brick pier and make sure the whole thing was properly supported. I hadn't costed for that work, but it had to be done.

Even on *Better Homes* we've had our surprises. In the Falmouth loft conversion a wall we thought would be solid turned out to be hollow. This meant extra expense and time lost. First, we had to get an engineer in to

make a new set of calculations for the wall that was to take all the extra weight. Then, a metal lintel was put across two load-bearing walls, with a timber plate on top to make fixing the floor joists easier. We used joist hangers (there are many different types and sizes) to fix the joists either side of the lintel. When you are working on an existing structure rather than building new, you have to be prepared for the unexpected and the potentially costly. You can minimise the pain by being prepared, and by employing an experienced builder who will know exactly what to do.

Getting the builders in will be less painful if you have an understanding of the work involved, the probable timescales and the amount of disruption that is likely. And finally, make sure your builders have plenty of tea – they categorise clients by the number of cups of tea they get.

House maintenance

A better home is a home that is well maintained. In this checklist I've listed some of the things that you should check when you first move into a new house, and at least once a year thereafter to ensure that the house is in good order. Find someone local who can do jobs that involve ladderwork – personal recommendations are the best way of finding someone, but the small ads in your local paper are also a good source. Money spent on regular maintenance is peanuts compared to the sums that will be involved if major problems are allowed to develop.

Chimneys

• Do you use your chimney? If not cap it off with a bit of lead. Chimneys are a major source of damp.
• Is your chimney standing straight?
• Is the brickwork in good condition, does it need re-pointing? There is a lot of weather up there. If your chimney falls over it will cause a lot of damage to the rest of the house
• Is the chimney to tile flashing in good condition? These sometimes get kicked up by the wind

Tile and slate roofs

• You should have access to the roof so that you can get out and check it
• It is also useful to check the roof from outside using binoculars
• Are there any cracked or missing tiles?
• Have any tiles slipped?
• Does the roof sag?
• Are the valleys and flat sections clear and in good condition? Is water gathering anywhere?
• Are the flashings in good condition?
• Are the ridge tiles complete and properly bedded into mortar?

Flat roofs

• These are especially prone to damage and have a limited life. Fibre-glass is a much better material than felt. It is about 30 per cent dearer, but it will last twice as long. It looks better than felt because you don't have to put gravel on it. You can walk on it. It won't crack and blister in heat. You can have it gel coated to any colour you want. It smells for a few days, but it is a fantastic product
• Are there splits, tears or signs of bubbling in the surface?
• Are the flashings in place and sound?
• You also need to check the roof from inside
• Is the loft properly ventilated?
• Does the loft smell damp?
• Are there any signs of water getting in – staining, damp patches?
• Is there any rot, mould or insect damage in the roof timbers?

Gutters and downpipes

• Are the gutters clear? Remove leaves and other debris
• Do the gutters sag?
• Are they securely fixed?
• Does the downpipe flow freely?
• Is there any sign of cracking or rusting?

Drains

• Does water flow away properly? Keep gulleys clear of debris
• Keep manhole covers and drain covers in good condition

Walls

• Check from outside first
• Are walls and openings straight?
• Are there any cracks in the façade?
• Is rendering damaged?
• Is the mortar in good condition?
• Are there any signs of damp penetration on inside walls?

Windows

• Windows are an important part of maintenance and will take up most of your maintenance time, especially if they are wood. Cleaning is part of good maintenance. If you don't clean them you get the build-ups that grow moss and that push them apart – then you have the start of rot
• Are the sills in good condition? Do they need repainting?
• Have the drip channels under the sills become blocked with paint? If there isn't a drip channel, fit a piece of hardwood beading
• Oil uPVC windows three times a year

Woodwork

• Is there any sign of cracking or rot?
• Is paintwork in good condition?

Electrical system

• It is important that all electrical fittings are in good order, so keep an eye out for damage and have it fixed immediately
• Are sockets damaged or loose?
• Are flexes frayed?
• Have you acquired more electrical goods during the year and do you need to have more sockets put in? A new computer may possibly need six or more sockets

Central heating

• Gas central heating boilers should be serviced once a year
• Is your boilder efficient? If it is old it may be time to replace it

On location with Better Homes

We really do have to work incredibly hard as we only have five days on location for each show. Day one is normally a Monday and is mostly taken up with Carol talking to the families who have to move out of their homes. A big crane is brought in so that they can get those overhead shots of Carol running between the two locations. We can't do any building work before the filming has been done – which can be a bit frustrating, as we want to get on. We rarely get started before three o'clock in the afternoon; sometimes it's six o'clock before we can go in and then we can't do much because we have to adhere to the regulations governing work and noise in a built-up area. Basically we have Tuesday, Wednesday and Thursday to get everything done, because Friday is taken up with filming. We get a bit of time in the morning because there is inevitably a lot of confusion with the crane being set up again – we use it to add finishing touches and arrange the furniture – 'cushion throwing', we call it. Then the families come back and their astonishment and delight makes all the late nights and hard graft seem worthwhile. And that's that until next time. What we achieve is amazing, but the team is brilliant and we all get on, and that makes a lot of difference.

Behind ths scenes – what the viewer doesn't see!

part two

entrances

kitchens

conversions

lofts

the projects

bathrooms

gardens

living rooms

bedrooms

'Kerb appeal' is an important part of selling a house, but how often do you stop and look at your home from the outside and try to see it as others see it? The exercise can be very revealing.

entrances

making an entrance

Most people focus on the inside of their home, yet it is the outside that makes the first impression on visitors and potential purchasers. A nondescript and neglected exterior colours our impressions of a home, even if the interior is immaculate.

Take a hard look at the front of your home from across the road. Does it look neat, cared for and welcoming, or is it untidy and ugly with dirty windows and peeling paintwork? How does it compare with adjacent properties? Is the front door easy to find? Perhaps the entrance is concealed by an extension or a garage. In some modern housing developments it can be very difficult to find your way to the front door because the properties vary in style and size, and they are all set at different angles and distances to the road. Often they are fronted by unfenced lawns, rather than individual gardens. If the front door isn't immediately obvious, visitors can feel confused and unwelcome. A clearly defined path is a good way of directing people to the front door, and a coat of brightly coloured paint will look cheerful and will also help to signal its location.

A canopy or porch makes the door look more important, and provides protection from the elements while you fumble with keys or visitors wait for you to answer the door. There are plenty of different styles, from a simple open-sided canopy to an elaborate conservatory-style structure. Choose something that complements the style, period and location of the building. Have a look at other houses in the street and remember that if you are in a conservation area or your building is listed, you will have to talk to the planning department before you make changes to the façade.

A pretty front garden or tubs of flowers or shrubs on either side of the door will look bright, cheerful and welcoming. Tumbling displays of lobelia, trailing geraniums and petunias look wonderful in spring and summer, while variegated ivy, dwarf evergreen shrubs and winter-flowering pansies can brighten the winter months. Good sized standard bay and box are expensive to buy but elegant.

The style and quality of the door and door furniture are a key element in the way that your house appears to others. Choose a good, solid door to match the period and style of your home – here again, a tour around the neighbourhood will help you decide what is appropriate. Architectural salvage merchants are a useful place to look for the 'right' door at a good price. A front door really does set the tone of a property; while a heavy panelled wood door emphasises the solidity and security of your home, a glazed door has a light, welcoming feel, and a flat, flush door with a glossy paint finish looks sleek and modern. Softwood doors need regular painting or varnishing to protect them from the elements.

Door furniture is expensive, but it is worth getting the best as it will last forever and look impressive. Unlacquered brass looks wonderful, but it needs regular polishing. Lacquered brass doesn't need polishing but the lacquer will wear off in time and the exposed brass will tarnish. The brass can, however, be cleaned and relacquered. Other choices include bronze (which is expensive), iron (which is

Checklist

traditional) and alloys, or aluminium which should be waxed or treated against oxidation. Letter-boxes (more accurately called letter plates), handles, knockers and numbers should match. Make sure the street number is large enough to be read from the street. It should be well lit at night.

Good locks are an important form of security and some insurance companies offer reduced premium rates if your door and window locks meet certain specifications. If there is a spyhole in a solid door, you can inspect callers before you open the door, while a solid chain allows you to open the door enough to talk to callers you aren't sure about. Your local crime prevention officer or neighbourhood watch coordinator are good sources of advice on home security.

FRONT DOOR

Is the front door solid and architecturally appropriate?

Is the paintwork in good condition?
Even hardwood doors need maintenance.

Are glazed panels well fitted, secure and clean?

Is the door furniture good quality and clean?

Can the door number be seen easily from the street?

Is the door secure with good locks, and does it open and close easily?

THE PORCH
Is this in good repair and painted?
Make sure that the junction between the house and the porch is watertight.

LIGHTING
Carefully postioned lights can transform a garden at night

An outside light is welcoming on dark nights, illuminates the door number and deters burglars.

THE PATH
Is the path covered with an attractive material and is it in a good state of repair?
Does it need weeding or sweeping?

Is the path well lit?

WINDOWS
Are the windows architecturally appropriate?

Are the window frames and the putty around them in good condition?

Check that windows and sheer curtains are clean.

BOUNDARY FENCES, WALLS, HEDGES AND GATES
Are fences in good repair and weatherproofed?

Are hedges trimmed and tidy?

Is the gate well-oiled and painted, and does the latch work?

GARAGE
Is this in keeping with the house?

Does the door need painting?

Check that the guttering and downpipes are clear.

Keep the door closed – it looks neater.

FRONT GARDEN
Is the grass cut and are the edges neat?

Could it be brightened up with plants and shrubs in pots, hanging baskets or window boxes?

Are dustbins clean and tidy?

Could they be stored somewhere else or be concealed behind trellis or hedging?

WINDOW BOXES
Are the sills wide enough to install window boxes?
Remember to water, trim and deadhead plants – dead and dying plants make a house look neglected.
Evergreen plants, such as ivy and box, add a splash of greenery in winter. Topiary balls and cones look neat and stylish.

'I want something that blends with the bungalow, *something that* **looks special** when you come up the close, and something that will give me *a lot of pleasure*'.

— JOYCE

the problem...

Paul and Joyce moved to Falmouth in 1978 where they ran a B&B until their retirement 18 months ago. They sold the business and moved to a pretty, two-bedroom, detached bungalow which they've spent the last year redecorating. A keen gardener, Paul spends as much time as possible in the garden, exercising his green fingers. Joyce is strictly an armchair gardener – the closest she comes to participation is watching Paul through the window! A conservatory will link the garden to the house and allow Joyce to supervise in comfort, 'If I'm in the conservatory he can get wet and I needn't', she says.

At the moment they have a tiny porch at the front door, but it isn't big enough to do anything except cut down on draughts, and possibly provide a place to leave umbrellas and muddy boots. They would like to replace this with a conservatory which would allow them to see and enjoy their lovely garden all year round. It would also add impact to the front of the house, make a grand entrance and considerably improve its 'kerb appeal'. For Paul and Joyce adding value is not a priority – this is their retirement home and they are going to indulge themselves. This is a 'lifestyle' improvement and the cost is a relatively small part of the equation.

ideas... The designer, Stephanie Dunning, decided that what they needed was a custom-built conservatory that would fit snugly into the corner between the bungalow and the garage. There are many different styles of conservatory on the market so it should be easy to find one to match the style and scale of your house. Standard shapes are rectangular, bay-ended or octagonal, and roofs can be lean-to, gabled or curved, with a choice of architectural embellishments such as lanterns, clerestories or finials. Kits come in standard shapes and sizes, but specialist firms will adapt them to suit your needs. Joyce and Paul wanted something that was modern but not too modern – and Joyce definitely didn't want 'a bobbly one'. Stephanie chose an elegantly restrained classical style that suited the scale of the bungalow.

Stephanie doesn't like south-facing conservatories – they get too hot and you need blinds which are costly, fiddly to use and can disrupt the clean lines of the structure. In this case the conservatory faces north-east and Stephanie has specified Pilkington K Glass for the inside of the sealed double-glazed units. This is a heat reflective glass which is 30 per cent more effective than normal glass units. The roof will be double-glazed, with blue-tinted solar control, toughened glass units.

Ventilation is important in conservatories to prevent condensation and the build-up of stale air. This design has ventilation integrated into the ridge, and Stephanie also specified an opening roof-light.

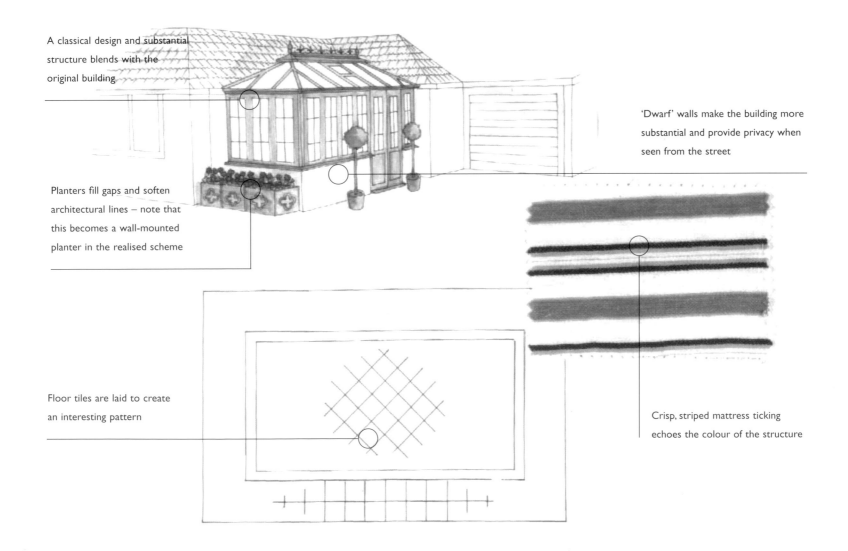

A classical design and substantial structure blends with the original building

'Dwarf' walls make the building more substantial and provide privacy when seen from the street

Planters fill gaps and soften architectural lines – note that this becomes a wall-mounted planter in the realised scheme

Floor tiles are laid to create an interesting pattern

Crisp, striped mattress ticking echoes the colour of the structure

ADRIAN & NEIL'S

DIY TIPS

Building a rough stone wall

Making a wall from a heap of randomly shaped stones is easy if you know how. The trick is to put plenty of mortar between the joints and let each stone find its niche. As you get a feel for the job, the stones seem to nestle down together and you get a smooth, professional finish

Add character to tarmac

Tarmac isn't the most beautiful material in the world, but it is hard-wearing, quick to lay and relatively inexpensive. Give it texture and colour by embedding small pebbles in the surface before it sets

the solution... Stephanie Dunning had to find a conservatory that would fit in with the style and scale of the bungalow, and wouldn't look like an afterthought. Initially, she wanted hardwood but Joyce and Paul were keen on the low maintenance qualities of uPVC. Until now uPVC conservatories have only been available in white, but Stephanie found a Cornish firm who offered uPVC in an almost limitless range of colours. The components are painted and heat sealed at the factory, and will not crack, peel or flake, so you can combine the colour of your choice with the low-maintenance qualities of uPVC. Stephanie chose a beautiful duck-egg blue, and was utterly converted.

The old porch was demolished and the foundations, concrete platform and low walls were built. Stephanie went for dwarf walls with glazing above, rather than floor to ceiling glazing, because the driveway sweeps up to the side of the house making this area highly visible from the road. The low walls give the structure a more substantial feel and also afford some privacy. 'I didn't want them to feel like they were sitting in a goldfish bowl, especially in the evenings', she says.

The conservatory was prefabricated off-site, so once the groundwork was done it came together remarkably quickly. The frame was erected on the walls and fixed into place. The roof arrived as a single unit. The whole team lent a hand to lower it into place and all of a sudden it looked like a complete building. Meanwhile the base walls were being plastered and skimmed, and the glazing was fixed in place.

The floor was then tiled in rustic-look tiling from Spain. The tiles were laid diagonally in the centre and square around the margins. A matching diamond-pattern border of small tiles was laid between the two areas to give a neat finish. This could have been a time-consuming and fiddly business, but fortunately the ready-made border is supplied on a gauze strip – so laying is quick and easy. A glazed structure can range from a greenhouse to a living room which is an integral part of the house or an extension of an existing room. In this case the room was outside the main structure, a transitional area between the inside and outside. Stephanie chose tough, frost-proof

tiles, so that Paul could use the room as a traditional plant house for potting, keeping tender plants in winter, and bringing on seeds and cuttings.

The low retaining wall on the right of the drive was moved back about a foot to ensure there was still access to the garage. Once the major components were in place and the really heavy traffic was finished, the driveway was torn up and re-laid with tarmac. Finally, all the outside walls of the bungalow and the conservatory were given a lick of paint, and the window frames on the main building were also painted.

Door options

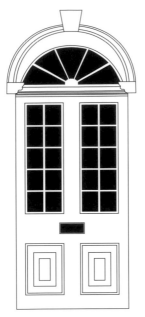

Georgian door
with fanlight above

Victorian panelled door

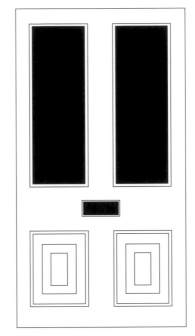

Panelled door with glazing

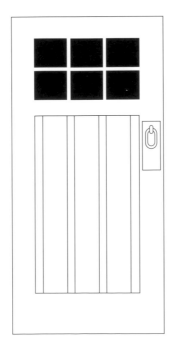

Arts and crafts-style door

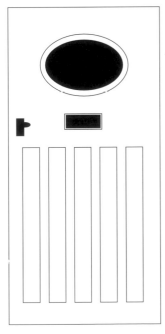

1930s door with oval window

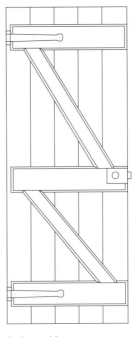

Ledge and brace
cottage-style door

Planning

- Check with the planning office first – planning permission is not usually necessary
- Kit conservatories come with plans and specifications which you can submit to the planning office
- Large, specialist conservatory firms often undertake to get planning and building permissions for you
- Planning regulations do not usually permit conservatories to be used for bedrooms, kitchens or bathrooms
- If you need to create a new opening you will need to consult the local building inspector

Construction

- Conservatories require a concrete base which should be damp-proofed and insulated
- The junction between the house and the conservatory must be properly weatherproofed with flashing
- Rainwater must be disposed of. Check with the building inspector to see if you are permitted to add the water to the house drainage system – if not you will need a soak-away in the garden

Living under glass

Although the Romans introduced the use of glass in windows, it wasn't until the early nineteenth century that the production of sheet glass was mastered. The combination of large, strong panes of glass and the flexibility of cast iron produced a revolution in building design and allowed Victorian engineers to erect complex structures easily, quickly and at very little cost. The combination of glass and iron was used for walls and roofs in railway stations, exhibition halls and art galleries throughout the country. The most famous glass building of all was the Crystal Palace built in Hyde Park to house the Great Exhibition of 1851 – and later moved to Sydenham in south London, where it was destroyed by fire in 1936. It was designed by Joseph Paxton (1803-1865) on a piece of blotting paper during a meeting of a railway company in Derby. (This original sketch is preserved in the print room at the Victoria & Albert Museum.) It was entirely constructed of standardised, pre-fabricated units. It was the largest building ever erected – 1,600ft (488 m) long and 770,000 square ft (71,610 sq m) in area. These developments in glass and iron structures coincided with a popular interest in plants of all types, but especially exotic species like palms, ferns and orchids. Every suburban villa had its plant house, while botanical gardens like Kew in London had magnificent light-filled buildings to provide a home for the species being brought back from faraway places by intrepid plant hunters. As Joyce and Paul's conservatory demonstrates, glass continues to provide a quick, cheap and very beautiful way of adding flexible space, and improving the appearance of your home.

'The bungalow is a well-maintained two-bedroom property and these are at a premium around here. It was valued at £78,000 when we started, and with the conservatory it is valued at £85,000, an increase of £7,000. The conservatory has added to the quality of Paul and Joyce's life, and has also added value to an already attractive property – if it came onto the market it would be snapped up straight away. The porch and conservatory gilds an already attractive lily.'

— Michael O'Flaherty

Stephanie Dunning's top tips
- Avoid building a conservatory on the south side of the house – you'll roast in summer
- Double glazing will retain heat in winter and will allow you to grow a wider range of plants
- Make sure your conservatory has plenty of ventilation

1 The dwarf walls provide a sill around three sides of the structure – useful for displaying plants

2 A wall-mounted water feature provides a visual focus and a soothing background sound

3 Ivy will trail down the walls, creating a natural green wall-hanging

4 Lantern style wall lights provide a subtle and welcoming light

5 These sturdy but stylish chairs are imported from Italy. Made from woven twine, they have a light and natural feel, ideal for a conservatory setting. Cushions pick up the pretty blue-green used for the conservatory

6 A wall-mounted window box softens the architectural form and will also help to screen the interior

7 The duck-egg blue used for the framework and glazing bars is attractive but not intrusive. The colour was applied to the uPVC components at the factory

8 Pebbles embedded in asphalt add colour, texture and interest

9 Coinciding roof-lines help unify bungalow and extension

Sally and Graham's ten-year-old house has **everything** – four bedrooms, a brilliant location, and inside it was beautifully decorated. **But** before you could appreciate all that, you had to traverse the neat but rather barren front garden. In the **'kerb appeal'** stakes it scored **zero** – *until Toby Buckland and his merry team took it in hand.*

the problem... Sally and Graham moved to their pretty cottage three years ago. Graham works at a school for children with special needs and Sally was a teacher until she retired. Inside, their house is spick and span, but their large front garden is in need of attention.

Graham has done quite a lot of work, laying herringbone pavers on the drive, creating a slab path and a well-groomed lawn – but as he says: 'I've turned it into the grounds of a crematorium. It is all a bit barren and needs livening up'. Sally believes that the front garden sets the tone

for the rest of the house; it provides a setting, and gives it what Michael O'Flaherty refers to as 'kerb appeal'. Well, their present, rather bleak garden certainly looks neat, but it has none of the charm of the English country garden which Sally could see so clearly in her mind's eye.

ideas... Sally wanted 'An English country garden please', and Graham liked the 'idea of a village pond with a weeping willow falling into it'. After a lengthy consultation, Toby Buckland decided to base the garden on a village green theme. His plan was to break up the relentlessly rectilinear geometry of the garden with changes of scale, shape, texture and height. A garden like this must work from several viewpoints – from the road, from the lower and upper windows of the house, and from points within the garden itself. The garden breaks down into three principal areas. From the entrance gates the paver drive leads to the garage, and a circle of granite setts arranged around a granite millstone marks the beginning of the paths that lead to the front and side doors. The front door and the route to it should be clearly signalled, or visitors will feel confused and unwelcome. The next area is the complex of ornamental water features on the right side of the garden. This is the core of the scheme and is designed to provide interest from every angle and in every season. The third area is the patio tucked away in a sheltered spot around the side of the house. When the planting around the pergola matures, it will screen this area and provide privacy.

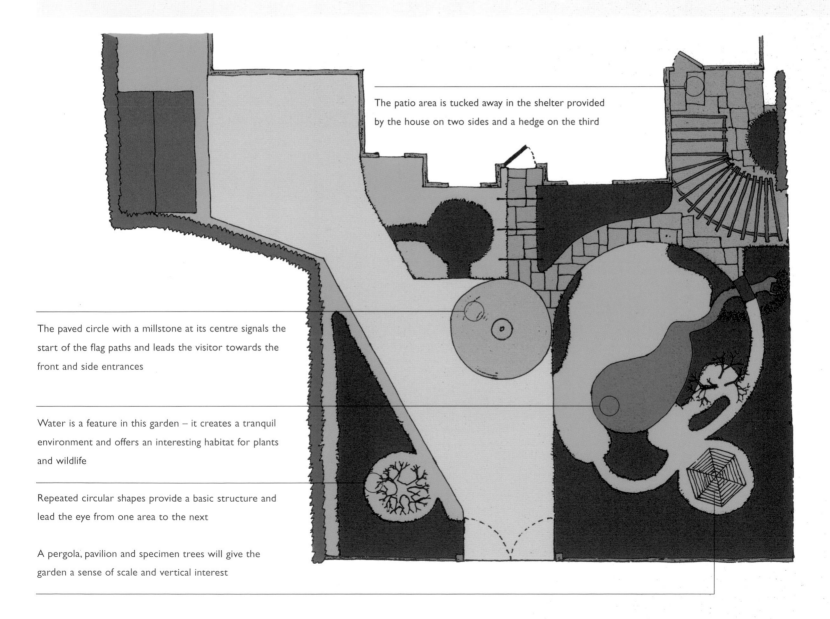

The patio area is tucked away in the shelter provided by the house on two sides and a hedge on the third

The paved circle with a millstone at its centre signals the start of the flag paths and leads the visitor towards the front and side entrances

Water is a feature in this garden – it creates a tranquil environment and offers an interesting habitat for plants and wildlife

Repeated circular shapes provide a basic structure and lead the eye from one area to the next

A pergola, pavilion and specimen trees will give the garden a sense of scale and vertical interest

ADRIAN & NEIL'S

DIY TIPS

Supplying power to the garden

If you need power in the garden – for lighting or a workshop – you must have it installed by a qualified electrician. Toby advises that power cables should be laid as deep as possible. Here they dug down three feet, back-filled with one foot of soil and then laid bright yellow warning tape. Anyone coming across this in the future will know that there are power cables one foot below. You should also run your cables close to the walls of the house or around the perimeter of the garden because that is where builders will expect to find services and will therefore dig with caution

Creating a dry stone wall

The trick is to find the right stone and move it around until it settles. Lay your stones out so that you pick and choose. You'll soon get an eye for what shapes slot together. If some seem a little unstable you can bond them at the back with cement like you would with a normal wall, but really gravity should be sufficient

the solution...

The location of all the main features was set out, the turf was removed and the hole for the pond and stream were dug. At the same time, trenches were dug for the electrical cable, so at times the garden looked like it had been used for tank manoeuvres. The pond was lined and the paths and other paved areas were laid. A major feature was the pergola near the patio by the back door. Sally had craved a pergola since a visit to Cyprus. Not only does it make a feature of the patio, but it will also provide privacy and shelter and make that area more useable. Six huge granite boulders each weighing around a tonne were distributed in and around the pond to improve the topography of the garden. Their sheer bulk gave the garden a sense of scale,

counteracted the flatness of the terrain and suggested wilderness and nature. A bold statement like this can transform a space and at relatively little cost.

Graham had expressed a yearning for a weeping willow, but Toby vetoed that as they are notorious for their vigorous and invasive root systems, and are not a good idea near the foundations of your house. Instead he chose semi-mature Himalyan birches (*Betula jacquemonti*), which have a similar delicacy, light green foliage and very white trunks which look striking in a winter or summer setting. When you are planting a new garden it is worth splashing out on a few mature specimens to give the planting a bit of a head start.

With the main structures and features in place, it was beginning to look like a garden, and the planting could begin. There was a large area to fill, even with much of the ground area taken up with paving and water. Toby allocated the plants around the beds and his team got on with digging them in. The eye finds symmetry disconcerting, especially in a natural setting, so it's important to remember to arrange your plants in groupings of uneven numbers, threes, fives, sevens and so on. This will have a more natural feel, and will produce drifts of colour along the edges. Don't plant bedding plants singly, they will look like blobs; think in terms of broad masses of colour and texture.

Toby has given structure to a flat, rectangular and rather boring space, using a framework of paved areas and paths, a pond and a stream, and the bulk of the granite boulders. A clever combination of natural materials including granite setts, an old millstone, some massive boulders, a timber pergola and wattle fencing provide texture and colour, and the natural and timeless feel that he felt Sally and Graham were after. In time the planting will provide mass, year-round colour and texture and will soften and blend the underlying structures. Even in its immature state the garden provided plenty to delight the eye, but when the team returned the following summer it had already begun to fill in and look established.

Outside lighting

Artificial lighting is an invaluable and often neglected aspect of a garden. In a large front garden it can be used to light the route to the front door at night – giving the house a bright, welcoming aspect for visitors. Courtesy lights with sensors will turn on automatically as people approach, providing useful illumination for visitors and a deterrent for would-be burglars. Ground level spotlighting can be used to highlight a few key features. Use low-voltage sets of mini-floodlights or mini-posts to create diffuse lighting around the garden, and especially in sitting or eating areas. Lights can also be used to illuminate water features, but they must be correctly installed by experts because the combination of electricity and water is potentially lethal.

Toby Buckland's top tips for gardens

- Think about where the sun rises and sets and position patios, features and plants accordingly
- Plant semi-mature trees if you are not planning to stay in the house for long, or you want to make an instant difference to your garden – but remember to keep well watered
- Use natural stone in gardens where you can, instead of concrete imitation stone, as it changes colour with changes in the light and moisture, is tactile and lasts forever
- Consider installing outside spotlights so that you can use your garden at night. Depending on the season the features you want to light will change – winter stems, eating areas, borders of bedding– so design flexibility into schemes with all seasons in mind

1 When the climbers have grown the pergola will screen the patio area

2 A waterfall brings the tinkling sound of moving water into the garden

3 The variety of stone surfaces is a feature of this garden and includes a dry stone wall, a bridge, a granite slab path and the huge boulders set into the pond

4 Semi-mature trees provide colour and scale while the rest of the garden grows in

5 In winter the red stems of Cornus or Dogwood will provide a splash of colour, the impact magnified by their reflections in the pool

6 Toby has softened the planting around the pool with *Stipa arundinacea*, a tufted grass with feathery plumes

7 A snaking mound of gravel gives the pool a natural and decorative edge

8 Wattle fencing gives a soft, rustic feel to the scheme

9 A rustic pavilion provides a secluded retreat and a focal point

Water features

Water has featured in all the great gardens of history. The gardens of ancient Persia were a refuge from the harsh desert conditions beyond the wall and a pool was always the centrepiece. Water was carried by subterranean aqueducts from distant foothills. Trees provided shelter from the burning sun and the play of shadows and light reflected on the water's surface was a theme in prose and verse descriptions of these oases of beauty. The gardens of Renaissance Italy featured elaborate cascades, fountains and sculptured basins. Probably the best known water gardens are those built for Louis XIV at Versailles. They feature canals, basins and sculptured fountains that still dazzle the visitor. Over one million gallons of water are required to supply the 50 fountains and 620 fountain nozzles for one hour. There has been a resurgence of interest in water features and they can now be incorporated quite easily into the smallest plot. To create the illusion of a natural millstream emerging from the fields beyond the garden, Toby placed a large pump in the pond. This pumps water up to a small reservoir behind the drystone wall so that water cascades over the stone weir.

Every household is different and makes very specific demands on the kitchen. Spend time getting the concept and layout right before you commit to spending a lot of money.

k i t c h e n s

planning your kitchen

A new kitchen adds value to a house and makes it more saleable, but the most important consideration is: will it make your life easier and more enjoyable? If the answer is 'yes', you need to set yourself a realistic budget based on your means, the value of the house and the length of time you intend to stay there. If you intend to move on in a few years you must think especially carefully about your expenditure. Although a new kitchen does add value to your home, it rarely adds as much as the kitchen cost. And remember that your successors may have very different tastes and needs and your dream kitchen may not appeal to them at all. Of all the areas in the home, the kitchen is the most responsive to fashion trends, and is therefore the most likely to date. An 80s country-style kitchen with rustic pine doors now looks as outdated as a minimalist stainless steel kitchen will look in a few years' time.

The kitchen is a complex workspace into which you have to fit several large items of different shapes and sizes – a cooker, fridge, dishwasher, work surfaces, storage space, sink – in the most efficient way possible. You are restricted by various factors including the shape and size of the room, and the location of structural elements like windows, doors and chimney breasts. Electric sockets and plumbing also have to be taken into account.

Preparing a meal can be broken down into four processes: food storage; food preparation; cooking; washing up. These processes are carried out most efficiently in a well-planned kitchen. Layout is more important than size – a small, well-planned kitchen will be much easier to use than a large, poorly planned one.

Time and motion studies have shown that certain kitchen layouts give the cook a logical work sequence with a minimum of legwork. The 'work triangle' is a concept which organises the main work areas so that the cook can proceed from one activity to the next, in an unbroken sequence. The sequence is fridge/worktop/sink/worktop/cooker and hob/worktop. This sequence works from left to right and is designed for a right-handed person. If you are left-handed you may want to reverse the order. The distance between each work zone should be at least 35in (900mm). The ideal total length is 23ft (7m). The dimensions of the triangle vary with the size and shape of the room, and the arrangement of the work zones, but the basic concept can be applied to any kitchen.

The six classic kitchen layouts are: the U-shaped kitchen, the L-shaped kitchen, the island, the peninsula, the single galley and the double galley. These layouts are described and illustrated opposite. Most efficient kitchens conform to one of these layouts.

Checklist

ACTIVITIES

Do you intend to eat in the kitchen – sometimes or all the time?

Do you want a proper dining area with a full-size table?

Will the children use it for homework?

Will the family 'live' in the kitchen – do you need easy chairs, a television or a radio?

Do you want to do washing and ironing in the kitchen?

SPACE

Is the kitchen large enough?

Can you acquire more space – from an adjacent room or by extending?

Can you create space by moving a large item like a washing machine, freezer or boiler into another area such as a utility room or a garage?

Are there too many doors and windows taking up valuable wall space? Consider blocking off redundant doorways

EQUIPMENT CHOICES

Cooker: free-standing, slide-in, built-in oven and separate hob? Extractor: vented out or recycling? Separate fridge and freezer? Microwave? Sink: single, double, extra half-sink? Waste disposal unit? Dishwasher? One drainer, two drainers, wall-mounted draining rack?

LIGHTING

Plan for:

general lighting, worktop lighting, spotlights, under cupboard lighting, lighting for the dining area

STORAGE

Which of the following do you want?

Corner cupboards with swing-out racks? Tall cupboards for brooms and other cleaning equipment?
Drawers for cutlery and utensils?
Undersink storage for cleaning materials.
Deep drawers or cupboards for pots and pans – ideally near the cooker?
Surface for toaster and coffee maker – away from the main cooking area?
Open, shallow shelves for jars of dry produce, bottles of oils etc?
Shelves for cookery books?
Narrow shelves for jars of spices?
Wine racks?

KITCHEN LAYOUT

Group dishwasher, washing machine and sinks together to simplify plumbing.
Group tall cupboards and units together so that they don't interrupt the work surface.
Place the sink under a window to give you a view as you work.
Make sure that there is a work area on either side of the cooker and the sink.
Avoid placing the hob under a window – the breeze may blow out a gas flame, and fabrics such as blinds or curtains may catch fire.

An L-shaped kitchen

Kitchen units and appliances are ranged along two adjacent sides of a room. This is a useful solution for a large room, especially if you want to incorporate a separate dining area.

A U-shaped kitchen

Kitchen units and appliances are ranged in a continuous sequence along three sides of the room. In a small kitchen make sure there is at least 2m in the middle. In long, thin rooms, or very large kitchens the work triangle should be restricted to the bottom of the U.

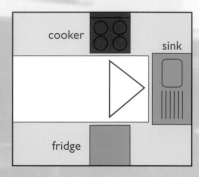

The island kitchen

An island can be introduced into a large U-shaped or L-shaped kitchen to give a more compact work triangle. A table that is used for preparation or a moveable butcher's block is technically an island. The island should be at least 60cm x 90cm (24in x 35in) and not more than 120cm square (47in).

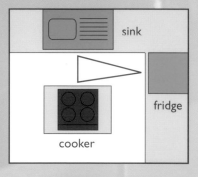

The peninsula kitchen

This is another way of creating a compact kitchen area in a large room. The jutting arm can be used as a breakfast bar or to house one of the key components.

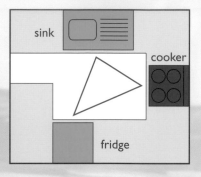

Double galley kitchen

If there are doors or tall windows at either end of a room you can arrange the units along facing walls. There must be at least 1.2m (4ft) between base units to allow doors to swing open and to allow access to under-worktop storage.

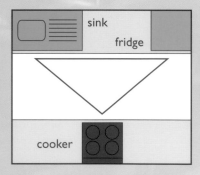

Single galley kitchen

In this plan the components form a single line giving a shallow work triangle. It can be slotted into a very narrow space – in a converted hallway for example.

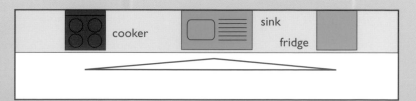

NOTTINGHAM | KATHY AND MARTIN'S KITCHEN

'We want it really modern and space age
... *a kitchen that nobody else has got.*'

— KATHY

kitchens

the problem... Kathy and Martin and their daughters Lisa, Jessica and Paula have lived in their three-bedroom semi-detached house for 13 years. They bought it from the council a year ago and since then they have decorated the entire house in their own highly distinctive style, with bright colours and bold design statements. All the rooms except the kitchen, that is. They are very clear about what they want – a kitchen that is 'really modern and space age ... a kitchen that nobody else has got', with lots of stainless steel and chrome and gleaming surfaces. The girls wanted 'something that says "wow!" when you walk in'. Kathy felt that it would increase the value of the house because a state-of-the-art kitchen is such a strong selling point. Kathy and Martin were fortunate in their designer, Orianna Fielding Banks, who is renowned for her funky designs which play off the qualities of different materials.

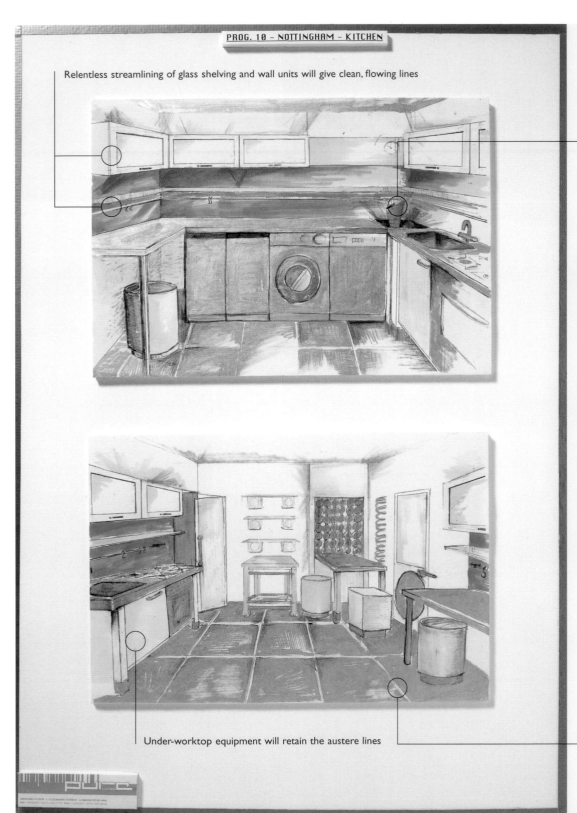

Relentless streamlining of glass shelving and wall units will give clean, flowing lines

This clever recessed storage area will use otherwise 'dead' space

Under-worktop equipment will retain the austere lines

Stainless steel tiles will contribute to the gleaming 'space age' look

ideas... One of the most important things a good designer must do is assess the client, and elicit from them what they really want. There is no point steam-rolling a client into agreement – they will never be happy. A glance at Kathy and Martin's house gave Orianna plenty of clues and as for Kathy's hair – 'I have had my hair all sorts of colours: red, pink, blue, and last summer I had it yellow which was rather embarrassing because it looked like a large dandelion and bees kept landing in it'. Her recent bright blue rinse was a visual clue which an alert Orianna took on board. Orianna decided to go for simple, clean lines and to set these off with stunning surfaces, materials and colours: stainless steel, sandblasted glass, acrylic, metallic lustre paints and lots of reflective surfaces. It's a style Orianna describes as 'modern with a serious twist'. The kitchen will be practical, colourful and fun – a place to eat, meet and entertain.

ADRIAN & NEIL'S

DIY TIPS

Fixing a batten

When fixing battens to a wall, people often pre-drill the batten and drill the hole in the wall afterwards. This can cause the batten to shift and twist. What you should do is drill straight through the batten and into the wall in one go, then you put the rawlplug into the hole and knock it in. Put the screw into the rawlplug, screw it in, and you have a perfect fixing

Fixing door furniture

Softwood frames are inclined to split when you fix hinges or locks. You can prevent this by chiselling out a snug seating for the metalwork. Work carefully, removing the wood to the depth you need to produce a snug fit

Safety

Wear a mask for dust-generating jobs like demolition

the solution... The existing units were stripped out, and the electrics and plumbing got underway. Builder Dave Wellman knocked a hole from the kitchen into the adjacent conservatory, and installed a supporting lintel. The aperture was to accommodate a 'push-me pull-you' table that could slide back and forth between the kitchen and conservatory.

Orianna had specified the dimensions of each of the kitchen units very precisely. She recommends that you measure your largest saucepan and your tallest jar to make sure that they fit into the storage space, and don't forget to allow for any new accessories you're thinking about buying. She had devised a wonderfully futuristic splashback using a blue, cast Perspex mirror. This wasn't fixed directly to the wall but was attached to battens to create a space to run all the electrical cabling. Always allow plenty of room for electrical cables, and gas and water pipes. The Perspex makes a brilliant splashback – it is the blue that Kathy wants, it will reflect the light back, and it is really easy to wipe down.

A kitchen is a heavy traffic area so flooring must be non-slip, easy to clean and hard wearing. Orianna chose stainless steel tiles which had an industrial, high-tech feel. Rubber matting was used to level off the floor and provide insulation. The ceilings and walls were painted with water-resistant paint so that they could be wiped down – essential in kitchens and bathrooms.

A continuous, sandblasted glass shelf was installed above the work surface echoing the horizontal lines of the work surface and the pale wood cupboards above. In the corner there is a cunning piece of design. Where the two surfaces meet you tend to get a dead area – under-counter shelves which are inaccessible. To exploit this potentially lost space, Orianna has dropped a box into

the work-surface and lined it with glass tiles which have an oxidised finish which is almost iridescent. This provides a neat compartment for bottles and other things which might clutter the worktop.

Next the gleaming space-age oven, hob, dishwasher, washing machine, fridge and freezer were installed – giving the kitchen that all-of-a-piece, high-tech, streamlined look.

Lighting in kitchens is often rather functional – here the combination of clever lighting and reflective surfaces creates a sense of airiness and space. It is a place where people will feel comfortable and want to linger.

A push-me pull-you table

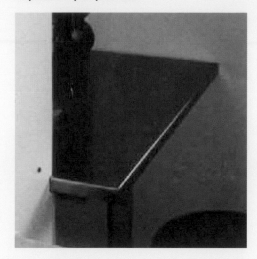

One of the many unusual elements in an unusual kitchen was a metallic table which could slide from the conservatory into the kitchen through a hole in the wall. This simple but efficient piece of furniture meant that the family could eat in the kitchen or the conservatory, but didn't have to waste space with two tables. Dave Wellman needed to knock a hole in the wall so that the table could run backwards and forwards. The wall above had to be supported on two four-inch lintels. He knocked out one side for the first lintel, leaving two bricks in the middle to support the wall above temporarily. Once the first lintel was in and fixed, they could carefully remove the bricks and fix the lintel in the other side. Then they could chop out the wall below. If you want to do something similar you should (a) first consult your building officer and (b) hire a professional builder. 'With this sort of structural work, money paid now is always money saved later,' says Welly.

Radiating style

In the past a radiator was simply a metal panel containing water that gave out heat. Now they can be an eye-catching feature, a design statement and a talking point. There is a bewildering choice available and looking through the catalogues or visiting a showroom is more like visiting an art gallery, with the brightly coloured and fantastically shaped radiators displayed like sculptures. To start with, these alternative radiators were aimed at the top end of the market and had dizzying price tickets. Now, however, many are available at quite sensible prices, although you can still get couture radiators designed to fit a specific space. In kitchens you need all the wall space you can get for equipment, shelving and wall-mounted units. Ladder, column and other vertical radiators are economical on horizontal space. Orianna installed an aptly named 'Hot Springs' radiator by Bisque Radiators in Kathy and Martin's kitchen.

**Orianna Fielding Banks' top tips
for kitchens**

• If you're building new storage, measure your largest saucepan and your tallest jar to make sure that they will fit into the storage space

• Kitchens are heavy traffic areas so choose flooring that is non-slip, easy to clean and hard wearing

1 **A sandblasted glass shelf combines transparency and texture**

2 **A Perspex mirror in a vibrant turquoise gives a large area of colour, reflects light and is easy to wipe down**

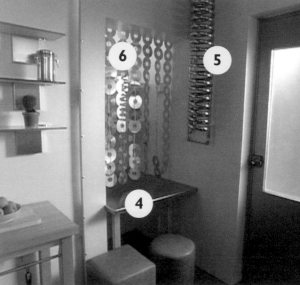

3 **Under-counter fridge, freezer and larder maintain the predominantly horizontal lines**

4 **A push-me pull-you table can be used in the kitchen or the conservatory**

5 **A vertical radiator uses valuable wall space efficiently, its sculptural lines are eye-catching and highly decorative**

6 **An eye-catching screen made from CDs creates dancing light and colour**

HALIFAX | AINE MARIE'S KITCHEN

A bit of thought and **a lot of work** transformed Aine Marie's kitchen *– and her life!*

kitchens

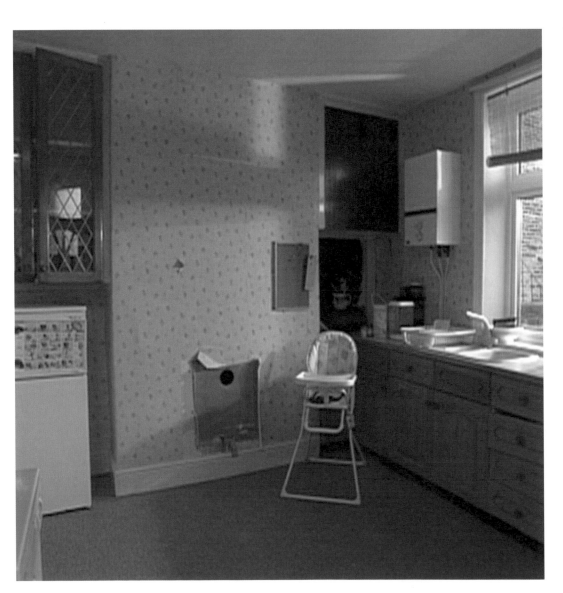

the problem... Aine Marie has lived in a typical turn of the century worker's cottage in Halifax, Yorkshire, for 18 months. She comes from this part of the world and her family still live close by. She has two children: Robyn, who is five and Sean, who is six months old. Aine works as a customer liaison officer. She loves living in this street but she passionately hates certain parts of her house, especially her kitchen. In fact, she hates everything about it: 'I never use it, it is badly designed, the wallpaper is horrible, the light switch is in the wrong place, the drawers are broken, the water heater is broken and when the toilet is flushed or the water is run, it screeches.' Apart from that, the kitchen was simply out of date, with worn out appliances and shelves and cupboards which are inconvenient and unattractive. When Aine is working in the kitchen there is nowhere for young Robyn to play. What she'd like is a comfortable family kitchen where they could have their meals, she could feed Sean, and Robyn could do her homework.

ideas... Stephanie Dunning decided to make this kitchen into a family room everyone could use. She wanted the kitchen to be stylish, practical and hard-wearing – a space where Aine could entertain guests, work efficiently and relax in comfort with her children. She decided to build an island to take the washing machine, and to knock out the chimney breast to create space for the oven and hob. This rationalisation will create space at one end for a table and chairs where the family can eat, and Robyn can sit and do her homework while Aine gets on with her chores without worrying about what the children are up to. The look will be traditional with a Belfast sink, a range-look treatment of the oven and hob, and Shaker-style units. The colour palette will be light and bright – pale floors and worktops and light yellow walls with an accent of contrasting 'Monet' blue.

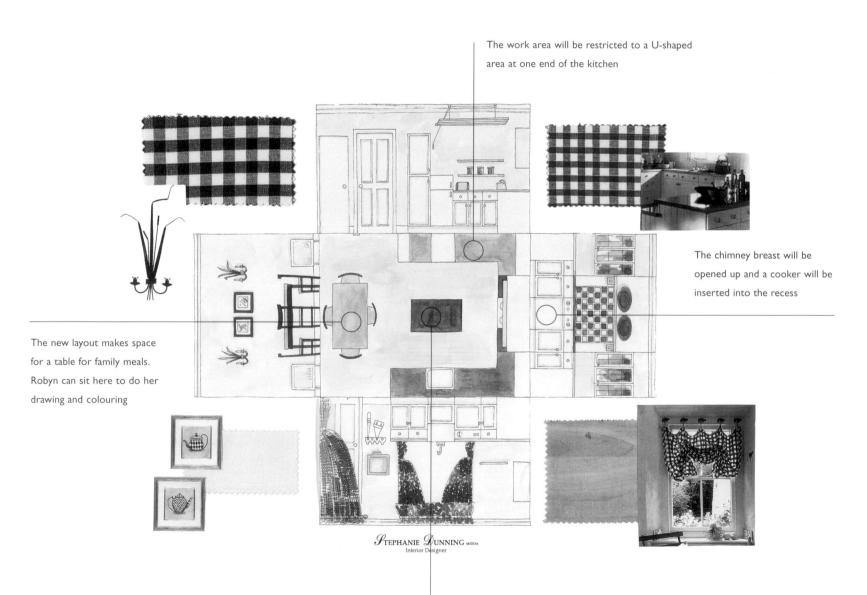

The work area will be restricted to a U-shaped area at one end of the kitchen

The chimney breast will be opened up and a cooker will be inserted into the recess

The new layout makes space for a table for family meals. Robyn can sit here to do her drawing and colouring

STEPHANIE DUNNING MIDDA
Interior Designer

An island will provide extra worksurface and a convenient location for the washing machine

ADRIAN & NEIL'S DIY TIPS

Safe and accurate hammering

Keep your thumb on the back of the hammer shaft – this grip gives you more control and prevents you bringing your hand back too far. And if you hold a nail between your fingers with the palm up it won't hurt quite as much if/when you hit yourself

the solution... Things always get worse before they get better, so the kitchen went from tatty to completely derelict as the units and carpet were ripped out, walls were stripped and Dave Wellman set about the chimney breast. A chimney is a substantial structure, so a lintel has to be inserted to support the chimney breast in the floor above. Opening up the chimney provided a neat niche for the oven and hob. Next they had to knock through the outside wall to provide venting for the new boiler which will replace Aine's 'screeching' and inefficient model. A great deal of time and effort had been expended at this stage and the kitchen looked like a building site. Be prepared for this if you take on a similar renovation – it can be very disheartening.

Aine remembers her family's old black range with affection. It was the heart of the family kitchen, provided constant hot water and they even used to dry their clothes on it. Stephanie didn't give Aine a range because it would be too expensive to run. Instead she has given her a wonderful slab of granite which has the blackness of the old range, is gorgeous to look at and very convenient – you can put hot pans on it and it won't burn. The granite is slotted into the chimney breast and a hole is cut out to take the hob – it's a slab of pure luxury.

A new tongue and groove laminated floor was laid, and a central island was built to make use of the 'dead' space in the middle of the room and keep the functional part of the kitchen at one end of the room. The washing machine was hidden away under the island. Stephanie installed Shaker-style kitchen units in a pale cream, uninterrupted runs of pale birch worktop, and a big, solid Belfast sink which is practical and has an old-world charm.

Lighting was provided by lots of twinkling downlighters recessed into a new ceiling. The walls were colourwashed with a sunny yellow, while the walls behind the hob were tiled with blue and yellow Provençal tiles. The transformation was complete. By assessing Aine's needs and making the most of the available space, Stephanie has created an attractive and efficient kitchen which is also a warm, welcoming and practical family room.

Kitchen layout

Stephanie has based Aine's kitchen on a variation of the classic U-shaped kitchen in which the units and appliances are ranged in a continuous sequence along three sides of the room. By grouping the working areas at one end of the kitchen, she has left the other end clear for a table at which Robyn can work and the family can eat. She has also kept the work area away from the two doors and out of the way of passing traffic. The island provides a useful location for the washing machine, and sensibly places it near the sink to simplify plumbing. By placing a tall cupboard and fridge at the end of one leg of the U she creates an uninterrupted work surface.

Blue and white

Blue and white is one of the most popular colour combinations in traditional kitchens. It has long been used in tiles and ceramics, from the intricate tile art of the Islamic world, to Chinese porcelain, Delft tiles and Wedgwood's jasper ware. The popular Chinoiserie design known as willow pattern did not come from the Orient, but was devised by Thomas Turner of Caughley in about 1780 in response to the fashion for Oriental-style objects and patterns. It was immediately copied by other manufacturers and by the nineteenth century the elements had become standardised. The now ubiquitous willlow pattern consists of a three-arched bridge, an overhanging willow tree, three Chinese figures crossing the bridge, a pagoda, two birds in flight and a boat. At the end of the nineteenth century no 'artistic' home was complete without a display of blue and white ginger jars and blue and white still accounts for more than 70 per cent of all commercial pottery production.

1   A tall cupboard and the fridge freezer are grouped together so that they don't interrupt the run of the work surface

2   A sink placed under the window gives Aine a view as she works

3   A bright, sunny yellow gives the kitchen a cheerful aspect – the colour is balanced by blue and white accents throughout

4   A 'portiere' curtain over the outside door will cut down draughts in winter time

Stephanie Dunning's top tips for kitchens

• Utilise the space. A utensil hanger is a great storage solution for small spaces

• If you have rough wall surfaces always line the walls with lining paper before decorating

• A vinyl wood-plank effect floor is great for kitchens – it's easy to clean, kind to the feet and forgiving of dropped china!

• If you like the idea of using granite in the kitchen, remember that is quite expensive. As an alternative try a manufactured granite-effect material. These are cheaper, easy to clean and almost as hard-wearing

5   Bulrush wall sconces provide atmospheric lighting in the table area; the decorative fittings separate this area from the more functional areas of the kitchen

6   Black marble on the island and in the cooking area are both practical and luxurious

7   Blue and white gingham is clean, crisp and timeless

8   Blue and yellow were the colours used in the artist Claude Monet's (1840-1926) sunny kitchen at Giverny

Claire and Colin wanted a kitchen that was **bright,** *airy* **and very contemporary,** and more storage space, and that is precisely what designer Genevieve Hurley gave them.

the problem... Claire and Colin met while working as representatives for Club 18-3O and moved to Swinton in Greater Manchester a year and a half ago when Claire was nine months pregnant with their daughter Lola. Colin now works on oil rigs and is away two weeks at a time, while Claire has given up working as a holiday rep to be a full-time mother. They both spend any spare time they have doing up their home and they've already 'done' the lounge, Lola's bedroom and their own bedroom. The next room on their hit list is the kitchen. It is cramped, badly designed and simply not to their taste, which is for the bright, colourful and uncluttered. The only item they actually want to keep is a wall-mounted utensil hanger in plain chrome and steel.

Small spots on a track
provide flexible lighting

An uninterrupted run of worktop gives clean
lines and plenty of preparation space.
The cooker is placed at the end of the narrow
kitchen to give an efficient work triangle

ideas... Genevieve Hurley, assisted by
Zoë Gingel had their work cut out, but
Claire and Colin had given them plenty of
clues. In the rest of the house they had
chosen bright colours, emphatic shapes,
clean lines and an understated, unfussy
look. They have two dogs and a very
young daughter, so practicality, cleanliness
and safety are also a consideration. They
had also expressed a strong preference for
the high-tech good looks of stainless steel
which is the look of the moment. It was a
relatively narrow space so Genevieve
decided to go for clean lines and
simplicity, given a bit of zest with a
vibrant apple green on the walls and
ceiling. By entirely reorganising the space,
getting rid of a tall fridge-freezer that
blocked a lot of light from one of the
windows and replacing it with a new
undercounter fridge she was able to bring
in more light and create a less cluttered
look. Even a relatively small kitchen can
be made to work well if it is carefully
planned. The kitchen is long and narrow
and Genevieve placed the cooker at the far
end, with the sink under the window on
the long side. This kept the door end free,
and allowed space for a really clever, wall-
hung fold down table.

ADRIAN & NEIL'S DIY TIPS

Filling with plaster

Often when you are filling holes with plaster, you find that the plaster falls out as fast as you put it in. The trick is to get the angle of the blade right. Hold the blade at about 45 degrees and press as you pull it across the hole. You'll find that you don't pull out what you have already put in. As the plaster starts to go off, put your knife into water and run it across the surface of the plaster to smooth it – it won't need quite so much sanding

the solution... The original fitted kitchen was out-dated and short on storage space – a common complaint in many homes. Because there weren't enough powerpoints in the kitchen, some of their appliances lived in the garage. Claire disliked the back door and the windows were rotting and falling apart. There wasn't really anything that could be salvaged so the kitchen was completely gutted – it only took 15 minutes to strip out the units, which were hardly attached to the walls at all. With the old units in the skip and the kitchen stripped bare Genevieve Hurley had a blank canvas to work with. A new ceiling was put in, rotten windows were replaced and the walls and ceiling were painted bright apple green,

with a lighter tone on the ceiling to give a sense of height. Claire and Colin like stainless steel so Genevieve sourced stainless a steel hob, oven, freezer, and dishwasher. She also found some stainless steel worktop savers – these are useful for putting hot pans on. Possibly the most exciting find was the aluminium tiles, which are handmade from recycled drink cans in Mexico. Not only do they look wonderful, but they are also ecologically sound because they re-use waste materials.

Genevieve included several rather special features in this kitchen. There was the integral water filter which means you can get cold water, hot water, or filtered water at the turn of a tap. A wall-mounted fold-away table provided a space-efficient work or eating surface – ideal for a rather narrow kitchen. A lockable kitchen safe was installed where poisonous and caustic cleaning materials could be stored out of harm's way.

A slate-effect porcelain floor finished off the room. The tiles have an uneven 'riven' surface which emulates slate and makes them non-slip, an important consideration in a busy kitchen.

The finished kitchen was sleek, practical and light-filled. Claire and Colin were absolutely delighted and couldn't believe how much Genevieve had managed to pack into what had seemed a very confined space.

Safety in the kitchen

Statistics show that your home is a dangerous place and the kitchen is the place where most accidents happen. If you have a good work triangle, plenty of well thought-out storage, and plenty of easy-to-clean work surfaces, your kitchen will be a safer place.

A modern kitchen is full of electrical appliances. Ensure that there are plenty of sockets, that equipment is in good repair, and that there are no trailing or frayed leads. If you are rewiring your kitchen or installing new powerpoints, have the electrical system tested by an NICEIC-registered electrician, especially in older houses.

Make sure that leads don't trail near heat sources, or trail over work surfaces where they can be grabbed by a small child. If you have a young family it is important to childproof your kitchen. A guard rail around the hob is a good idea, and choose solid wide-based saucepans and use them on the back burners if small children are around.

Deep frying is particularly dangerous and causes a great many kitchen fires. If the pan does catch fire turn off the heat and cover the pan with a lid, a heat-proof plate, a fire blanket or a damp cloth. If you exclude air the fire will go out. Don't throw water over the pan, don't open a door or window and don't try to carry the pan outside. Leave the pan to cool before you remove the cover.

If you have young children fit childproof locks on cupboards and drawers. A lockable safe cage under the sink can be used to store poisonous household cleaning products – they are available from good DIY stores and are easily fitted.

1

1 Slate-look porcelain tiles have a 'riven', non-slip surface

2 A stainless steel lighting track with mini-spots looks high-tech, and is very practical. You can add more spots if necessary

3 Shiny metallic tiles look sleek, clean and contemporary, and have a pleasing light-reflective quality

4 A fold-away table and wall-mounted stools are space saving solutions for a rather narrow space

Genevieve Hurley's top tips for kitchens
- If you need new powerpoints contact an NICEIC-registered electrician
- Fold-away tables are great for small kitchens
- Buy a door kit from kitchen suppliers or good DIY shops to hide away appliances
- If you've got children invest in childproof locks

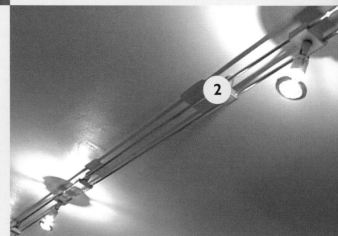

2

Tiles for kitchens

The main choice is between hard finishes and soft finishes. Hard finishes include ceramic, terracotta, quarry slate, stone, marble, terrazzo and recently metallic tiles. Hard tiles are extremely durable, though they tend to be more expensive and more difficult to lay than soft finish tiles. They can be cold, hard on the feet, and terminal for dropped china or glassware. Soft finishes such as vinyl, linoleum and cork are softer, warmer underfoot and generally less costly than hard finishes. They are hardwearing, easy to lay and easy to clean but they don't offer the same strength and longevity as most hard tiles. Because they are quieter underfoot, they are ideal for flats.

Before you decide on a particular type and style of tile, you need to check that it is suitable for its intended position and application. For example, some hard tiles are slippery when wet and therefore aren't suitable for use in kitchens or bathrooms. The nature of the floor is also important. Some floors aren't strong enough to bear the weight of quarry tiles, while other floors are so uneven that they will require a lot of costly preparation before a tiled floor is laid. Soft tiles tend to be more forgiving in this respect than hard tiles. Some tiles, like stone and rough terracotta, are best laid by an expert. It is worth having a chat with the retailer – tell them what you want and where you want to use the tiles, and they will advise.

Get some samples of your chosen tiles so that you can see them in situ – check them in natural and artificial light before making a final decision. If you have to buy several boxes of tiles, check the code number to make sure that they are all from the same batch – colours sometimes vary between batches. If you have to buy from two batches then mix them up so that you don't get a sudden change of tone. Most retailers have a sale or return policy so that you can return unused boxes of tiles. It is a good idea to keep some spares in case of damage.

Often gritting your teeth and finishing an ongoing project is the best way to add value to your home... **and improve your lifestyle.** Lucky Ashley and Julie had the *Better Homes* team to sort out their unfinished kitchen for them.

the problem... Ashley and Julie have known each other almost all their lives and have been married for 12 years. Ashley is a funeral director and Julie is a registered child-minder. They share their deceptively large terraced house with their three young daughters Natalie, Amanda and Jordan, Ashley's sister and a dog, and not surprisingly the house has become rather cramped. It is the first house they have ever owned and they have lived there for about two and a half years. Ashley has embarked on a lot of decorating jobs but he hasn't always had the time or money to finish them. Off the kitchen there is a damp and dingy breeze-block extension which Ashley was intending to make into a utility room. The kitchen is a complete wreck and Ashley takes total responsibility for that – a job started and not finished. It is cold and bleak, with concrete floors – a stoical Julie says she has survived by wearing lots of clothes, running in very quickly and running out again. So not a kitchen to linger in. But with David Wellman, Kieran Kelly and twin Adrian to take things in hand, hope is restored.

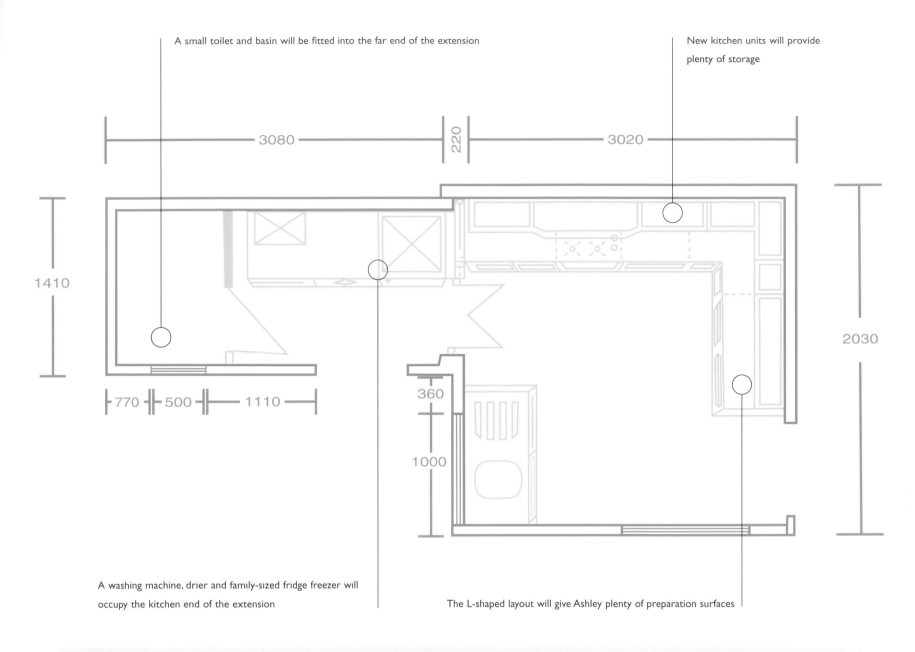

A small toilet and basin will be fitted into the far end of the extension

New kitchen units will provide plenty of storage

3080

220

3020

1410

770   500   1110

360

1000

2030

A washing machine, drier and family-sized fridge freezer will occupy the kitchen end of the extension

The L-shaped layout will give Ashley plenty of preparation surfaces

ideas... Ashley and Julie are very taken with the clean, timeless good looks of the American Shaker style. Ashley, who used to be a chef, is the family cook. He loves to have people over for dinner and yearns for a good preparation area, and a working space that is open and light and plenty of storage.

Julie is good at puddings and indeed considers herself 'a pudding person ... but I couldn't do a full-blown dinner party'. They'd like to end up with a bright, practical kitchen, a downstairs toilet, and a utility room for the washing machine and drier. Welly decides to use the essence of the

Shaker style as the basis for his design – simple lines, simple materials and a restricted palette of colours. The basis of the utility room and cloakroom is already there – it's simply a question of wiring, plumbing, plastering, fitting, fixing and decorating!

ADRIAN & NEIL'S DIY TIPS

Fitting units to non-square walls

Walls are never square even in a new-built house. However, the brackets supplied with most units allow for this by permitting adjustment back and forwards as well as up and down

Hanging a door

When you check the size of your frame make sure your door is about ³/₁₆in (3mm) smaller all the way around because that allows for shrinkage and expansion

Filling holes

An easy-fill joint filler goes on really quickly and is easy to use. Because it sets faster than plaster, you can sand and decorate really quickly

Gaps between wall and skirting

There are often gaps between the wall and skirting boards, especially in old houses. The way to get around it is to run filler along the gap and smooth it with your finger. Once it is painted you won't know it is there

the solution... The kitchen was stripped bare. The team decided that installing a downstairs loo at the far end of the extension was feasible – Welly knew it would add value to the property and improve the family's lifestyle. A stud wall and door were built to separate the loo from the rest of the room (complying with building regulations) but no actual partitions were put up between the kitchen and utility room. All these changes were first discussed with the local building inspector. The kitchen and extension were rewired and the sockets put in place – Welly made sure there were enough double sockets to meet all their requirements. The bare concrete walls were dry-lined and skimmed, and glazed terracotta tiles were laid on the floor – these are tough and easy to clean, important in a kitchen with a door onto the garden and a household replete with children and animals. A combination boiler was installed to provide heat and hot water efficiently, cheaply and when you want it.

Ceramic tiles for kitchens

Ceramic tiles are hardwearing, water-resistant, easy to clean and available in an infinite range of finishes, colours and patterns. They can be used on walls, floors, worktops and in fireplaces. They range from cheap and cheerful to hand-made tiles with serious price tickets. Tiles are sold singly, by the square metre (yard), or in boxes of various quantities.

Wall tiles are available in plain, patterned and textured designs. In coordinated ranges 'field tiles' may be complemented by individual 'dècor' tiles with smooth or relief designs; tile panels or plaques; border tiles; and dado and cornice tiles to give an integrated look.

Tiles for worktops and fireplaces are heat-resistant. Floor tiles are thicker than wall tiles and are fired at a higher temperature to make them stronger. They may be glazed or unglazed (unglazed tiles must be sealed before use). Border and inset floor tiles are available to add interest to the main floor tiles.

Welly chose a white Shaker-style kitchen, with a beech worktop which is light and has a warm, natural look. The knobs on the cupboard doors are the same wood to give a coherent look. The area between the worktop and the wall-units was tiled in Shaker-blue glazed tiles, the muted blue relieving an otherwise austere scheme.

The transformation was complete and Ashley, Julie and the girls were thrilled. The cloakroom meant that the girls didn't have to keep running upstairs, the utility room provided space for storage and laundry, and Ashley had a kitchen fit for a chef.

Kieran Kelly and David Wellman's top tips for new kitchens

- Plan your kitchen as a working triangle with the sink, cooker and fridge at its points
- Consult a CORGI-registered professional before you move gas appliances or plumbing
- Tiles are easy to keep clean. Choose a style and colour to complement the colour scheme. But if you're fitting them yourself remember to do a 'dry' practice layout first
- Install dimmer switches to create mood lighting – bright for when children are doing homework, subdued for evening entertaining
- If you're building a downstairs loo check building and planning regulations. These will include rules on ventilation, hygiene and access

1 The Shaker palette included a range of strong but muted colours, like the blue selected for the wall tiles

2 White units, a pale beech worktop and simple door knobs have the unornamented beauty which is the basis of the Shaker style

5

4

Shaker style

The Shakers or Shaking Quakers were a Christian sect founded in England in 1747 and in America in 1774. They lived an austere communal lifestyle, adhering to ideals based on plain living, scrupulous honesty and craftsmanship. They produced furniture which is characterised by respect for materials, purity of line and unadorned surface. From the beginning, Shaker craftsmanship was appreciated by those in the World, as the Shakers called all non-Shakers.

The best-known items of Shaker furniture are their chairs. Ladder-back dining chairs known as slat-back, straight, or side chairs were exceptionally graceful. They had three slats in the back and tall slender back-posts topped by characteristically rounded finials. Maple was the most popular wood with the Shaker craftsmen and the seats were made of tape, cane, leather or woven straw. Shaker chairs are still popular and can be found in the high street as well as in more specialist outlets.

The peg rail is another typical Shaker product. They were installed in all Shaker houses 2m (6-7ft) from the ground. At intervals of about 30cm (1ft) pegs were fixed to the rail so that objects could be stored out of the way. Chairs were hung upside down to keep the seats dust free. The Shakers produced beautiful oval boxes which have become a symbol of shaker design. They had curved sides which were cut from maple, walnut or cherry and steamed into shape. Swallow tail motifs cut into the sides were designed to stop the wood from splitting, but are also a beautiful embellishment. The top and base were cut from pine.

3 Always have double sockets in a kitchen – you can never have too many sockets

4 Pale ceramic floor tiles reflect light and contribute to the light, airy feel

5 A utility room adjacent to the kitchen is a real bonus, and will be a good selling point

The living room is primarily a place for the family to relax in comfort, but as one of the most public rooms in the house it is also a place to express your sense of style. Usually it is the room which most accurately reflects your tastes and personality.

living · rooms

a space for living

A well-used living room takes a lot of wear and tear and needs to be redecorated or completely refurbished from time to time. Start by making a list of the features in the room that please you and those that you find unsatisfactory. Has the room got a visual focus, does it lack style, are you short of storage for your rapidly increasing CD collection? List the items you want to get rid of – a tired sofa, for example – and those that you want to keep.

Next decide on a style. Magazines are a great source of inspiration. Think about the way that you use the room. If it is a real family room in which the children play and everyone gathers to watch TV, then an informal style may be most suitable. If, however, your kitchen is the heart of the house and the living room is a quiet retreat or a place to entertain guests, you might choose a more formal look. Once you have decided on a look you can prepare a sample board as described on page 24.

Walls

The walls are the largest block of colour in the room and what you do with them will set the scene for the rest of the scheme. Wallpaper is available in a huge array of colours and patterns. It gives the room a very finished appearance and can hide blemishes in the surface of the plaster. On the downside, it can be costly and it takes skill to hang it well. Paint may be a cheaper and easier solution, and the colour ranges are improving all the time. Paint may highlight imperfections in the wall surface, although 'broken' colour techniques like colourwashing will camouflage irregularities.

Floors

The floor is another large block of colour and texture, and the floor covering will be one of the most expensive elements in the scheme, so it is important to make the right choice. Fitted carpets are warm, practical and available in a bewildering range of colours, patterns and textures. The texture and quality of a carpet are determined by the way it is made, and the finish applied to the fibre tufts or pile. Carpets may be woven, tufted or bonded. Woven carpets like Wilton and Axminster are traditionally the strongest and most expensive carpets. In tufted carpets, tufts of fibre are stitched into a backing material – they are cheaper than woven carpets but the quality can be excellent. Bonded carpets are made by bonding the pile fibre to a woven or foam backing – they are the cheapest carpets available, but the quality has improved in recent years.

Natural floor coverings have become increasingly popular in recent years. Although they have been around for centuries, they can give a room a very contemporary feel. Jute is soft to the touch but it is the least hard-wearing of all the fibres and is best in low-traffic areas like bedrooms and studies. Seagrass, so-called because it is grown in fields that flood with seawater, is a hard-wearing matting. It does not take a dye and is only available in natural shades which range from pale yellow to russet. Coir is made from coconut fibres softened in freshwater. It is fairly hardwearing, but is quite prickly to the touch. Sisal is produced from the leaves of the Agave Sisalana plant and takes dyes well. It is durable and available in a wide range of textures.

Sanded and polished floors, or wood-block flooring has a clean, contemporary feel, and can be softened with rugs. Some of the projects in this book have used tongue and groove laminate floorboards – these are pleasing to the eye, inexpensive, easy to lay and easy to clean.

Windows

Window treatments are an important way of establishing a style and mood. Lined and interlined curtains in a quality fabric give a sense of luxury and provide good insulation. Elaborate headings can look fussy, but may be right in a period-style room. For a restrained, neat appearance, go for curtains in plain, neutral colours finished with formal headings and pleats. Roller blinds in a plain colour look elegant with dress curtains. For a contemporary look choose blinds in a plain colour and curtains with very little gather and no pelmets. If you need sheers, choose the plainest and go for cream, rather than white. Muslin hung flat is a popular solution to the problem of concealing your interior from prying eyes.

Storage

Storage is as important in the living room as anywhere else and, as we accumulate more belongings, it becomes ever more important to have 'a place for everything, and everything in its place'. Alcoves are an obvious place for built-in shelving and they can take a lot of clutter and so help to streamline your room. Make the lower shelves wider to take the hi-fi and television. The upper shelves can be narrower for books and ornaments. A wood moulding can be used to frame the shelf unit and give it an architectural feel. The whole thing can then be painted to blend in with the doors and skirtings.

Checklist

ACTIVITIES

Is it a real family room, do the children play and do their homework there?
If so, you need storage for toys and a surface for them to work at.

Do all the family gather there in the evening?
If so, you need to plan some appropriate seating.

Is this where you watch TV and listen to music?
Provide locations and surfaces for TV, video and music system – also check number of sockets and locations.

FOCAL POINT

Does the room have a focal point, such as a pretty fireplace, or French windows overlooking the garden?

Would you like to put in a fireplace?

SEATING

How many sitting spaces must you provide?

Do you prefer soft 'lounging' furniture, or more formal 'upright' seating?

Do you want a matching suite or do you prefer mix and match?

Do you eat meals there, at a table or on your knee?
Often, sometimes or occasionally?

Would you like to have a computer in there?

STORAGE
Do you have: books, videos, tapes, CDs, ornaments?
Provide shelving, storage units, display cabinets.

LIGHTING
You will need task lighting for activities such as reading, crafts, homework. Wall lights and side lights can provide atmospheric background lighting for entertaining and relaxing.

Have you got enough room to have two sofas facing or placed at right-angles to each other?
See 'Sofa options' on page 91

Do you need a sofa bed?

STYLE/ATMOSPHERE
Would you like the living room to be:
casual and comfortable
elegant and restrained
bright and modern
minimalist and cool?

EXISTING FURNISHINGS
Will you keep:
curtains, carpet, sofa or other major items?

Barry and Denise had a lovely lush garden, with striking topiary and year-round greenery, **but the layout of their house didn't really allow them to make the most of it – *until Kitty Edwards-Jones and the* Better Homes *team came along and* brought house and garden together.**

the problem... Barry and Denise have lived in their house in Northenden in Greater Manchester for just over a year, with their children Jenny and Mark. Denise is an assistant cook and Barry is a bus driver. Barry works long hours but has found time to work on the house, supervised very closely by Denise. The have a pretty garden with some fine trees and shrubs. They did have a beautiful fish pond until the neighbour's cat went on a killing frenzy. The sight of fish heads scattered all over the lawn was too much for Denise and the pond was filled in. They are a sociable couple and love to entertain, but the living room is small and feels cramped. They would love to have more living space, and they'd really like to find a way of improving the access to the garden. So over to designer Kitty Edwards-Jones.

Curving false walls in the corners will accommodate Barry's beloved hi-fi and television systems

ideas... Kitty immediately set about finding a way of opening up the living room and integrating the garden with the house. She decided to take her inspiration from the garden which is very green, with simple shapes provided by topiary trees. The living room will incorporate flowing, organic lines, and cool, airy colours. An opening will be broken through to the garden and a conservatory will link the house with the garden. A curved wall will integrate the stereo units, the video and the huge television and will give a feeling of flow through the room. Barry 'lives for his music and TV' and the new living room will accommodate these interests in a modern and stylish way without making them the centre of attention.

An elegant conservatory provides extra space and a retreat when the weather doesn't encourage sitting out in the garden

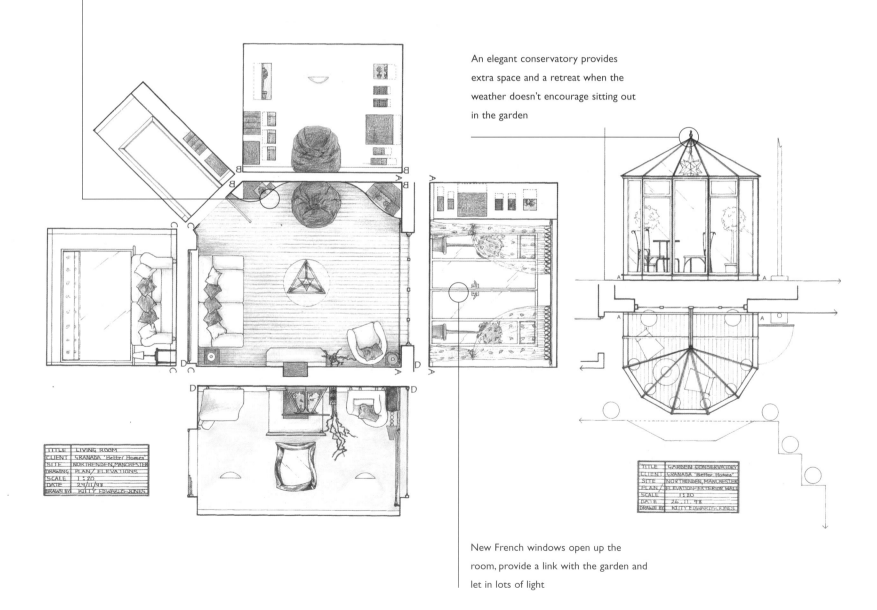

TITLE	LIVING ROOM
CLIENT	GRANADA 'Better Homes'
SITE	NORTHENDEN, MANCHESTER
DRAWING	PLAN/ ELEVATIONS
SCALE	1:20
DATE	29/11/98
DRAWN BY	KITTY EDWARDS-JONES

TITLE	GARDEN CONSERVATORY
CLIENT	GRANADA 'Better Homes'
SITE	NORTHENDEN, MANCHESTER
PLAN/	ELEVATION-EXTERIOR WALL
SCALE	1:20
DATE	26.11.98
DRAWN BY	KITTY EDWARDS-JONES

New French windows open up the room, provide a link with the garden and let in lots of light

the solution...

The builders move in and the living room is gutted – the old fireplace comes out, the walls are stripped and the floral carpet Denise dislikes so much goes into the skip. Under the carpet, Kitty finds a sheet of lino – 'a piece of social history' – and that is put aside for anyone who wanted it. The window comes out and the opening is enlarged to accommodate the

With Barry and Denise's carpet gone, the team found some lino dating from about 1939. Kitty was fascinated because 30s design is one of her special interests. Lino has a long and interesting history. In the seventeenth and eighteenth centuries linseed oil was applied to cloth to give it a smooth, hardwearing film. Floorcloths were tough and were used as floor covering and as protection for expensive carpets. Sometimes oilcloths were decorated and in 1694 a patent was granted for printing oilcloth and by 1804 it was being manufactured in continuous lengths. Originally Linoleum was the trade name for a type of floorcloth patented in 1860 by Frederick Walton. But it is applied more generally to any floor covering with a jute canvas foundation covered by oxidized linseed oil and other materials such as pine resin, wood flour, cork, lay and chalk. Early lino was printed, but in 1880 the pigments were introduced into the composition which meant that the decoration did not wear off. Linoleum was a popular floor covering until the 1950s, when various types of vinyl flooring became popular. Made from natural materials, linoleum is experiencing a revival. Wonderful, complex one-off designs can be created using laser technology, though these are not cheap. Linoleum is hardwearing, warm and soft underfoot, water resistant and easy to clean.

new French windows. The work starts early in the morning so that the doors can be fitted before the end of the day. The conservatory was a supply and fit system and was assembled in a day by the specialist team. The design is simple, chosen to echo the curves in the living room, and to sit comfortably with the proportions of the house and the size of the garden. You don't necessarily need planning permission for a conservatory – if you keep a wall or doors between the living room and the conservatory, it is technically a garden room and doesn't count as an extension. But do check with the planning and building regulations departments of your local authority just to make sure.

Richard installed a new ring main and sockets, and put the speaker wires under the floor and behind the false wall. The wall was constructed using sawn two-by-two timber for the carcass and ply for the boxed shelves. Ply has much better load bearing qualities than MDF. The wall contains compartments for all of Barry's kit, as well as niches for displaying objects or plants. Then plasterboard is cut into panels to take it around the curve and the

ADRIAN & NEIL'S

DIY TIPS

Planing wood

If you haven't got the confidence to use a hand plane use a rasp instead. It has a cutting edge but it is much safer

Chaise longue

Knole sofa

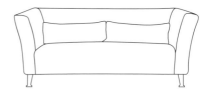

Modern mininalist sofa

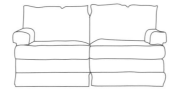

Cottage comfort

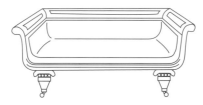

Regency-style 'Grecian' couch

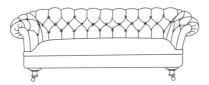

Chesterfield

Pocket curtains

Pocket curtains are a delightful way of personalising sheer curtains. You can make them by sewing pockets onto lengths of sheer fabric, but Kitty sourced some fabric with ready-made invisible pockets. She found some fabric leaves – you can get these in some good haberdashery stores. The leaves were a little bright so she toned them down by immersing them in an infusion of tea. She left them for about four hours, removed them, left them to dry flat and them slotted them into the pockets in the curtain fabric. For a scented curtain pop sprigs of dried herbs into the pockets – lavender, and rosemary are pretty, and a few bay leaves will provide a different motif. Look for things that have a good silhouette and look interesting when seen against the light; sparkling buttons and beads also work well.

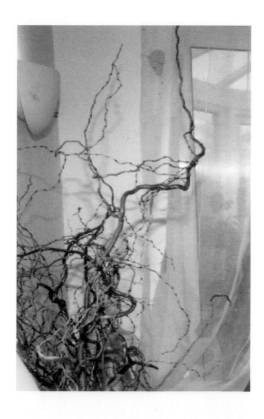

entire thing is skimmed to create a curving surface, which is smooth and pleasing to the eye.

Much of the success of the scheme depends on the clever use of lighting. The central pendant was removed, and uplighters were installed on three walls. Tiny halogen lights in the display niches illuminate the objects and contribute to the ambient light in the room. The French windows and the window on the facing wall bring plenty of daylight into the room, which is reflected in the overmantle mirror.

Meanwhile the pale beech floor was laid in both the living room and the conservatory, the direction of the boards drawing the eye through the rooms to the view of the garden. A chunky fireplace in creamy Bath stone is installed, and supplied with a gas flame fire. The curved walls are painted in a creamy textured paint which echoes the colour and textures of the stone fireplace. The walls around the fireplace are washed in a very pale shade of aquamarine. The same colour is used for the inside of the niches in the curved wall. This use of colour gives the room a bright, airy and unified look.

The *coup de theatre* is a wonderfully sculptural fish-tank table in beech wood which seems to open out like the petals of a flower in the centre of the room. Kitty hopes it will console Denise for the loss of her fish pond. At night it creates a gentle pool of watery light.

1 Niches with spot lighting provide an eye-catching setting for plants or ornaments

2 The organic, flowing lines of the room are echoed in this stylish standard lamp. The dado rail was removed to create an uncluttered wall and an illusion of height

3 A curving false wall accommodates Barry's music equipment and TV neatly and beautifully

4 A creamy natural stone fireplace with a sinuous overmantle mirror provides a focus for the room

5 Pale beech laminated flooring gives the room an airy feel. The direction in which the boards are laid has been chosen to draw the eye towards the garden

6 A pyramid-shaped 'fish-tank table' was designed and made to compensate Denise for the loss of her fish pond

7 French windows and a conservatory with glazing right down to the floor allow an uninterrupted view of the garden

Kitty Edwards-Jones's top tips for creating a room with a light and airy feel

• If you remove your dado rail it will give the impression of higher ceilings

• If your ceiling is low remove any central pendant lights and install flush ceiling lights or recessed downlighters. Use wall lights with dimmer switches, and introduce table lamps and uplighters for atmospheric lighting

• Paint ceilings white and use natural colours to lift the feel of a room. Use matt emulsion when painting walls, and eggshell or satinwood on skirting, window frames and doors as this provides a softer look

• Strategically place a large mirror in a room to reflect light and energy

• For a calm and relaxed environment remove all clutter

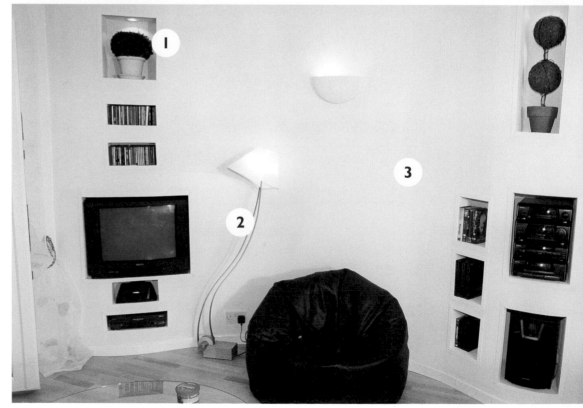

Jackie and Jo felt they weren't making
the best use of their home in beautiful Port Sunlight.
But with the help of designer Stephanie Dunning and the Better Homes team
they soon had a 'better home'!

the problem...
The Hawkins family, Jackie and Jo and their children Julie, Phillip and Amy have lived in their four-bedroom, semi-detached house in Port Sunlight Village for four and a half years. They have got a huge living room at the front of the house and a small, rather cramped kitchen at the back. They don't use the front entrance because the house faces onto the busy Chester Road. Instead access to the house is through the back door and the already congested kitchen, so poor Julie has to put up with a lot of toing and froing as she works. Serving meals is difficult because there are two doors between the kitchen and the living room where the family eat. The family would like to rationalise the use of space in the kitchen and living room, and have direct access between the two areas. They think that knocking the two rooms together will utilise the available space more effectively, make Jackie's life a bit easier and make the access to the house much more welcoming.

ideas... Stephanie Dunning agreed with the basic plan. She decided to block in the original kitchen and living room doors and make a new opening which would merge the kitchen and living room spaces. Port Sunlight is a conservation area and all the houses are Grade II listed, so plans had to be submitted for planning permission and listed building consent, as well as building regulations approval. Allowing the two areas to flow into one another will make them seem bigger and lighter, and both areas will become more accessible and useful. Julie can prepare meals in the kitchen without feeling shut away, and the whole family will be able to eat comfortably at a table in the living room. The existing layout suited the lifestyles of the late nineteenth century, but what is required today is a fluid and flexible family living area.

Jackie and Joe don't have any preconceived ideas about colour or style – so in theory Stephanie has *carte blanche* to do whatever she wants. But she is determined to give them something they will really like and resorts to all sorts of designer tricks to elicit their tastes. She looks at the choices they have made elsewhere in the house, and shows them pictures from magazines, advertisements and catalogues to see if they trigger a response. The scheme she devises is bright and modern, but at the same time refers to the history of the house and the architectural significance of the area.

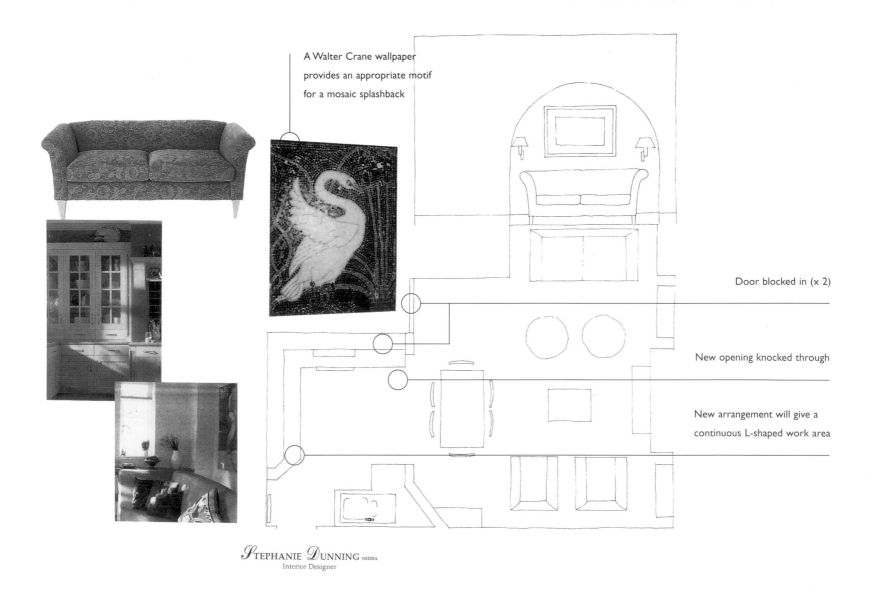

A Walter Crane wallpaper provides an appropriate motif for a mosaic splashback

Door blocked in (x 2)

New opening knocked through

New arrangement will give a continuous L-shaped work area

$\mathcal{S}$TEPHANIE $\mathcal{D}$UNNING MIDDA
Interior Designer

ADRIAN & NEIL'S

DIY TIPS

Cleaning your brushes

If you've used an oil-based paint like gloss, your brushes should be cleaned in white spirit. If the paint is water-based like emulsion you should wash the brushes in water. Emulsion paint dries quickly, so don't leave brushes or rollers lying around or you'll ruin them. If you don't have time to wash them immediately, stand them in water

Looking after your roller

Using your paint roller again tomorrow? Well don't bother washing it, simply put it in a plastic bag and tie it tightly with an elastic band to ensure that no air gets into it. It will be ready to use in the morning

the solution... The builders move in and the existing fittings and equipment are removed from the kitchen and the living room is stripped. Stephanie's plans involve a lot of major structural work and Geoff Brandt, a structural engineer, is brought in to advise on the technicalities of knocking the rooms together. An opening is created and a steel lintel is inserted to support the new archway. The existing doorways are blocked up and the fireplace in the living room is opened up and completely remodelled. A hole is drilled in the outside wall to provide venting for the washing machine – a necessary precaution to avoid condensation. When the rooms were opened up it was possible to appreciate the spaciousness of the accommodation and the generous ceiling height – a lofty 9ft (2.7m).

New kitchen units are installed, the revised layout providing a continuous run along two sides of the room. New wood flooring laid throughout provides a visual link between the kitchen and living areas. In the living room Stephanie's new fireplace creates a central focus for the room, while bookcases in the recesses provide much-needed storage.

Interestingly, Stephanie did some of her designing on the wing. For example, she had originally intended to open the fireplace to the height it would have been in the days when it accommodated a range. But when she saw the opening she realised the proportions didn't work and brought the lintel down, creating a more compact and pleasing shape. Similarly, she had intended to key the height of the archway to the original picture rail, but decided that taking the supporting lintel right up to the ceiling enhanced the sense of space and airiness. And the truth is, she was absolutely right – but, as Stephanie says, 'trust me, I'm a designer!'

Port Sunlight

Port Sunlight Village was built over 100 years ago by the soap magnate and philanthropist William Hesketh Lever (later Lord Leverhulme) to house the workers at his local soap-making factory. More than 30 architects (including the then unknown Edwin Lutyens, 1869-1944) contributed to the project and the village is a wonderful cocktail of architectural styles: there are art nouveau tulips in white plasterwork, Gothic windows, gargoyles, barley sugar chimney pots, elaborate brickwork, ornate mouldings, half-timbered gables and overhanging eaves. But despite the pot pourri of architectural devices, the village has a wonderfully harmonious feel. With fewer than 900 homes on a 130-acre (52 hectare) site, Lever was trying to create a rural idyll in an urban setting at a time when urban poverty was a major concern for those with a social conscience. He also provided a hospital, school, art gallery, gymnasium and swimming pool in an effort to improve the quality of people's lives. Port Sunlight was one of the first places in the country to have electricity. Today all the houses are Grade II listed and the village is a conservation area.

Donna Reeves made an Arts and Crafts style splashback to go behind the cooker. She took a motif from a Walter Crane wallpaper, enlarged it several times on a photocopier, traced it on to board and then worked her mosaic over the template – simple really! She chose a Walter Crane (1845-1915) design because the painter, designer and illustrator was a follower of William Morris and a leading light in the Arts and Crafts movement.

**Stephanie Dunning's top tips for
an open plan kitchen/living area**

- Design the kitchen ergonomically so that you
  have a working triangle with the fridge, sink and
  cooker at each point
- Position the preparation area so that you can
  keep an eye on the kids or watch television
  while preparing meals
- Make sure there's good lighting over the work
  surfaces and preparation areas
- Keep clutter to a minimum so it's easier to keep
  the rooms clean
- Recycle
- Have plenty of shelving for books, games, hi-fi
  and videos – if they are to hand they are easily
  used, and easily put away

I **A Farrow & Ball red is warm and
   welcoming in the kitchen**

2 **A stylish fireplace with a gasflame fire –
   but no mantelpiece. No mantelpiece,
   no clutter!**

3 **Cream walls make the living room light,
   bright and airy**

4 **Tight upholstering emphasises the
   pleasing lines of the settee and
   armchairs, and looks neat**

5 **Side lights shed pools of illumination –
   which is kinder and more interesting
   than an even, all-over light**

The Arts and Crafts Movement

The Arts and Crafts movement originated in the mid-nineteenth century as a reaction against industrialisation, mass production, the loss of craft skills, and the increasing use of inappropriate decoration. Its proponents wanted to revive the handicrafts and skills of the Middle Ages and improve the standards of decorative design. William Morris (1834-1896) believed that beautiful objects should be functional and skilfully handcrafted from the finest materials. Most decoration was superfluous. The intention of the movement was to make beautifully designed everyday objects available to everyone. Unfortunately, the ideals of the Arts and Crafts movement were inherently self-defeating, since the use of intensive hand-labour and the best materials made the finished products prohibitively expensive. Nevertheless, the ideals expounded by William Morris and others have profoundly affected succeeding generations of designers, and mass-produced versions of Arts and Crafts designs remain popular. Ironically, the mass-production they decried has made their designs available to all.

Bedrooms need the same rigorous planning as any other room, yet they often get left to last because 'we only sleep there'! But in these hectic times it is important to have a beautiful, relaxing and comfortable place to retreat to at night.

bedrooms
making the most of your bedroom

Your bedroom is the most personal room in the home, and is probably the only place where you can shut the door on the world, relax and be yourself. As it is primarily a place to sleep, it must be comfortable and relaxing. Choose a decorative style and colours that give you real pleasure, whether it is simple, streamlined and understated, floral and romantic, or exuberantly theatrical. If it is a sleeping-only room then you can allow the bed to dominate, keep other furnishings to a minimum and choose decorations which will normally be seen under artificial light. If the bedroom is also used as an office or a living room you may want to disguise the bed, and the decorative scheme should be designed to look inviting during the day as well as at night.

Storage

Life will be much easier if you have a well-organised storage system in your bedroom. A little time spent analysing your needs and planning the storage will mean that you can lay you hands on your clothes quickly and the morning scramble will be less stressful. Built-in cupboards which become part of the architecture of the room provide plenty of storage without appearing to intrude into the room spaces and are the best solution in a small or crowded room. Free-standing wardrobes, chests of drawers, dressing tables and blanket boxes look attractive, can be moved around and are often quite cheap. For cheap and stylish storage, buy second-hand furniture and paint it to create a coordinated yet individual look.

Window treatments

You need privacy for changing and undressing, and darkness if you are to sleep soundly. Choose window treatments to suit the situation – a bedroom in a ground floor flat at the front of a building will probably need some sort of screening during the day, but you can get away with something simpler if the bedroom is at the top of the house and not overlooked. Voile and muslin curtains prevent those outside from seeing in without cutting out too much light and there is a bewildering range of styles and fabrics to choose from. For a contemporary look, use plain muslin hung flat; for a period look, choose a lace panel. At night when the lights are on, you need curtains or a blind for complete privacy. Unlined curtains will not provide the complete darkness most people need to sleep, especially if there are street lights outside the window. Fully-lined and interlined curtains will cut out light and provide good heat and some sound insulation. Blackout linings are a cheap and effective alternative. In a Victorian house shutters may be an appropriate

solution, and provide extra security as well. Window treatments are an important part of the overall look of a room – choose elaborately draped curtains with decorative headings and shaped pelmets for a formal bedroom, and simple curtains and plain blinds for a more contemporary look.

Lighting

Background lighting should be soft and warm to create a relaxed and comfortable atmosphere. Choose bulbs which give a warm light. You will need task lighting – reading lights by the bed and good lighting by a mirror so that you can apply make-up, fix your hair, or shave. Make sure that storage areas are well-lit – lights inside a large wardrobe are very practical. A full-length mirror in good light is also useful.

Checklist

USAGE
Is this the 'master' bedroom?

Will it be used regularly, or is it a guest room?

Is it a child's room? Will it be used for play and study?

Will it be a dual-function room – a bedsitting room, or a bedroom/office?

FIXTURES, FITTINGS AND FURNISHINGS
Which fixtures and furnishings will you keep?
bed; wardrobe; curtains; bed-linen; carpet; light fittings; other?

What style of bed do you want?
(see 'Bed options' on page 111)

Do you want sanded and sealed floors or carpets?

FEATURES
What features would you like to highlight?
windows; decorative plasterwork (ceiling rose, cornice); fireplace?

What features would like to hide, lose or camouflage?
Melamine fitted cupboards; ugly windows, a textured ceiling?

WASHING FACILITIES
Do you want an *en suite* bathroom?
Consider installing a washbasin or shower cubicle in a guest room, *au pair* or adolescent's room to relieve pressure on the bathroom?

Is there a water supply nearby?

STORAGE
Is there enough?
Do you want more free-standing units such as wardrobes, dressing tables and chests of drawers?
Do you want an off-the-peg built-in storage system?
Are there any alcoves or recesses you could have cupboards built into?
Do you want a walk-in wardrobe or dressing room?
Is there room for drawers or other storage under the bed?

LIGHT
Does the room get the sun in the morning or evening?

Do you like sleeping in darkness or do you like some light filtering in?
If you like total darkness, think about heavy curtains or blackout linings.

OTHER USES
Do you need space for an ironing board, a sewing machine, computer?

Do you need somewhere quiet to read/study?
Plan task lighting

Do you need a place for a hobby – painting, patchwork, crafts?

What facilities do you need near the bed?
Radio?
Clock?
Alarm?
Reading light/s?
Television?
Video?
Music system?

'Thomas and David are in **soccer heaven** since John Cregg, Suzie Horton and the *Better Homes* team made them a *dream bedroom* / **play-area** / *shrine to football* in the loft of the family home.'

the problem... Teachers Steve and Clare moved to their three-bedroom terraced house in Smethwick a year and a half ago. The house is fine – the trouble is they have both been married before and, between them, they have accumulated a total of five children aged 5–13. When the entire family is in residence, the house is full to bursting.

They really, really do need more space, and the obvious place to find it is in the loft. Extending into the loft would solve their space problems, please the boys – and the girls – and definitely add value in an area where good-sized family homes are at a premium.

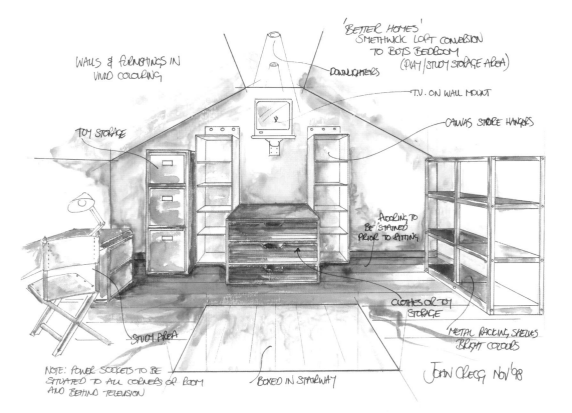

'BETTER HOMES'
SMETHWICK LOFT CONVERSION VIEW TO STAIRWAY

JOHN CREGG NOV '98

6 LOW VOLTAGE DOWNLIGHTERS
RECESSED AIRFLOW ALLOWED AT PITCH

VELUX NO. 2

ONE OF TWO VELUX ROOF LIGHT

ALBION

ASTON VILLA SHRINE

TONGUE & GROOVE FOR EXTRA SUPPORT STRENGTH

VILLA F.C.

WEST BROMWICH ALBION SHRINE

ASTON VILLA F.C.

TONG'D GROOVE FLOORBOARDS STAINED GREEN

STAIRWAY TO LOFT BOXED IN FOR FIRE REGULATIONS & BUILDING REGULATIONS

ASTON VILLA ACCESSORIES FROM VILLA PARK

DESK TOP & SUPPORT FROM HOMEBASE + ACCESSORIES FOR OFFICE AREA

WALLS & FURNISHINGS IN VIVID COLOURING

'BETTER HOMES'
SMETHWICK LOFT CONVERSION TO BOYS BEDROOM
(PLAY/STUDY STORAGE AREA)

DOWNLIGHTERS

T.V. ON WALL MOUNT

TOY STORAGE

CANVAS STORE HANGERS

FLOORING TO BE STAINED PRIOR TO FITTING

CLOTHES OR TOY STORAGE

STUDY AREA

METAL RACKING, SHELVES BRIGHT COLOURS

NOTE: POWER SOCKETS TO BE SITUATED TO ALL CORNERS OF ROOM AND BEHIND TELEVISION

BOXED IN STAIRWAY

JOHN CREGG NOV '98

ideas...

When John Cregg arrived to discuss possible solutions he discovered an open, draughty loft which stretched across three houses with no walls in between. Dividing walls would obviously have to be built, and this was one of the aspects of the proposed conversion that John had to discuss at length with the local planning and building regulations departments.

There are very strict regulations concerning what you can and can't do in a loft area, especially if it is going to be used as a bedroom. As Dave Wellman says on page 35, it is a good idea to contact the planning department at a very early stage, even before you commission any drawings or plans. John also made a very important discovery – Thomas is an Aston Villa supporter and David supports West Bromwich Albion. This bit of information set interior designer Suzie Horton thinking and she devised a decorative scheme that would reflect the boys' interests, and incorporate their team colours – Aston Villa's claret and blue and West Brom's blue and white.

ADRIAN & NEIL'S

DIY TIPS

Contain the dust and mess

If you are doing heavy building work or DIY at the top of the house, keep the doors downstairs shut so that the mess is restricted to the stairways and the hall

the solution...

People sometimes think that a loft conversion simply involves laying boards over the joists, plasterboarding the ceiling and getting the paints out. But there is an awful lot more to it than that. The joists in the loft are designed to hold the ceiling up, not to bear the weight of furniture, or of people walking over them. Most loft conversions involve putting in more joists to provide adequate support for a floor that you can walk on safely – your building regulations officer will advise you of their requirements. In this case John also had to brick up the access to the neighbours' lofts – this was necessary to comply with fire regulations, as well as to provide privacy. He had to bring natural light into the loft and this he did by installing Velux roof windows. Again, it was not simply a case of putting a roof-light in; he had to find one that would open fully and provide a means of escape in case of fire.

The next problem was providing access from the floor below – you can't simply put in a loft ladder. You must have a proper staircase that meets fire regulation requirements (see page 142 on Conversions). John's design created a large bulkhead in the loft area – this was necessary to give people coming up the stairs sufficient headroom, and also to provide a fire wall. He made it extra sturdy by using a timber construction because it was inevitable that the children would clamber over it.

All in all it was a tremendous undertaking. The scaffolding was erected, the ceiling knocked through to create an opening for the staircase, the electrics were rewired and the fire walls were built. Slates were removed from the roof and openings created for the double-glazed roof windows.

Insulation is important in a loft, so the roof was lined with insulating materials. A special foil-backed plasterboard was used – this will provide some fire-proofing and insulation, and prevent condensation. The staircase arrived pre-assembled and was quickly installed, then the handrail and balusters were fitted.

With the structure of the new room in place, Suzie and the team could get on with decorating. The tongue and groove floorboards were stained a vivid green, chosen to conjure up the green sward of a football pitch. The product used was a waterbased stain and sealant.

Suzie had chosen a vibrant orange for the walls and ceilings. Although it's a rather striking colour, it is perfectly balanced by the large expanse of green on the floor, and by the

claret and blue, and blue and white enclaves by the boys' beds. For a final flourish, Suzie created brightly coloured cutouts of the boys – playing football of course. A wall-mounted television, colourful furniture and plenty of shelving completed Thomas and David's retreat!

Using woodstains

The advantage of woodstains is that they colour the wood without losing the grain and the feel of the natural material. There are a huge range of products on the market, some aimed at the professional market, others targeted at DIYers. Some woodstains are colourants only, others are combined with a varnish. When you are applying a woodstain to new untreated softwood floorboards, you will find that the wood is very absorbent and you have to work quickly to avoid the stain drying with hard edges. You may find it helpful to moisten the surface first – if you are using a water-based stain use water, if it is oil-based use white spirit. Twin Neil used a quick-drying water-based stain, a small roller and worked quickly and plank by plank to avoid hard edges. If you are using any solvent-based products work in a well-ventilated space and wear a mask!

Suzie's drawing tip:
Transferring a favourite logo

If you have been inspired by Suzie's decorative ideas, you too can create exciting paintings in the children's bedrooms – or better still get them to do it themselves. You don't have to be good at drawing, you simply enlarge the logo on a photocopier and transfer it to the painting surface using trace-down paper – a kind of carbon paper. If you want a really huge motif you can enlarge it several times, section by section, and then tape the separate bits together.

Bedrooms for school age children

Children have different needs at different ages. When they start school their room will probably need re-arranging and possibly altering to accomodate new interests.

Storage is important because children are avid collectors, and if the storage is well organised there is just a chance that you'll avoid a descent into complete chaos. Narrow shelves are useful for displaying toys, collections and soccer ephemera. Tins, wicker baskets, glass jars and plastic storage boxes can be used for small objects; and large plastic stacking bins for larger objects. They'll also need shelves for books, and for special objects like fish tanks and computers. Label the different storage areas. Cork pinboards are useful for year planners, notices and for display of cards and posters. Hanging space for clothes becomes more important for school age children. Place rails at a height they can reach. Beds and storage systems can be combined with drawers under beds, or desks and storage placed under platform beds. Thomas and David have storage boxes that can be rolled under their

beds. It is surprising what can be fitted into a small space with a bit of careful planning – and there is an outside chance that a child with a place for everything may keep things tidy.

Children have an ever-increasing homework load and they need to have a place that is conducive to study. Young children can work at the kitchen table or in the living room, but as they get older they need a private space. Make sure that they have good light and a chair that encourages good posture. These days computers, TVs, videos, and games machines are all part of the technical wizardry that children seem to take for granted, so you may need to get extra sockets put in.

When children share a room, as Thomas and David have to, it is a good idea to give each a clearly defined area. Here the staircase separates the two areas, and Suzie Horton underlines the division with the clever use of paint. Providing separate lighting will cut down on arguments about keeping the light on to read, or trying to sleep.

John Cregg's top tips for a loft conversion

- Talk to the experts. Professional advice is essential for all loft conversions
- Remember to stand on the rafters when accessing an unconverted loft
- Reinforce the existing rafters with joists, to bear extra weight, before you lay a floor (you cannot just lay down planks – building regulations need to be adhered to!)
- For safety and building regulation reasons you must erect partition walls if you are converting a space in an open terrace
- For valuation purposes, a loft conversion accessed by a ladder only counts as storage space. The room must have a fixed staircase to count as an extra room and add value to the property
- Always check with the building regulation department of your local authority before installing Dormer or Velux windows. In certain areas, these windows are banned on the front of buildings and in some places they are banned completely

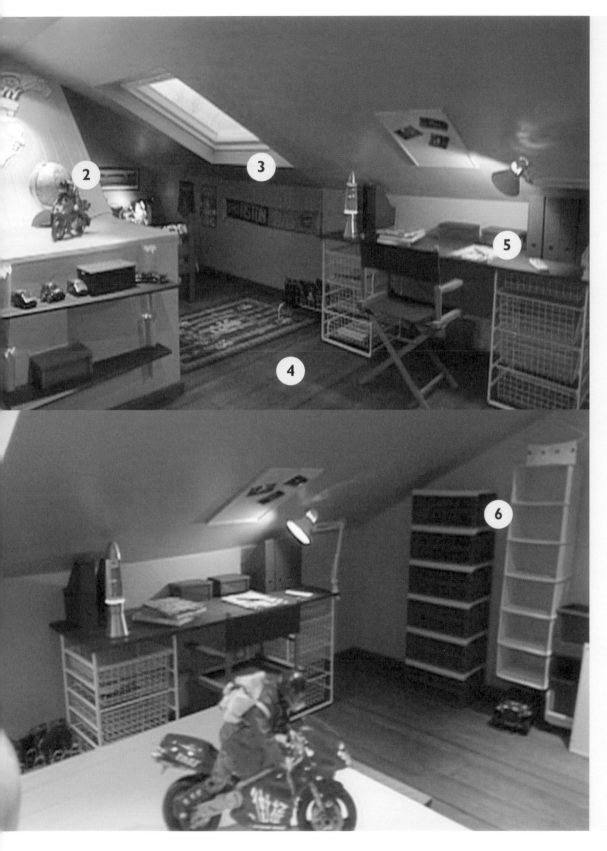

1 Suzie's mural of the boys in their team's strip. Thomas's area in Aston Villa's claret and blue. David's area in West Brom's blue and white

2 Bulkhead strengthened with timber can be used for sitting, storage or display

3 Contrast colour taken around the inside of the window reveal

4 Stained floorboards balance the vibrant walls and conjure up the green grass of a football pitch

5 Desk area for homework

6 Metal shelving and canvas hanging units provide cheap storage

Alison didn't want much in her bedroom
only *more wardrobes, an office* – *and all looking like the Sistine Chapel.*
Well, Genevieve Hurley, Zoë Gingell
and the *Better Homes* team gave her **just that!**

the problem... Alison and Geoff share their two-bedroom house in Port Sunlight Village with their daughter Kizzy. Like all the houses in the village, it is grade II listed. They have lived there for 18 months and have redecorated most of the house, and it looks absolutely stunning. Alison has a good eye and they both have a very clear vision when it comes to colour and decoration. The bedroom, which is the only room they haven't tackled, looks very sad by comparison with the rest of the house. It is inconvenient, doesn't have enough hanging space for clothes, and an assortment of wardrobes and chests of drawers made it look cluttered and bitty. Like so many people today, they make multiple demands on every room in their home. Alison has a market stall, and a handicraft business which she runs from home and she needs somewhere to work, make phone calls, put a computer and get a bit of peace and quiet. Geoff, who is a mature student, also needs a computer for his assignments and essays and a quiet space to study.

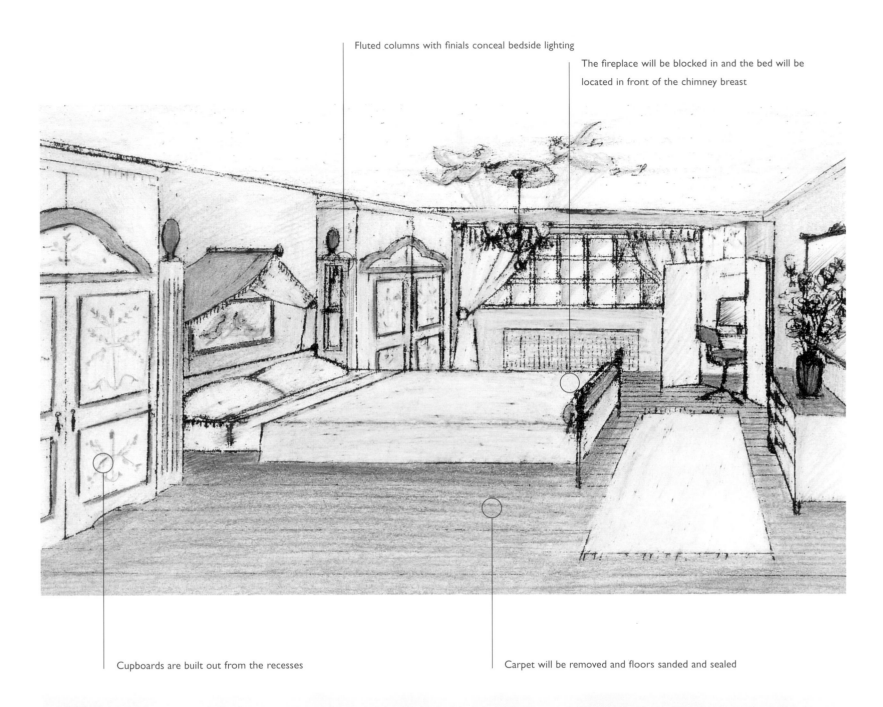

Fluted columns with finials conceal bedside lighting

The fireplace will be blocked in and the bed will be located in front of the chimney breast

Cupboards are built out from the recesses

Carpet will be removed and floors sanded and sealed

ideas... Genevieve Hurley was the project designer, and her task was to find more storage space, create a work space, and give the room an integrated look which would reflect the couple's very particular decorative style. Alison and Geoff wanted a Renaissance feel with lots of gold, cream and cherubs! Genevieve decided on an elegant and romantic look with creamy paintwork, classical columns concealing the bedside lighting, and a simple canopy over the bed. The ceiling was high, so for a final flamboyant flourish Zoë Gingell painted putti and fluffy clouds spiralling around the ceiling rose.

ADRIAN & NEIL'S DIY TIPS

To get a smooth finish with a floor sander

When you are sanding a floor, start by going across the grain using a rough sandpaper. This will get rid of the main humps and bumps. Then change to a finer grade sandpaper and work with the grain – this will give a smooth finish and eradicate the marks produced by the first rough sanding

Undoing a radiator

Use two pairs of pliers to undo 8mm central heating pipe, this will prevent you from fracturing the pipe

the solution... The first stage was to clear the room, take up the rugs, strip the wallpaper and block up the fireplace. A double bed takes up a lot of floor space, so its location will determine the layout of the rest of the room. Genevieve Hurley changed the alignment of the room by placing the bed in front of the chimney breast. Hanging space for clothes was created in the recesses, exploiting an otherwise redundant architectural feature and giving the room a pleasing sense of symmetry. Note that chimney breast recesses are fairly shallow, so the cupboard fronts project forward from the line of the chimney breast – to be useful the cupboards should be deep enough to accommodate the width of a coat hanger.

The radiator was moved to make space for the workstation in the corner. It is often suggested that the best place to put a radiator is under a window, so that the warm air rising from the radiator will mix with cold air coming in from the window. But as Carol pointed out, when floor-length curtains are closed the warm air goes up behind them and not into the room. This is less of a problem in a bedroom, because the heating is generally off during sleeping hours. Of course, if you use blinds instead of curtains then this is no problem.

The mini-office was built into a corner under the eaves. Because of the location the structure is not simple, but the varied angles and changes of plane make it disappear into the background.

It is important to get the wiring sorted early on, so Genevieve has indicated exactly where all the lights, sockets and switches should go. It is a good idea to get TV aerials and speaker cables laid in at this stage. They can be concealed under the floor, behind skirting or conduiting, or chased into the walls to give a neat, streamlined finish. And don't underestimate the number of sockets you will need – even in a bedroom. Alison and Geoff need several for the computer and its peripherals.

The floorboards were sound, so Genevieve decided to sand them. Natural wood floors are popular, low maintenance and will add to the saleability of the house. You can either hire a specialist contractor or hire a sander. Sanders use several grades of sandpaper and what you use will depend on the condition of the floor and how it has been treated in the past. Here the boards were fairly uneven, so Zoë started with a coarse paper working across the boards to get them flat. Then a fine paper was used, working along the grain to produce the smooth finish that Genevieve wanted. You'll need a small hand-sander to get right up to the edges and into corners. The floorboards were stained with a pale woodstain and sealed to keep them clean and easy to maintain.

Then Zoë went to work with paint and brush. The walls were painted in a Farrow & Ball antique-look white emulsion paint. All the woodwork, cupboards and furniture was painted in a similar creamy shade. Door panels and the fluting on the bedside columns were picked out in a muted blue-green, and the same colour was used to create a tracery of stylised foliage on the doors. Crackle glaze was used to give an antique feel to the decorations. Zoë then set about creating the cherubs that Alison had set her heart on.

The team had moved into a room with no particular style, furnished with a mish-mash of furniture. By the end of five days, they had transformed it into an elegant, clutter-free space with plenty of storage, a coherent look and a wonderfully romantic mood. Alison and Geoff were absolutely delighted with everything, but the computer provided by *Better Homes* was the icing on the cake.

Bed options

The bed is the most important piece of furniture in the bedroom, and as you spend approximately one-third of your life in bed it is worth choosing one that is comfortable and attractive.

Futon

A flexible bed design from Japan, the pallet base and cotton-wadding mattress can be folded to create a low sofa. Ideal as a put-you-up or in an adolescent's bed-sitting room

Bunk bed

Useful in children's rooms

Platform bed

Ideal in a room with high ceilings; gives work space underneath

Slatted wood framed bed

Clean and airy for a contemporary look

Four-poster

For a traditional look. Dress with gorgeous fabrics, or choose plain checks for a Scandiavian-style room

Old-fashioned iron and brass bedstead

Gives a traditional look to a bedroom

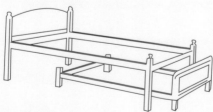

Sleigh bed

An elegant historic style

Shortcuts to decorative painting

Classical motifs painted by Genevieve on the cupboard fronts echo the Renaissance theme and help tie the scheme together. Dover Books publish a huge range of period pattern books. If you decide to have a go yourself, find a design you like, and enlarge it by photocopying it – several times if necessary. Stick the template together with tape and transfer it to the surface using trace-down paper – it resembles carbon paper and is available in large sheets from art and craft suppliers.

If you are feeling really ambitious you could also tackle the cherubs in much the same way. Find some picture reference – again Dover Books have a wonderful archive of images – and photocopy them up to the size you want. Transfer them with trace-down paper. The trick is to use a limited palette of colours. Choose a good mid-tone – here it was the cream used on the walls – and use a small paint brush to apply that to the image. Now darken the mix by adding a touch of black or raw umber acrylic paint. Use this darker tone for the shaded areas. As the image will only be seen from a distance you can work quite freely. Now use white to add touches of highlight here and there. You will be surprised how effective the results are! If you are not convinced practise on a piece of lining paper prepared with a coat of white emulsion.

Truckle bed

Provides a solid guest bed. In the past, servants often slept on truckle beds in their master or mistress's bedroom

THE WIRRAL | ALISON AND GEOFF'S BEDROOM

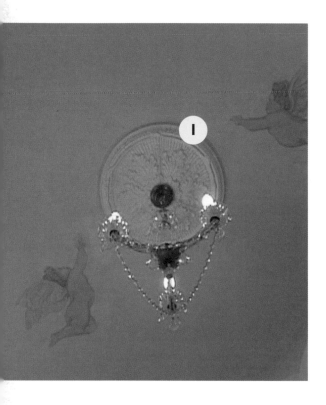

**Genevieve Hurley's top tips
for small bedrooms**

- Install fitted wardrobes and/or shelves in alcoves
  to increase storage space
- Move the radiator underneath the window for
  more efficient heating and to use wall space
  most effectively
- Use a light coloured wood stain on floorboards
  to make the floor area appear large
- Choose light colours and a monochrome
  colour palette for the walls to enhance the size
  of a room

1 On the ceiling the painted cherubs
   that Alison wanted – the ceiling and
   ceiling rose have been antiqued to
   blend everything together and give it a
   period feel. A dainty chandelier
   is in keeping with the grandeur of the
   room, but not overwhelming

2 A large mirror is a brilliant way of
   amplifying the light in a room

3 An existing chest of drawers was
   painted to make it blend into the
   room scheme

4 The radiator was slotted under
   the window to free up wall
   space elsewhere

5 Cupboards built into the recesses
   either side of the chimney breast
   provide much-needed storage

6 Bedside lighting is concealed within
   faux columns with fluted decoration
   and finials

7 A corner cupboard conceals a mini-
   office – complete with lighting and
   plenty of sockets. The TV is housed
   neatly in a shelf over the 'office'

8 Sanded, stained and sealed floors are
   light, hardwearing and cheap. They
   also give a home a period feel

The Renaissance

The term 'Renaissance' or 'rebirth' describes
the intellectual and artistic revival which
occurred in Florence in the early fifteenth
century. It reached its highpoint in the early
sixteenth century, by which time it had spread
to the rest of Europe. One of the characteristics
of the period was a revival of interest in the art
and literature of the Greek and Roman
civilisations. In the visual arts, this
was manifested by a deliberate imitation of
elements taken from classical architecture,
motifs from classical decorations and a desire
for naturalism in art. In this sense the
Renaissance was a classical revival.
Architectural devices like columns, pilasters,
capitals and mouldings will give a room or
furniture a classical flavour and these are
readily available in a variety of materials
including plaster, wood, plastic and papier
maché. The putti used in Alison and Geoff's
bedroom often appeared in Renaissance panel
paintings and were also depicted in *trompe l'oeil*
decorative schemes on walls and ceilings.

A cold, badly planned and old-fashioned bathroom is uncomfortable and unappealing, yet your bathroom can usually be updated at very little cost.

bathrooms

planning a bathroom

The best way to start the day is in a warm, well-lit bathroom with constant hot water, and cisterns that flush instantly and fill quietly. And if you don't have to queue while the rest of the family prepare to meet their public, it will be even better. British bathrooms are frequently old-fashioned, inefficient and uncomfortable, and sometimes stay that way because people don't realise just how easy it is to update them. A bathroom can be completely transformed for a fraction of the money you might expect to spend on a kitchen.

When planning a new bathroom you must consider the plumbing arrangements, and in particular the location of the soil stack. If you are relocating the bathroom or installing a new one, place it as near the existing soil stack as possible. In most homes you'll find that rooms that require a water supply are grouped together or stacked above one another. If you are planning to change the drainage in the house contact your local Building Control officer.

When planning a bathroom you should allow for 'standing room'. This is the space needed beside each item for activities like undressing, drying yourself, or using the loo. If the room is too tightly packed it will be difficult to use. Make a scale plan using gridded paper, as suggested on page 22, and indicate the standing room. Allow a minimum of 27½in (70cm) by the bath and in front of the shower. Allow a space 27½in (70cm) wide by 43in (110cm) deep by the basin and WC. Note that these spaces can overlap as you only normally use one function at a time.

If the bathroom suite needs replacing choose white – it never goes out of fashion and always looks stylish. Old cast iron baths can be given a new lease of life with a coating which is guaranteed for two years. If the bath is antique you could have it sand-blasted and re-enamelled, but this is expensive.

Bathrooms must be warm to be comfortable. A plumber or heating engineer will be able to calculate the correct radiator size using formulae based on volume, location and use. Consider a heated towel rail for background heating. If you want constant heat talk to a plumber to see if the rail can be supplied from your water heating system. An oil-filled electric towel rail with thermostat is easier to install because it requires no plumbing. Note that it must be connected directly to the electrical circuit – it can't be plugged into a switched socket – see 'Safety' opposite.

Bathroom suites are available in a bewildering range of styles. Take the most basic unit – the basin – for example. This can be wall-hung, with the pipework concealed behind the wall, or a pedestal design which rests on a vertical pillar. Inset basins are set into countertops, while semi-inset basins are recessed into built-in units. Undermounted basins are set under a stone or marble surface and accessed via a hole in the surface. An integrated basin is one in which the counter and basin are from a single moulded unit.

Checklist

PROBLEMS
Is the existing bathroom:
too small?
outdated?
cold?
in the wrong place?

GOOD POINTS
List good features such as the view,
comfort, a pretty window or the
generous size

USAGE
**How many people use the
bathroom: children, *au pairs*,
lodgers, parents?**

CREATING EXTRA FACILITIES
Consider installing:
an *en suite* bathroom
a separate toilet
a separate shower room
a washhand basin in a bedroom
a spa bath

BATHROOM FITTINGS
**Is the bathroom suite attractive and
in good condition?**

HEATING
Is the bathroom warm enough?

WALLS AND TILING
Are these dry and free from mould?
Is the grouting in good condition
and waterproof?

WATER SUPPLY
**Is the water pressure adequate
for showers?**

**Is your hot water storage tank
big enough?**
Most storage tanks provide only enough
hot water for one or two baths at a
time. If you have a large household you
could consider installing a larger tank to
alleviate the problem

SHOWER
**Do you want an above the bath
shower? If so do you want:**
a shower-mixer tap?
an independent shower unit?

Is there room for:
a separate shower cubicle?
a separate shower room?

VENTILATION
Is the bathroom well-ventilated? If not,
you will certainly get problems with
condensation and mould. Note that most
authorities now insist that extractors are
installed in all new bathrooms.

SAFETY
Water and electricity are a lethal
combination and wiring regulations are
designed to ensure that bathrooms are
completely safe. All socket outlets, except
shaver-supply units, are banned in
bathrooms. It should be impossible to
touch a wall switch while standing in
water or touching a tap – so most
bathrooms cannot have light switches or
switched socket outlets. Lights must be
operated by a pullcord switch or a wall
switch which is outside the bathroom.
Don't take risks with electricity – it
simply isn't worth it. Use a qualified
electrician and never use an extension
lead to use electrical appliances in the
bathroom.

If there are children in the household, fit
a lock that can be opened from the
outside with a screwdriver in an
emergency, or place a bolt on the door
above child height. Thermostatic controls
on showers will avoid accidental scalding.
Medicines should be locked away in
childproof cabinets.

Shower options
*'People travel abroad so much now that they
have very high expectations. Britain has the
world's worst water pressure, so spend that
little bit extra and get a power shower. If you
have a shower you want to be pinned up
against the wall.'*
— *Michael O'Flaherty*

As Michael says, people do expect an
invigorating shower, not a feeble trickle.
Ensuring that you have sufficient water
pressure for your shower can be a
problem – but it is easily solved with the
help of a good plumber. Even if water is
pressure is adequate in the bath and
basin taps, you may find that pressure in
the shower is totally inadequate. This is
because the spray head is too close to
the water level in the cold water storage
tank. If your shower operates on a gravity
system there should be at least 2 metres
(6½ft) between the shower head and the
water in the tank – ideally. The higher the
'head of water', the greater the water
pressure. There are several ways to
ensure that you achieve the shower
pressure you want.

You can raise the cold water storage tank
to increase the head of water. This
involves building a platform in the loft
and extending the pipe-work and is not
always practical. Or you can place the
shower room at a lower level in the
house, but this is not always possible or
desirable. You could fit an independent
electric shower heater fed with cold
water from the rising main. This is not
the perfect solution, because the flow of
the shower will depend on the time it
takes to heat the water. And when
anyone runs a tap fed by the rising main
the water pressure will drop. The best
solution is to install a shower with a
separate electric pump. These are
entirely automatic once installed. You
need a minimum unboosted flow rate of
0.5 litres of water per minute, but this is
not difficult to achieve and a qualified
plumber can advise you.

The taps in the washbasin have 'fallen out with each other', the kitchen floods when the hot water tap is turned on, and the décor is well past its sell-by date. **It was time to call in the Better Homes team and designer Stephanie Dunning to work a little magic.**

the problem...

Pam, Ray and Millie have lived in their house in Swinton for just over two years. Ray works for a laminate company and Pam is a housing manager. Ray, who is a skilled joiner and carpenter, has done a lot of work on the house, but the bathroom has been left until last. It is small, inconvenient and very dated. The taps in the basin have 'fallen out with each other' as Pam says, and the kitchen floods when they run the hot tap.

They have to wash in the bath or transfer hot water from the bath tap to the

washbasin. The bathroom really lets the house down, so improving it is bound to add value and make the house more marketable, but more importantly it will seriously improve their lives. It is easy to see why Pam and Ray are so willing to hand over the keys of their house and let Dave Wellman and his aides rip their bathroom apart.

ideas... Designer Stephanie Dunning agrees with Pam and Ray's assessment of the situation – the bathroom definitely needs a serious revamp. When she's had a look around she can also see that removing the wall between the bathroom and toilet and merging the two rooms will give them a more attractive and flexible space. Pam and Ray have fairly conservative tastes – they like a rather traditional English country house look, with a touch of Victoriana. It is a gentle, easy-to-live-with look that has never lost its appeal, and each generation interprets it in its own way.

Pam was quite determined that she didn't want 'anything black or purple' – she has obviously seen rather a lot of other television makeovers and didn't really like what she saw. They'd like a white, free-standing bath with claw feet, but more than anything they want taps that work and hot water. Stephanie is quietly confident that her scheme will meet all their requirements and improve the value of their home.

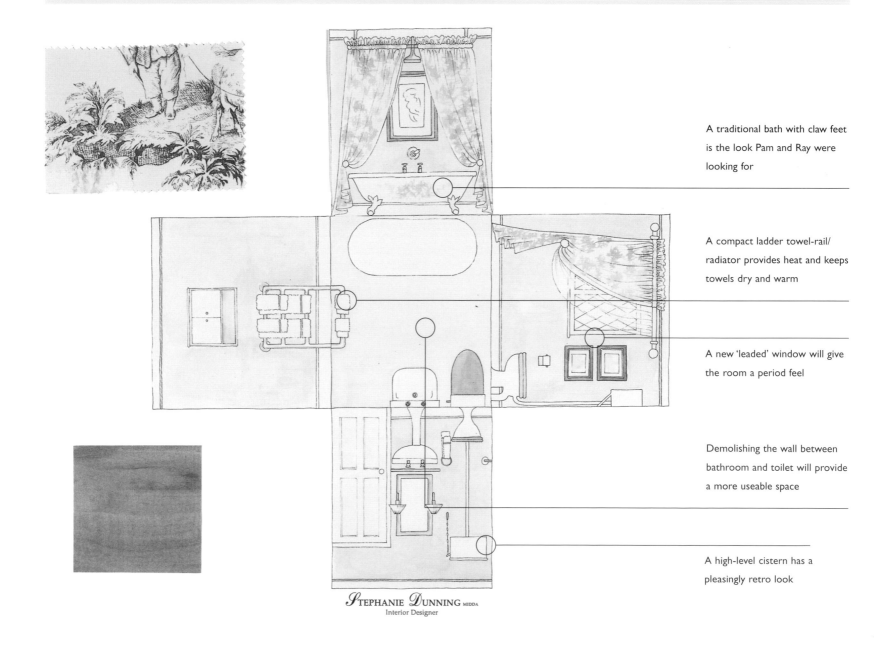

A traditional bath with claw feet is the look Pam and Ray were looking for

A compact ladder towel-rail/ radiator provides heat and keeps towels dry and warm

A new 'leaded' window will give the room a period feel

Demolishing the wall between bathroom and toilet will provide a more useable space

A high-level cistern has a pleasingly retro look

STEPHANIE DUNNING MIDDA
Interior Designer

ADRIAN & NEIL'S

DIY TIPS

Positioning a mirror

It is important to get the task lighting in a bathroom right. If you want to use the mirror to apply make-up or shave, you must place the light between you and the mirror. If it is behind you a shadow will fall across your face and make it difficult to see what you are doing. If the light is above, the light will fall across your nose and you'll get strange shadows under your eyes and your nose

SAFETY TIPS

Cross-bonding

Electrical safety requires that non-electrical metal fittings in bathrooms and showers should be linked together with an earth cable. The earth cable should be connected with metal clamps. Cross-bonding ensures that if any stray electrical wires should touch the pipes, the electricity will go to earth and not through you

the solution...

Before you can make a better home you have to trash it first. All the sanitary ware was removed, the electric immersion heater for the shower was taken out and the blockwork wall between the bathroom and the toilet was demolished. The window was replaced with a leaded window more in keeping with the new design. Stephanie liberated even more space by removing a central heating water tank and hot water storage cylinder from the bathroom, and installed a new and much larger tank and cylinder in the loft above the bathroom. Bathrooms must be well ventilated to cut down condensation and damp, so an electric ventilation unit was installed.

The floor was covered in plywood to provide a smooth base for the pale woodstrip floor covering. The walls were filled and skimmed, and lined ready for decoration. A dark blue basecoat was applied and then the walls were dragged in white to create a softly textured effect.
The technique is simple. When the basecoat is dry, apply a wash of thinned white paint to a section of the wall. While it is still wet drag a long-bristled brush through the glaze, working from the top of the wall down to the skirting. Wipe the dragging brush on a piece of cloth every now and then to prevent the paint building up in the bristles. Work in narrow bands to avoid the glaze drying before you have dragged, or better still make it a two-handed job with one person applying the glaze and the other dragging the brush through to create the striations.

If you need a break, stop at an architectural edge like a corner or a recess, then the junction between the sections of paint won't show. If you haven't tried the technique before, practise on a piece of lining paper before you start and experiment with colour combinations. Once you get a feel for it you'll find that like a lot of decorative paint techniques it is quick, simple, and very effective.

Once the walls had been decorated, the white bathroom suite and the towel rail/radiator could be installed and the bathroom really began to come together. The free-standing bath has claw-and-ball feet, and taps in the centre rather than at one end. Using thinned blue paint, Stephanie painted a *toile de Jouy*-style scene along the side of the bath, which gave the scheme a pleasingly coordinated look. A hooped curtain rail is sited above the bath to take shower curtains which will completely encircle it. The shower curtains are made from the same *toile de Jouy* fabric as the window curtains, but are lined with a waterproof fabric.

Decorative paint effects

Decorative paint effects are a quick and easy way of transforming a home and giving it a unique and handcrafted look. Many of these techniques are actually very simple indeed and quite forgiving if you do go wrong. And if you really lack confidence, there are plenty of kits that make it so easy that it is impossible to go wrong. Paint effects fall into broad categories.

The *faux* or false techniques replicate another material, like marble, stone or wood, in paint. Because you are trying to reproduce a very particular effect, these techniques can be more demanding. However, if you refer to a book or use a kit you'll find that some are actually very easy once you have mastered a few basic tricks of the trade.

The broken colour effects like sponging, dragging, ragging, stippling and colour-washing give a painted surface depth and a softly generalised texture. You can decide how much pattern or contrast you want and if you don't like the effect you can simply add another layer of glaze. A good tip for beginners is to avoid strong contrasts of tone – the results can look rather blotchy and crude. Two tones of the same colour is a good starting point.

Some of the most entertaining paint techniques fall between the decorative and the illusory. Fantasy marbles in colours never found in nature are designed to amuse rather than deceive. Other methods, such as rubbing or distressing, deliberately disrupt a paint finish to suggest the sort of wear incurred after years of use. This instantly gives any surface a sense of history, regardless of its age. This is a very effective tool for those wanting to match an existing historical style.

Toile de Jouy

These pictorial designs were developed in 1770 at the Jouy factory near Versailles, in France, and depict happy, bucolic scenes replete with merry milkmaids and their swains, shepherds watching their sheep, or lovers strolling arm in arm through the countryside. The fabrics are printed in a single colour on a white, off-white or creamy background, and the colours are soft and mellow, based on the original natural dyes. Pinks and pinky-reds, blues and rusts, earth green, brown and black are the traditional colours. The misty colours of the fabric and the pale backgrounds combine to create an elegant effect which looks lovely in formal bedrooms or living rooms, but also suits a cosy cottage style. Because the prints tend to be large in scale, they work best on large areas like curtains, flat blinds and bedspreads where the whole pattern can be seen. If you do use them on smaller objects like cushions, position the motif centrally and make sure that it still reads when it is cropped. Stephanie recreated the design on the side of the bath.

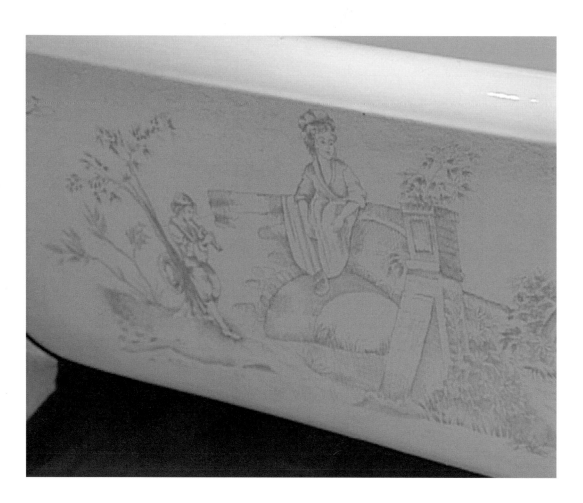

Stephanie Dunning's top tips for bathrooms
- If you can, move your water tank into the loft
- Install an electric ventilation system to cut down condensation and damp and allow air to circulate freely

1 Pretty wall lights with fabric shades have a nicely period feel. Stephanie has sourced chrome rather than the more usual brass

2 A silver gilt mirror is in keeping with the cool, pale colour scheme

3 A dragged paint effect on the walls and the cabinet creates a gently antiqued look

4 Chrome taps and shower in a traditional design match the shelf and other fitments

5 *Toile de Jouy* print looks fresh and has the right period feel

6 A hand-painted motif on the side of the bath echoes the *toile de Jouy* print

7 Leaded windows have a traditional feel

Extending into the loft can be an ideal way of finding the extra space you need, but some lofts cannot be converted, or are difficult and expensive to convert.

lofts
exploiting your loft space

Start by getting a professional such as an architect or a builder to look at the loft space and tell you whether a conversion is feasible. In traditionally constructed houses, roofs were made on site from a complex structure of wooden beams. A traditional loft space is a forest of beams – rafters (sloping beams that support the roofing material), purlins (horizontal beams that tie the rafters), and struts (timbers that brace the purlins against the ceiling joists of the floor below). However, it is usually possible to make a room space by relocating some of these components. In houses built since the 1960s, roofs are often supported on lightweight, factory-made trussed rafters. The way these triangular timber frames are erected and braced means that removing any one element can seriously weaken the whole structure. Converting a loft space in this kind of structure is difficult and can become very expensive.

If your loft lends itself to conversion it may prove to be the simplest and cheapest way of enlarging your house. You won't have to sacrifice any garden area or build foundations, and the building work can usually be confined to the loft area until the point at which the staircase is installed. This should mean that dirt and disruption in the rest of the house are kept to a minimum. Keep doors leading into hallways closed during working hours to isolate the dust and dirt.

Get in touch with the planning department and tell them broadly what you intend to do. If you aren't intending to raise the roof level, or put dormer windows in the front roof you probably don't need planning permission. However, it is always best to check and you certainly will need planning permission if your building is listed, in a conservation area, a national park or an area of outstanding natural beauty. If there seem to be no planning problems you could call in an architect who can draw up plans. Alternatively you could get a builder in to discuss your plans and give you some idea of the possible costs - and problems. Remember that you will need building regulations approval if the conversion involves structural alternations. Building regulations are concerned with the safety of the structure, access, ventilation, fire-proofing and means of escape, and waste disposal. Fire regulations for a loft are very stringent, especially if it is going to be used as a bedroom.

Loft rooms can be used to provide extra sleeping quarters, a playroom for the children, a quiet home office away from the rest of the house, or a small guest suite or granny flat. With their sloping roofs, low walls, interesting angles and wonderful light lofts can make delightful and unusual living spaces. The three lofts in this section have been converted to give: two bedrooms, one with an *en suite* bathroom; a granny flat; one bedroom with an *en suite* bathroom. The designers really have managed to fit a quart into a pint pot.

Checklist

PLANNING PERMISSION
Start by talking to the local planning officer

BUILDING REGULATIONS
You will need building regulations approval if the conversion involves structural alternations

ACCESS
A proper permanent staircase makes the room feel part of the house rather than an afterthought. Ideally you should fit the staircase in without sacrificing space from a bedroom. Staircases to lofts are the subject of special fire safety regulations

way of taking power into the loft. Generally it is best to install a new ring main circuit. Plan the location of lighting and power points early on, and make sure you have enough sockets. These days, particularly with the proliferation of computers, you can't have too many

VENTILATION
Ventilation is important in a loft space. If moist air condenses in the insulation material in the roof, it will become ineffective and you risk getting dry rot in the roof timbers. Ventilation can be provided by opening windows or installing eaves ventilators

HEAD ROOM
Ideally you need a head height of at least 7ft 6in (2.3m) over a large area of the loft. This gives a really usable space. A low ceiling means that a loft room can only be used by children and this limits its potential added value (see 'Adding Value' on page 16)

FLOORING
The floor will probably need to be strengthened. The fact that a loft has been boarded for storage does not mean that it will take the weight of furniture and people. A builder, architect, surveyor or engineer will tell you if additional joists are needed. The floor must meet fire safety requirements

WINDOWS
The room will need some natural light. This can be provided by skylights which are set into the roof and lie flush with the roofline. Dormer windows are vertical and the dormer structure juts out from the slope of the roof and have their own ceiling. Dormers require structural alterations to the roof and are therefore more expensive than skylights, but they create more useable space. It may be necessary to make the window a means of escape to meet fire regulations

SOCKETS AND LIGHTING
Your needs will depend on the intended function of the new room. A professional electrician will advise you on the best

FIRE PRECAUTIONS
Special safety features are required in a loft conversion, particularly if the original structure is more than one storey high. They are designed to ensure that if there is a fire people do not get trapped in the loft. These requirements make loft conversions more expensive – but of course they are essential. The stairwell must be fireproofed and boxed in from the rest of the house. There should be a fire-resistant door between the loft room and the rest of the house. The floor must also meet a 30-minute fire resistance standard. There should also be an alternative means of escape, such as a window, which is accessible and large enough to climb through

INSULATION
The walls and roof require good thermal insulation, but it must be designed to prevent condensation – see above. A vapour barrier made from a material such as reflective foil building paper or polythene will prevent moisture getting into the insulation materials which therefore will prevent any condensation

HEATING
Consult a heating engineer to see if you can extend your central heating system into the loft. If your boiler does not have the capacity for this you could consider the option of installing night storage heaters. However, find out if they will fit into your budgetary situation

'Sometimes 17 workmen don't turn up,
a supporting wall isn't,
and the entire house needs rewiring –
but do Kieran Kelly and Dave Wellman panic?
of course not!

the problem... Andrew and Lisa and their sons Stephen and Mark have lived in their stylish and beautifully maintained semi-detached bungalow for four years. Andrew works as a carpenter at a local shipyard and Lisa works in a supermarket. At the moment the boys have bunk beds in a shared bedroom, but as they are growing up and support different football teams, they need their own bedrooms. If Stephen and Mark had a room each they'd have somewhere to entertain their friends, and their parents would get a bit of peace. As Andrew and Lisa have already built an extension on the back of their home, the only unexploited space is in the loft. In an ideal world they would like two bedrooms which would solve their space problems and certainly add value to their house.

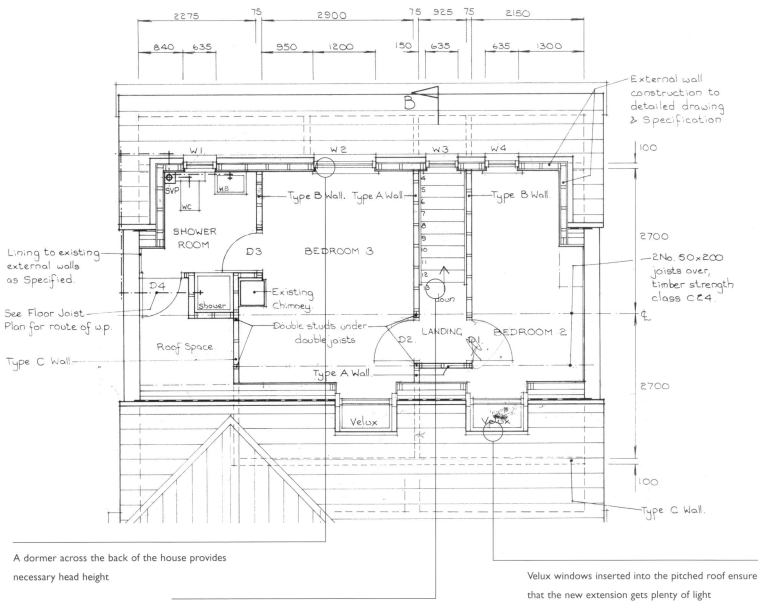

2275   75   2900   75 925 75   2150

840   635   950   1200   150   635   635   1300

B

External wall
construction to
detailed drawing
& Specification

W1   W2   W3   W4

100

SVP
WC
HB

Type B Wall.   Type A Wall.   Type B Wall.

SHOWER
ROOM

2700

Lining to existing
external walls
as Specified.

D3   BEDROOM 3

2 No. 50 x 200
joists over,
timber strength
class C24.

D4

Shower   Existing
Chimney.

See Floor Joist
Plan for route of w.p.

₵

Double studs under
double joists

Roof Space.

D2   LANDING   D1   BEDROOM 2

down

Type C Wall.

Type A Wall.

2700

Velux   Velux

100

Type C Wall.

A dormer across the back of the house provides
necessary head height

Velux windows inserted into the pitched roof ensure
that the new extension gets plenty of light

The new stairway comes up between the two bedrooms

ideas... Kieran Kelly has been given the task of solving Andrew and Lisa's problems. He is feeling quite ambitious: 'We are going to turn it into a three-bedroom bungalow with an extra shower room', he says. He plans to create two bedrooms in the loft, one with a shower room en-suite. A large dormer will be have to be built at the back of the house in order to get sufficient headroom. The design will be restrained with neutral colours and interesting textures, to tie in with the rest of the house. Well not entirely; the second bedroom will be a bit different! But I'll let you find out what that is for yourself when I've finished the project.

the solution... Loft conversions involve major structural work, so it is important to discuss all your plans with the planning and building regulations people well in advance. You will also need professional help to specify all the structural work.

On the first day scaffolding goes up and a hole is made in the ceiling of the boys' room to provide an opening for the stairs. It's quite usual to 'lose' a small room to gain permanent access to an upper floor, so the boy's room will become part of the hallway. Kieran and Welly had a few problems to contend with – some of the workmen failed to turn up and a wall they thought was solid turned out to be hollow. But problems are there to be solved and new bodies were press-ganged locally and Dave Wellman brought in an engineer to re-work the calculations and re-specify the structural work. A metal lintel had to be installed between two load-bearing walls and a plate went into the opposite wall. A timber plate on top of that provided fixings for the new loft floor joists. Joist hangers were used to fix the joists to the lintel.

The roof was stripped of its tiles. The dormer window frames were pre-fabricated offsite and a gaggle of carpenters appeared to fit them. The entire house had to be rewired to meet safety regulations – electricians Richard and James had been sorting out the problem from day one, so by the time the structural work was done they were well within schedule.

The loft floor was laid, new rafters were fitted and the ceiling was plasterboarded. Up on the roof the roofers started to apply roofing felt and tar to provide a waterproof layer. Then the roof tiles went on. The walls were skimmed ready for the decorators. The stairs for the loft arrived pre-formed and to everyone's relief fitted first time. The shower room was fitted out and plumbed and then the decorators could get to work. It was all hands on deck to meet the tight filming schedule – at one time there were six men in the small shower room, all busy painting.

A sand-coloured berber carpet was laid throughout the attic floor, maximising the sense of space and light – it will also be warm underfoot, and will minimise the noise transmitted to the floor below. In the tiny shower room a toilet, handbasin and shower have been installed – everything is plain white to reflect Andrew and Lisa's rather austere taste. The iron bedstead with its gothic arches is a quirky touch. Window treatments are plain with blinds, a metal curtain rod, and simply gathered drapes in a crunchy, cream fabric. A set of botanical prints in a cool green relieve the expanse of wall.

ADRIAN & NEIL'S DIY TIPS

Applying varnish or stain

When applying woodstain or varnish to fiddly areas like balusters you can eradicate your brushstrokes by wiping the surface with a damp cloth as you work

Using a neutral palette

These no-colour colours are highly valued by designers who constantly dip into their palette of taupe, beige, stone, biscuit, fawn, camel, buff and mushroom — descriptive names which try to pin down the subtlest of colour nuances. They are quiet colours which provide undemanding backgrounds for brighter, more strident colours. Used together, they create harmonious relationships and a stylish, timeless and uncluttered look.

They work especially well when textures are piled on textures. In Andrew and Lisa's loft pale walls and a warm neutral carpet are combined with the textures of cane, wicker and slatted blinds, accented with the crisp black tracery of the gothic-style bed. Nature is a rich source of 'colourful' neutrals. On the seashore you'll find the pearly pinks of seashells, the myriad greys, beiges and browns of water-smoothed pebbles, and the sparkling whites and knocked-back yellows of the sandy shore. Elsewhere the landscape provides the warm greys of granite, the bluer greys of slate and limestone and the buffs and beiges of sandstones. From field and hedgerow we can take the tawny shades of straw and sun-bleached grasses, autumn leaves and sawn wood.

Living with orange

Orange is a bright, insistent colour which needs to be handled with care. It has gone in and out of fashion, appearing in the design schemes and fabrics of Art Nouveau and Art Deco, and surfacing again in the psychedelic 60s. Often it is used in a slightly neutralised form as burnt orange or bright terracotta. In the little loft bedroom it is teamed with hot reds and bright yellows: the glorious colours of New England in the Fall. The room is bathed with light from a Velux in the roof and a window in the opposite wall, so that the colours dance and sparkle.

The bright colours are relieved by neutral carpets and pale wood furnishings which also provide a visual link with the hallway and the room across the hall. A touch of blue in the desk door provides a cool contrast.

Dave Wellman and Kieran Kelly's top tips for loft conversions

• It's normal to 'lose' a small room in order to gain permanent access to an upper floor. In this case the boys' room became an addition to the hallway

• Always check local planning and building regulations before starting any structural work

• Be prepared for hidden problems and setbacks, like having to get the house rewired

1. A dormer roof gives height and space, and the windows bring in light

2. Wicker storage baskets are functional and provide texture in a neutral scheme

3. A desk under a window is a quiet and well-lit spot in which the lucky occupant can work

4. Pale neutral colours are easy to live with, and have a clean, airy, timeless feel

5. A tiny *en suite* shower room makes the attic storey more self-contained and is a real bonus

6. A gothic-style iron bedstead creates a crisp line in the minimal surroundings

7. Hot with hot creates a sizzling colour scheme. Here burnt orange is teamed with a knocked-back red

8. A single bed fits neatly beneath the eaves

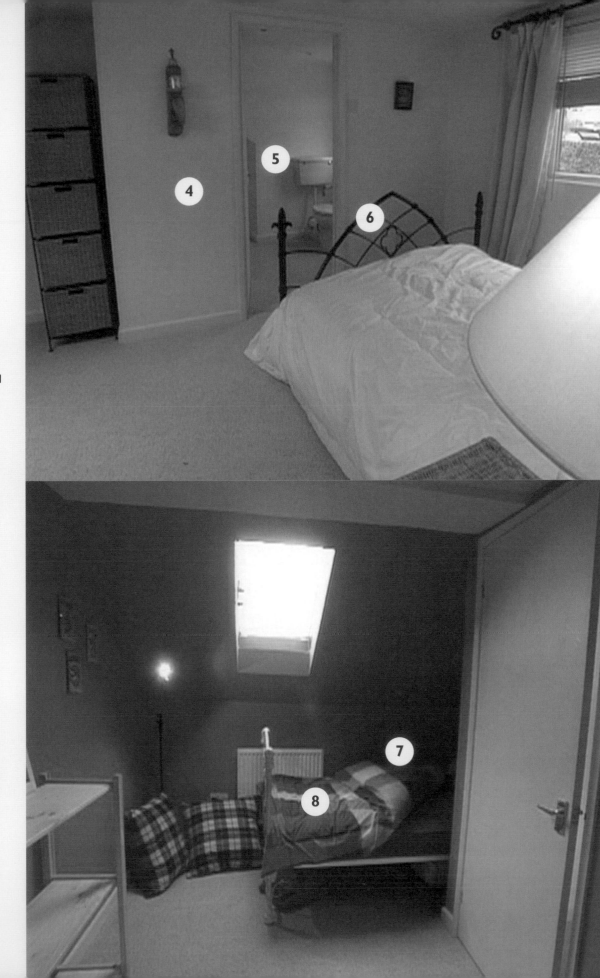

This project created a self-contained granny flat in a detached house, solving a common family dilemma. **About 8% of households have one parent living with them, so there is a tremendous demand for this type of accommodation.** In this case, however, *it was the younger generation who were going to live in the 'granny' flat.*

the problem...

Jean, her daughter Jeanette and husband Terry share a spacious detached house in Newbury with Dougal the dog. Terry is a printer and Jeanette is in the process of starting her own business. They are saving to buy their own place, but they would like a bit more privacy, a shower room with a toilet and some storage. At the moment Terry and Jeanette have a bedroom, a shower room and a very small living area. The house belongs to Jean and she is quite happy with the idea and thinks 'it would put quite a lot of value on the house because there are so few granny annexes around, and it would be quite unique to this area'. This sort of flexible accommodation would be suitable for a second family, an *au pair* or nanny, or a teenager who has not yet left home. Jeanette and Terry aren't intending to live with Jean indefinitely, and once they find a place of their own, Jean's mother is planning to move in with her – so it really will become a granny flat.

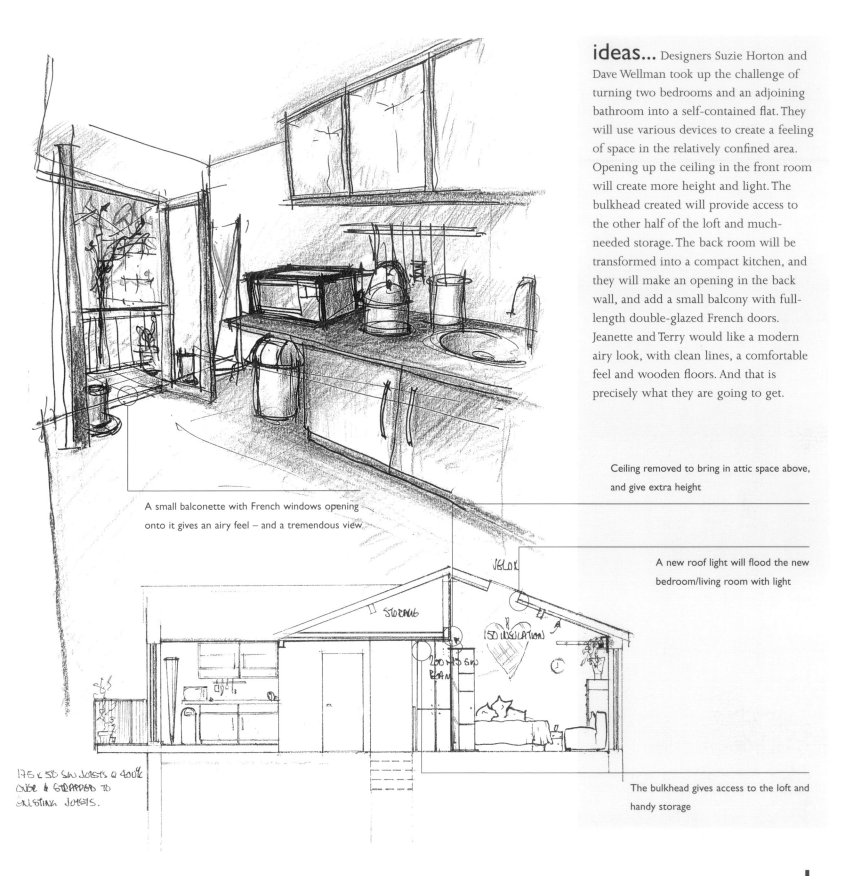

ideas... Designers Suzie Horton and Dave Wellman took up the challenge of turning two bedrooms and an adjoining bathroom into a self-contained flat. They will use various devices to create a feeling of space in the relatively confined area. Opening up the ceiling in the front room will create more height and light. The bulkhead created will provide access to the other half of the loft and much-needed storage. The back room will be transformed into a compact kitchen, and they will make an opening in the back wall, and add a small balcony with full-length double-glazed French doors. Jeanette and Terry would like a modern airy look, with clean lines, a comfortable feel and wooden floors. And that is precisely what they are going to get.

Ceiling removed to bring in attic space above, and give extra height

A small balconette with French windows opening onto it gives an airy feel – and a tremendous view

A new roof light will flood the new bedroom/living room with light

The bulkhead gives access to the loft and handy storage

ADRIAN & NEIL'S DIY TIPS

Fire safety

Fire safety is especially important in dwellings with multiple occupancy and regulations are stringent. Check with your planning department. Every house should be equipped with smoke detectors

Employ skilled contractors

The construction of the balcony involves metal, gas and a welder. Always use the right person for the job. It is not worth cutting corners

the solution...

the solution... The first step was to remove the ceiling and ceiling joists in the front room in order to take height and space from the loft above, and create a sloping ceiling. A roof light was inserted in the attic roof and the roof was insulated, plasterboarded and skimmed.

At the back of the house, the window is removed and the opening enlarged to make a space for the French windows. Next, the team set about constructing the balcony which will project over the garden, but at an angle so that they overlook Jean's garden rather her neighbour's. Welly explained that there were several construction options. They could have supported the balcony on columns in the garden, but that would have been cumbersome and intrusive. It could have been bolted to the wall but that would not have been secure. In the end they went for a cantilevered structure, with the balcony supported within the main building structure.

The uPVC French doors were prefabricated and slotted easily into the frame. The French windows really open up this part of the flat, and create a long vista through the kitchen.

In the bed-sitting room a fold-away bed is installed, a brilliant idea when space is at a premium. The back room was fitted out as a kitchen with neat units, wall storage, a sink and a top of the range cooker/microwave oven. The existing bathroom was made slightly larger and given a new suite and accessories.

Pale fitted carpet was laid throughout to give a light, unified look. A lilac border gave a neat finish and a splash of colour.

Making the most of a small space

• As much as possible should be built-in

• A fold-down bed liberates space during the day

• Choose compact bathroom fittings

• Dispense with a draining board – a wall-mounted plate rack would work well and economise on workspace

• Glass shelves in storage cupboards allow you to see what is on the upper shelves

• A single mixer tap takes up less space than separate hot and cold taps

• Use a good microwave rather than an oven and hob

• Take all your key measurements when you go looking for items, and ask advice

• Bring in as much light as you can – it makes a small space feel bigger and airier

• The French windows and a roof light enhanced the sense of space in this conversion

**Suzie Horton and Dave Wellman's tips
for self-contained accommodation**
- Ensure that you have adequate fire and
  smoke alarms in your home
- Fold-away beds are great when space is
  at a premium

Roof lights and windows

If you decide to exploit your attic by converting it into a useable space, or by taking the space into the room below as Suzie Horton and Dave Welman have done in Jeanette and Terry's flatlet, you will need windows that fit into the slope of the roof. In the past these were single-glazed and metal framed structures that could be propped open with a metal bar. In the past 50 years, roof windows have become more sophisticated and are just as convenient as the windows you fit into vertical surfaces. They are substantial, double glazed and can open in a variety of ways. Roof windows are normally pivoted in the centre, but top-hung windows give a bigger opening and can be used as a means of escape. It is important to control heat and light in a loft room, and blinds in various styles and finishes are available. Blackout blinds are sensible if the room is for sleeping in, while thermal blinds control heat. The Velux roof window in Jeanette and Terry's bedroom was too high to be opened and shut manually, so an electronic system was installed. A remote control can be used to open and shut the window and control the blinds and a sensor ensures that the window shuts automatically if it rains.

1 The bracket-mounted television saves space

2 The carcass, doors and butcher's worktop were bought separately and assembled to create the look Suzie was after

3 The balcony was designed at an angle so that it overlooks Jean's garden

4 A chair will fit on the wider part of the balcony

5 French windows open up this wall and make the flatlet seem light and spacious

6 Pale carpet is used throughout to make the spaces flow into one another – it also reflects light

'It is a funny shaped loft with the chimney stack right in the middle
– I think that **they are going to have to make a feature of that,**'
Spencer said, and how right he was.
Designer Orianna Fielding Banks made a virtue of a necessity
and designed *sleeping, washing and storage* **space**
that pivoted around the central stack.

the problem...
Sarah, Spencer and their daughter, two-year-old Georgia, live in Newbury in a modern semi-detached house which has two bedrooms and a box room. They both work for the same company although Sarah works part time at the moment. They love having friends to stay and desperately want more space.

They would like to transform the cobwebby attic into an extra bedroom with an *en suite* bathroom. This would allow them to use their small bedroom as an office or rather a shrine to Arsenal. They have considered extending to the side or the back of the house, but felt that the loft space would give them something more unusual, and would avoid eating into the plot on which the house stands. Getting an extra bedroom while retaining the size of the garden will certainly add value to their home. With Orianna's help they will get something very special indeed.

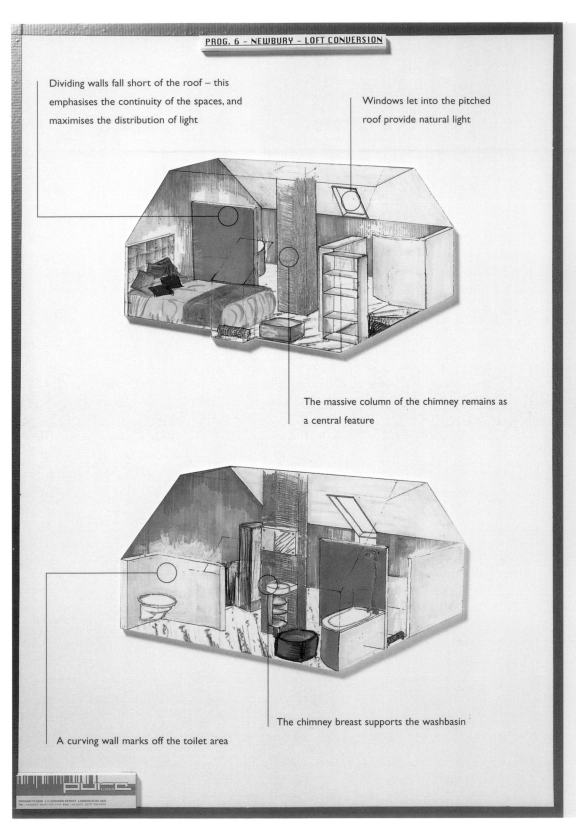

Dividing walls fall short of the roof – this emphasises the continuity of the spaces, and maximises the distribution of light

Windows let into the pitched roof provide natural light

The massive column of the chimney remains as a central feature

The chimney breast supports the washbasin

A curving wall marks off the toilet area

ideas... Orianna is faced with an attic space which is interrupted by a massive chimney stack. She decides to incorporate this large architectural feature into the design, using it as a natural pivot and divide. She will use sweeping lines and organic shapes to create spaces that flow naturally into one another. Normally an *en suite* bathroom has straight walls, right angles and a door. Here there are no doors and the dividing walls don't quite reach the ceiling. Nevertheless, each area is clearly defined and the completed conversion will be light, modern and a delight to use. The proposed scheme will use the space creatively and, above all, it will work. The look will be contemporary with lots of pale wood and chrome.

the solution...

The raftered truss construction of the roof was a problem, and a substantial amount of structural work had to be done to meet building regulations. The rafters and joists had to be completely reworked to clear the space for the conversion.

Everything downstairs is cleared away before work starts in the loft. On the roof, tiles are removed and an opening is cut for the two windows which will be inserted into the roof. Sturdy frames are constructed to support the windows and the prefabricated units are installed. If you are converting the loft for use as a bedroom, make sure the windows have blackout and thermal blinds.

You will need a proper fire-proofed staircase if a loft room is going to be used as a bedroom, and these take up space. This staircase ascends from the boxroom, so Sarah and Spencer have had to sacrifice part of that room to gain the space in the loft but the remaining space is still useable. The staircase was custom-built off site and delivered as a complete unit.

The low dividing walls are erected to delimit the various sections of the space, and the pale ash plank flooring is laid. The figuring is lovely, and its light colour reflects the light received from the windows in the roof and contributes to the airy feel.

Lighting was an integral part of Orianna's design. In a multifunctional space it can be used to underline functions and define different areas. Mood lighting is required in some areas, whilst task lighting is required in others. Lights dotted along the dividing walls provide soft background light and wash the roof space, drawing attention to its height and gabled construction.

The chimney breast was panelled in mirror-like stainless steel to create a reflective column. A pedestal wash-basin was fixed to one side. In this way Orianna ensures that the stack is fully integrated into the scheme.

ADRIAN & NEIL'S DIY TIPS

Clever floorboarding

In a small area dramatic flooring has an impact. Laying the wide planks diagonally underlines the freeflowing nature of the scheme and the non-rectilinear nature of the space

Working with the eccentricities of the space

A loft room may be one of the few areas of a home that you will be able to design from scratch, but its inherent irregularities can be a real challenge. The combination of sloping ceilings and walls of varying heights makes it hard to find the line at which the walls end and the ceiling begins, and low ceilings make it difficult to fit ready-made furniture. You can take a number of design routes. One solution is to build in furniture to exploit the odd shapes and create a clean, streamlined look. An all-over colour scheme will blur the junctions between walls and ceilings and give the space a coherent look. Alternatively, you can do what Orianna has done and make a feature of the eccentricities of the space. She has used lichen green for the walls, bedcoverings and bath base, and white for the ceiling – the junction between light and dark highlights the unusual geometry of the space, creating an ever-changing pattern of green against white, or green against pale wood. The strangeness of the volumes, shapes and angles is enhanced by the images reflected in the mirrors set into the central chimney stack.

Treatments for loft windows

Getting the right balance of privacy, light and shade is difficult in any room, but is especially so in a loft room with roof lights. Because these windows are turned directly to the sky, they receive more light and heat than normal windows, and both can be a problem. Some form of curtain or blind is necessary to cut out light at night and to minimise solar heat gain during the day. The manufacturers of some ranges of roof lights make roller, Venetian or pleated blinds especially for roof lights, with tracks or fixings at the sides to hold them in position. They also produce blackout blinds and thermal blinds which deflect heat during the summer, and retain heat within the room in winter. Alternatively, you could make a curtain with a channel at the top and bottom; thread narrow rods through the channels and fix these above and below the window. If the window is set low in the roof you could hang floor length curtains from a pole above the window, then catch them behind a second pole at the angle where the sloping roof meets the wall. Sunscreen fabric made from fibreglass yarn filters the glare without cutting out much light. Dormer windows can be treated like normal windows.

Orianna Fielding Banks' top tips for loft conversions

- Blackout blinds and thermal curtains are a good idea, and can normally be ordered with the window
- Use flooring and lighting to create the right mood in multifunctional rooms

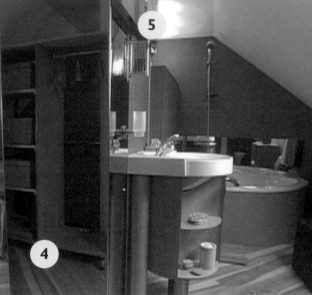

1 Concealed lights behind the bed provide atmospheric illumination

2 Walls fall short of the roof, giving an airy spacious feel, allowing the entire area to share natural and background light

3 A compact 'Flowform' radiator by Bisque Radiators is good-looking and space saving

4 A mirror on the chimney stack reflects light and draws attention to the juxtaposition of angles and lines

5 Lights along the top of the walls washes the roof space

Cellars, basements and garages offer opportunities for conversion to different uses. If you have any of these spaces it is worth seeing if they can be used to provide the additional accommodation that you need.

conversions
basements, cellars and garages

Many older properties have a basement or cellar. The basement was the lowest floor of the house and was wholly or partly below ground level. Natural light was often provided by windows onto outside 'areas'. The kitchen and scullery were generally located in the basement and they were usually connected to the upper storeys by a normal staircase, although many townhouses had separate 'tradesmen's' entrances via the front area. Cellars were intended for storage – of coal, foodstuffs and wine – and sometimes ran under part of the house only. In some Georgian and Victorian terraces the cellars run out under the pavement so that the coal man could deliver coal to the cellar through a hatch in the pavement.

Basement conversions

Basement conversions don't usually pose too many problems. Internal walls are sometimes knocked down to create through kitchen-dining rooms but this requires building regulations approval, and engineering costs will be incurred if load-bearing walls are involved. The basements of town houses are sometimes converted into separate flats, but remember that any change of use requires planning permission.

Cellar conversions

Making a cellar habitable can be difficult and expensive because they are often damp, poorly ventilated, have no natural light, and the ceiling height may be too low for normal uses. Nevertheless, a cellar does represent potential additional usable space so it is worth looking at your options. You will probably have to damp-proof floors and walls, and plaster or dry-line the walls and put in a ceiling. It may also be necessary to install mechanical ventilation, and you may need a new staircase in order to meet building regulations. You will also have to upgrade the power supply and install heating.

Garage conversions

Garage conversions are increasingly popular, but remember that future purchasers may regard the lack of a garage as a negative feature. Nevertheless, a garage that is attached to the house, or is within the main structure of the building can be converted to a workshop or a utility room fairly easily. If you want to create a really habitable living space, such as a children's playroom or an office, the work involved will be more substantial – the exact nature of the work will depend on whether the garage is detached, attached or an integral part of the dwelling. You may have to put in a damp-proof membrane, and insulate and dry-line the walls and ceiling. The front opening of the garage will have to be reduced in size, blocked in or partially blocked to create window and door openings. These should match the style and

proportions of those in the main dwelling. You may also need to create access to the main house. The power supply will also have to be upgraded and you will have to decide how you are going to heat the space.

The best garage conversions belie their humble origins. Externally architectural features like windows, doors and the roofline should blend harmoniously with the main building. Clever landscaping and planting can disguise the part of the driveway which is now redundant. Internally, changes of level, new windows and doors which give views onto the garden, and decorations which conceal the original proportions can all help to give the new room a character of its own. The *Better Homes* projects show that it is well worth hiring the services of a designer or an architect if you want a stylish and convincing conversion. It is worth seeking advice at an early stage – from the planning department and from a design professional – even if you've done this sort of thing before. You will find that the rules vary from one area to another, and they are constantly being updated.

Checklist

BASEMENT
Is your basement wholly or partly below ground level?

Does it have natural light?
Could you increase the light by enlarging window openings? You may require planning permission to change the size of these. Building regulations approval will be required if you want to put a new opening in a load-bearing wall. Could you excavate the ground outside to give more light or give access to the garden?

Does it have good access – from the main house, or from an area at the front?

Could it be converted to make a separate 'granny' flat?
A change of use would require planning permission

Are the internal walls structural?

Could internal walls be knocked down to create a big kitchen dining area?
You would need building regulations approval and the services of a structural engineer

CELLAR
How big is it – does it run under the entire house?

Does it project beyond the house – under the street?

Are there signs of damp on floor or walls?
You will probably have to damp proof floors and walls, and plaster or dry-line the walls

Is there a ceiling?

Does it smell musty?
This can be a sign of dry rot

Is untreated wood in contact with bare earth?

Is there a power supply?

Will you need plumbing?

Is it well ventilated?

Is there any natural light?

How high is the ceiling?
You may need a new staircase in order to meet building regulations

Could you excavate an 'area' to bring light into the basement?

GARAGE
Is the garage attached to the house?

Could you extend over the garage?

Is the garage integral to the house?

Is the garage detached?
You may need planning permission if there is a change of use – check with your planning department

Has anyone in the neighbourhood converted a garage?
Investigate how they have done it and what they have got.
Avoid creating a room that looks too obviously like a converted garage. Landscape the area around the converted garage and the driveway so that its original function is no longer obvious. Relate proportions and architectural features like windows and doors to the main building.
An attached or detached garage will not have cavity walls or roof insulation. You will require building regulations approval to bring the thermal insulation up to the required standard

John Cregg and Eugenie Van Harinxma set out to turn a neglected basement into a **bright, multifunctional family room** that could be used as a *playroom, dining room, guest bedroom, office, studio or sitting room.* A lot to ask? Well, aided and abetted by the *Better Homes* team,

they managed it brilliantly.

the problem... The Mallinsons are Nigel and Tracey, Lee, who is 13, Aaron, who is 11 and Nicole, who is seven. They moved here five years ago. Nigel works for a courier service. He often works night shifts and finds it difficult to sleep during the day when the children are at home. Tracey works part-time as a dinner lady and shop assistant. The family has grown fast and the house has become very crowded. They have a cellar which is used for storage. They'd like somewhere for the children to play, do their homework, and engage in their many hobbies. They'd also like to be able to put up the occasional guest. Converting the basement into useable living space would solve a lot of their problems and definitely put value on the property.

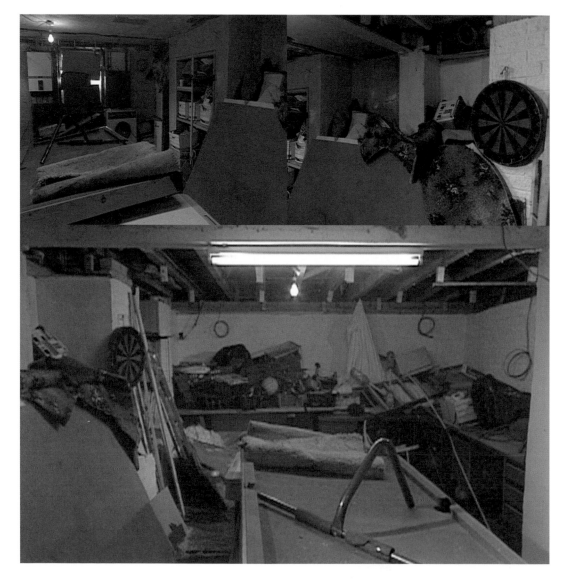

John Cregg and Eugenie Van Harinxma's task is to design a multifunctional room that can be used for a whole range of activities by the whole family. To maximise the space and give the room a streamlined look, they will line the entire space with cupboards containing shelving and other storage. The wall of doors will also conceal a brilliant foldaway bed and a built-in office area. The basement gets very little natural light so the designers will combine carefully planned lighting with pale flooring to make the most of the available light, and a matching pale grained effect on the built-in units.

A small window gives some natural light

A fold-down bed will occupy the end wall

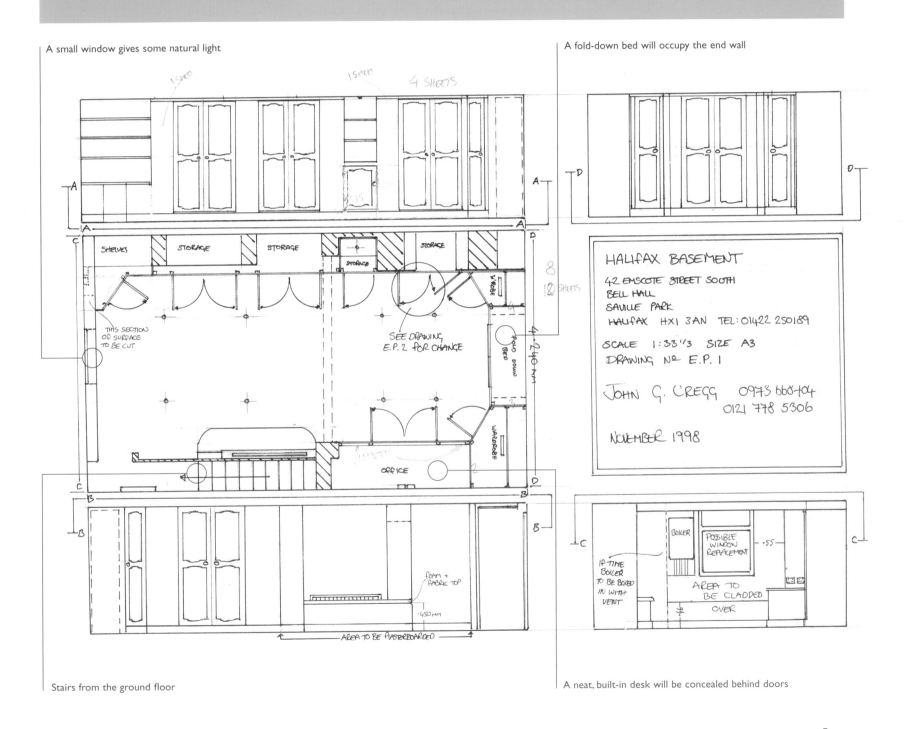

Stairs from the ground floor

A neat, built-in desk will be concealed behind doors

the solution... The first step was to clear the cellar of the household 'stuff' that had found its way there over five years. The ceiling was in poor condition and had to be removed. The cellar is where boilers, meters and all the other unsightly but essential services tend to be located. John had to arrange for gas pipes to be moved by a Corgi-registered gas fitter and for gas and electric meters to be moved. All these things take time to organise. When all that had been sorted the real work could start. A combi boiler was installed and radiators plumbed in.

A new ceiling was put up. The entire basement was rewired for lighting and powerpoints – never underestimate the number of powerpoints you will need.

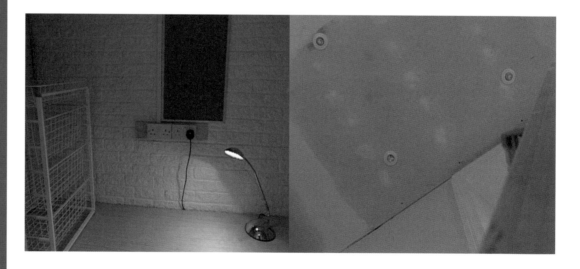

Once these basics had been dealt with work could start on the complex jigsaw of shelves and cupboards. Every bit of useable space was exploited. There were wardrobes for clothes, recesses for display, shelving for books, videos and toys, a workstation, and a foldaway bed. This involved an enormous amount of meticulous planning, and a great deal of skilled, hard work. But the results are magnificent. A huge amount of carefully designed storage space has been created, and once the cupboard doors go on, all you see is a continuous wall of pale wood.

John selected a tough, plank-style, laminate flooring. It looks like wood, but is a resin-based composition with the wood-effect applied photographically. It is easy to lay, child-proof and can be cleaned with a damp cloth. Its light tone was chosen to match the colour of the cupboard doors, giving the room an integrated and harmonious feel. By moving everything onto the walls, John and

ADRIAN & NEIL'S DIY TIPS

No-nail flooring

Wood-effect laminate flooring is easy to lay. A foam-like material, which is supplied on a roll, is laid onto the floor. This provides a seating for the boards and acts as sound insulation. The tongue and grooved boards are laid and glued at the joints. Easy!

Eugenie have kept the floor space clear, leaving plenty of room for a large dining table and chairs.

Nigel and Tracey will be able to entertain and have dinner parties, and the children will have somewhere to run around, play and make a noise without disturbing the adults.

Little light is admitted by the single window, so colour and lighting is important in this basement area. The pale tone on the walls and floors are light-reflecting, while the lovely aqua chosen for the exposed walls has a bright and airy feel. Low voltage spots provide overall lighting, with pools of light provided in recesses.

Hide-away beds

Beds take up a lot of the floor area, so a bed that folds away neatly is a brilliant way of releasing valuable floor space. Guest beds like fold-down beds, and truckle beds which slide under an existing bed, are a useful way of providing occasional sleeping facilities but the wall bed is a particularly neat solution. Although it is not a new idea, it has experienced a revival in recent times because it meets the need for multifunctional spaces. The beds have a subframe which is fixed to the floor and the wall. When not in use, the bed swings up into the subframe and stands vertically against the wall. When you want to use it, you pull it down on to the floor. The bed in Nigel and Tracey's basement swings down in this manner, and is concealed behind doors when not in use. It is not necessary to strip the bedding off as it is held in place by a strap. A similar arrangement was used in Jeanette and Terry's granny flat.

Considering a new boiler

There are many reasons why you should consider installing a new boiler. It will be much more efficient than a boiler which is 10-15 years old, even if it has been regularly maintained. An old boiler is probably only operating at about 50 per cent overall efficiency. Better designs and advances in technology have improved performance. New boilers are also more flexible – fanned flues mean that boilers don't have to be located on the inside of an outside wall – they can be installed in lofts, garages, and inside cupboards.

Combination or 'combi' boilers take up less space than traditional boilers because they do not have a hot water storage cylinder and do not need feed and expansion tanks in the loft. Combination boilers are efficient because they produce hot water as you need it. Replacing your old boiler may save money, allow you to improve your room layout and save space.

John Cregg's top tips for this type of cellar conversion
- Hide-away beds are great for when guests come round
- Cellars normally get little natural light, so keep the colour scheme as bright as possible

1 **A new combi boiler will supply water and heating cost effectively**

2 **Aqua is a cool, receding colour which opens up a space**

3 **This table nearly ended up on the skip but was salvaged by Eugenie. It can be used for dining, working or crafts**

4 **Pale floors reflect light**

5 **A swing-down bed can be stored vertically and concealed behind doors**

6 **A spot-lit recess is an ideal place to display a collection of artistically painted models**

7 **Recessed low voltage halogen spots give brilliant, daylight illumination**

8 **Eugenie colourwashed and grained the cupboards to create a limed effect that matches the laminate floor**

A blacksmith's workshop with up-and-over garage doors,
a corrugated roof and a large oil tank didn't look at all like a garden room –
but designer John Cregg was undaunted.

the problem... Janet and David both work in the travel industry and met 15 years ago when David came to work in Janet's office. Their beautiful three-bedroom cottage used to be the blacksmith's house and they have been busy doing it up since they moved in a year ago. The outbuilding which is attached to the cottage used to be the blacksmith's workshop and forge and has a very industrial look.

It is a large space which is used as a garage and store, and contains the oil tank for their oil-fired heating system. They'd like to convert it into a summerhouse from which they could enjoy their lovely view and their garden. The conversion would improve the quality of their life, and certainly add value to the property. It wasn't something they'd considered doing when they bought the house a year ago, so it really would be a bonus as far as they are concerned.

Tongue and groove cladding will be applied to walls

to create a garden house feel

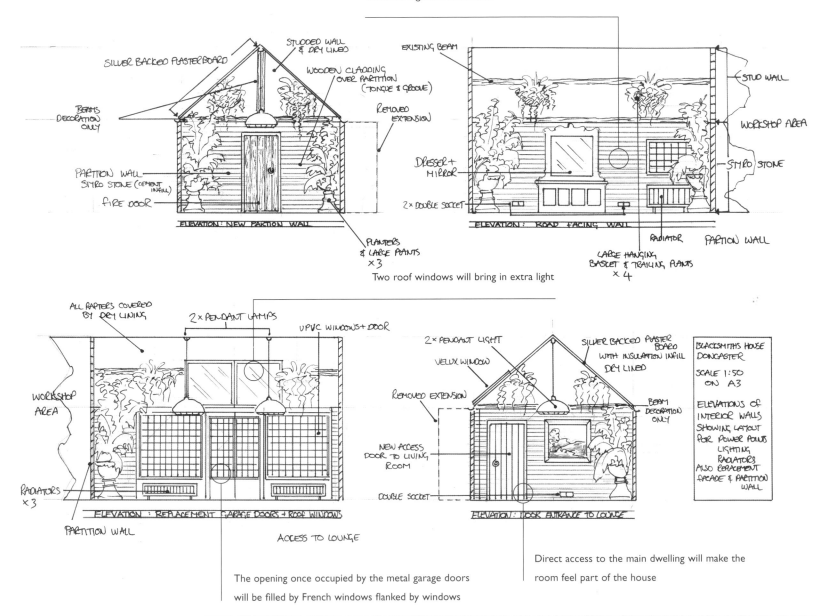

SILVER BACKED PLASTERBOARD

STUDDED WALL & DRY LINED

WOODEN CLADDING OVER PARTITION (TONGUE & GROOVE)

BEAMS DECORATION ONLY

REMOVED EXTENSION

PARTITION WALL STYRO STONE (CEMENT INFILL)

FIRE DOOR

ELEVATION : NEW PARTION WALL

EXISTING BEAM

STUD WALL

WORKSHOP AREA

DRESSER + MIRROR

STYRO STONE

2 x DOUBLE SOCKET

ELEVATION : ROAD FACING WALL

RADIATOR

PARTITION WALL

PLANTERS & LARGE PLANTS x3

LARGE HANGING BASKET & TRAILING PLANTS x 4

Two roof windows will bring in extra light

ALL RAFTERS COVERED BY DRY LINING

2 x PENDANT LAMPS

UPVC WINDOWS + DOOR

2 x PENDANT LIGHT

SILVER BACKED PLASTER BOARD WITH INSULATION INFILL DRY LINED

VELUX WINDOW

WORKSHOP AREA

REMOVED EXTENSION

NEW ACCESS DOOR TO LIVING ROOM

BEAM DECORATION ONLY

RADIATORS x 3

DOUBLE SOCKET

PARTITION WALL

ELEVATION : REPLACEMENT GARAGE DOORS + ROOF WINDOWS

ACCESS TO LOUNGE

ELEVATION : DOOR ENTRANCE TO LOUNGE

BLACKSMITHS HOUSE DONCASTER

SCALE 1:50 ON A3

ELEVATIONS OF INTERIOR WALLS SHOWING LAYOUT FOR POWER POINTS LIGHTING RADIATORS ALSO REPLACEMENT FACADE & PARTITION WALL

The opening once occupied by the metal garage doors

will be filled by French windows flanked by windows

Direct access to the main dwelling will make the

room feel part of the house

ideas... John Cregg's plan is to split the existing outhouse in two. The area adjacent to the house will become a summer-house while the other half will remain as a workshop – it will also accommodate the oil tank which must be moved. A door will be knocked through from the main house so that the summer-house can be accessed without going out of doors – it will become part of the main house and will be useable throughout the year. He also intends to introduce lots of natural light by putting glazed doors and glazing where the two garage doors were.

A pair of roof windows will bring in further light – the room will be like a conservatory or indoor garden. Looking at the existing building it is hard to visualise the transformation, but John obviously has the vision thing and is quietly confident.

ADRIAN & NEIL'S DIY TIPS

Successful plastering

The biggest mistake people make is putting too much plaster on at once. It is much better to apply a little at a time; or as the project plasterer advised – 'get in an expert'

Wheeling your barrow safely and easily

If you straighten your back and pull your arms up all the weight falls on the front wheel and you have more control. Correct posture will protect your back and avoid back strain

Laying floors tiles correctly

Laying tiles along a straight edge isn't foolproof. It is much better to use a right-angle to check that everything is square. Work from one end and sort out the tiles around the edges later

the solution... Some heavy duty work had to carried out in the workshop – a lot of shifting, smashing and demolition – definitely a job for the boys, Neil and Adrian. The oil tank had to be moved to the far end of the space to make room at the 'summer-house' end. Health and safety requirements stated that it should be located behind another wall. The next big job was removing the metal garage doors and their frames – specialist work requiring heavy-duty cutting equipment and definitely best left to the experts. An opening was made into the main house, providing access to the living room. A single thermal block wall was built across the middle of the building to separate the workshop area from the summer-house area. Tongue and groove cladding was applied to give it a rustic or old-time New England feel. Extensive areas of timber must be treated with two coats of fire retardant paint, allowing two hours between applications. New windows were fitted to front and back, the roof was insulated then drylined with silver-backed plasterboard, and skimmed. Oil filled electric heaters, insulation and double glazing will ensure that the summer-house will be cosy and warm all year round. New electrical circuits were put in providing several double sockets, and outlets for two large pendant lights. Ceramic tiles were laid onto the existing concrete.

Tongue and groove panelling

Wood panelling is an attractive, flexible and varied finish for a wall. Here it was used to cover the rough walls of what had been an industrial workshop. Because it is a natural and traditional material it is especially suited to garden rooms, and chalet-style structures. There are different types of timber for cladding. Tongue and groove can have a narrow or wide V between the boards, a wide V, or a double V (to create to appearance of narrower panelling). In shiplap each board has an L-shaped edge and a curved edge so that the channel between the boards has a curved and straight side. Tongue and groove panelling also works well in traditional kitchens and bathrooms. In wainscoting timber was applied vertically; matchboarding is usually applied horizontally. Panelling can be washed with thinned colour, distressed or given a solid matt covering. Extensive areas of panelling must be given a fire-retardant finish – special paints were used on the walls of David and Janet's summer-house for this purpose.

Plant maintenance

Healthy house plants add freshness, colour and a breath of the outdoors to the home, and are a must in a conservatory or garden room. Read and keep the care labels carefully; some plants have very specific needs. Most plants like an even temperature during the growing season and light, but prefer to be away from direct sunlight. Pale-leaved plants need more light than dark-leaved ones. Plants grow towards light so turn them occasionally to maintain even growth. Plants with thin leaves, such as ferns, need a high level of humidity and thrive in bathrooms and kitchens, though they'll be happy elsewhere if you spray them daily with tepid water. Plants with thicker, tougher leaves are more resiliant and can tolerate a drier atmosphere.

Take care not to overwater your plants – more house plants die through overwatering than anything else. Feed plants regularly during their growing season, but don't feed dormant plants. A new potted plant will have sufficient food in the compost for about two months. Concentrated multi-purpose liquid and soluble powder fertilisers are suitable for most plants and are easy to use and effective. Large leaves should be cleaned once a month using tepid water or rain water. Wipe tough glossy leaves with a damp cloth or sponge. Alternatively, use proprietary products such as spray or leaf wipes, available from garden centres.

**John Cregg's top tips
for this type of conversion**

- Always start by speaking to the building inspector at the local authority. The building inspector is not there to be obstructive, but will give you sound advice that could help you avoid any pitfalls and potentially save money
- Remember that if the new work doesn't comply with regulations, the building inspector has the power to stop the work or make you restore the building to its original state
- A building that has never had central heating or has not been inhabited for many years, such as a barn, is likely to have some damp problems. Always check for dampness and take the appropriate preventative measures; for example, install damp proof course, renew damp plaster and renew or repair the roof before any interior work starts
- If you plan to knock through a wall, check to see if it is load bearing. Always check with a structural engineer or surveyor first
- Plants can make all the difference to a summer house. Spend some time researching perennials and other plants that provide year-round colour
- Double glazing will increase your choice of plants

1 **Bright yellow paint on the wood panelled walls is a lovely sunny colour for a garden room**

2 **Terracotta-red ceramic tiles are tough and easy to clean**

3 **Beams give the room an old-world charm**

4 Pendant lights on long flexes shed large pools of light

5 Roof windows provide plenty of natural light – an ideal habitat for hanging baskets and specimen plants

One of the surprises of the *Better Homes* TV series is the extent to which a well-designed and well-presented garden can improve the quality of your life... and add value to your home.

g a r d e n s

creating glorious gardens

Gone are the days when a garden consisted of a neatly manicured lawn surrounded by an orderly border. Today's garden is an extension of the home – a place in which the children can play, and the grown-ups can relax and entertain. The ideal garden is easy to maintain, looks wonderful from every viewpoint and in every season, provides an attractive setting for the house, and doesn't reveal all its delights at once. The successful garden gives pleasure every day – you catch glimpses of it through windows and doors, wander into it to relax with a cup of coffee or read the paper, and sit out on the terrace to catch the last glimpses of the setting sun. If your garden fails to meet any of these criteria, it is time to take a long hard look at it and to devise a strategy to ensure that it becomes an essential part of family life. Start by working through our checklist – this will help you identify the way you would like to use the garden, the things you like about it now and the things you would really like to change. This will provide a framework for your garden plan.

Plan your garden as you would any other part of the house. Draw a scale plan on gridded paper – just as you would for a room (see page 22). Indicate north and south. Draw existing structures to scale; include walls, house extensions, sheds, paved areas and steps. Mark gates and doors, indicating the arc of their swing. Use a blue pencil to lightly hatch in areas that are mostly in shade, and use a yellow pencil to indicate sunny areas. This will help you to choose eating and sunning areas, and will also help in planning your planting.

Now you can begin to plan the new scheme. Start with the hard landscaping – this will give you a basic framework to build on. Draw in new walls, fences, buildings, paved and concreted areas, and decking, then plot the location of lawns and bedding. You need to plan a garden for all seasons, so indicate the possible location of the evergreen trees and large shrubs that will give the garden structure, interest and colour in the winter months. With the skeleton in place you can start to flesh it out with blocks of smaller shrubs and perennials. Think of your garden as a series of pictures which are revealed one after another as you wander through. Don't forget to consider how it will look from ground floor doors and windows, and from windows on the upper storeys. Every viewing point should have a focus, so that the eye is led into, over and around the 'picture' in a leisurely way.

Scale is an important aspect of garden planning. If everything is the same size and has similar textures, the garden will lack interest. Changes of height and leaf size are as important as orchestrating your colour scheme. You can even use scale to create a false perspective – make a small garden feel larger by placing large plants near the house and smaller ones further away, or make a long thin garden seem shorter by placing some large shrubs or trees at the far end. Above all think broadly – plan blocks of colour and texture. Scent is one of the most seductive aspects of a garden so remember to include scented plants in your

scheme. Plant them so that those which release their perfumes during the day are placed where you will get the benefit of their fragrances, and plant night scented varieties around the area where you sit out or eat in the evening.

The gardener must plan not for today or tomorrow but for years ahead. It takes at least three years for a garden to grow in and five years to fully mature. But a cleverly designed garden will begin to work straight away. The hard landscaping will give it form, and a few mature specimen trees and shrubs and fast growing plants will provide colour and begin to soften the contours. Allow your garden to evolve in phases, so if there are flourishing plants that don't feature in the final scheme leave them there until the new plants have begun to establish. Use tubs, pots and hanging baskets to provide temporary splashes of colour in bare areas, and hide ugly features with fast-growing climbers.

Checklist

What do you want from your garden?
Something beautiful to look at? A retreat? A source of flowers, vegetables or herbs? A play-area for the children? An outside space for pets? A place to eat out of doors? Somewhere to sunbathe? A place to garden?

What features do you want in the garden? Your list could include:
lawn, patio, barbecue, water feature pond (dangerous if there are small children), pergola, sundial, permanent seating, workshop, potting shed, garden room, conservatory, storage for deckchairs, sandpit, climbing frame swimming pool.
List these in order of priority – just in case you can't accommodate them all!

USERS
Who is going to use the garden?
adults, children, animals, elderly people, disabled people

SIZE
If your garden is large consider dividing it up into different areas.
If it is small think about paving the entire area

LAWN
A lawn is relatively high maintenance but provides a pleasant surface for children to play on

PRIVACY
Is your garden visible from neighbouring gardens, or overlooked by adjacent properties? If you feel exposed, consider trellis or hedge screening around the sides. A pergola or trees can also give privacy

LIGHT AND SHADE
The distribution of light throughout the day will determine planting and the positioning of play areas, patios, garden rooms and furniture

GROWING CONDITIONS
Soil type, drainage, climate and exposure to light will determine which plants will thrive in your garden. Is your soil acid or alkaline? Use a testing kit to find out – take samples from different parts of the garden. You can modify the nature of your soil by adding lime or organic matter. Are there are any hot spots or frost pockets?

GARDENING
Are you:
a committed gardener?
someone who uses the garden as an outside room?
Do you garden a little but often, or have periodic onslaughts?
Design the garden to suit your gardening style. If you are a lazy gardener make a low-maintenance garden with no lawns and plenty of ground cover to minimise weeding

LIGHTING
If you intend to eat in the garden regularly you should consider some form of artificial lighting. Low voltage lights can also be used to highlight spectacular plants and to create drama and mood

EATING OUT
Do you intend to eat out of doors?
Ensure there is easy access to the house and kitchen
Allocate space for a barbecue

STYLE
Do you want:
an old-fashioned cottage garden?
Something more formal? A modern 'designer' garden?
Formulate your ideas by visiting friends' gardens and gardens that are open to the public. Study books and magazines, watch TV and visit gardening exhibitions

Sue and Phil's garden was almost entirely redundant – they couldn't see it, they didn't use it and it contributed nothing to the appearance of the house. Designer **Kieran Kelly** and garden designer **Ginni Gillam** put their heads together *and came up with a scheme which* changed all that.

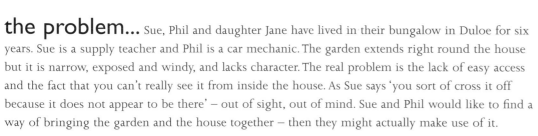

the problem... Sue, Phil and daughter Jane have lived in their bungalow in Duloe for six years. Sue is a supply teacher and Phil is a car mechanic. The garden extends right round the house but it is narrow, exposed and windy, and lacks character. The real problem is the lack of easy access and the fact that you can't really see it from inside the house. As Sue says 'you sort of cross it off because it does not appear to be there' – out of sight, out of mind. Sue and Phil would like to find a way of bringing the garden and the house together – then they might actually make use of it.

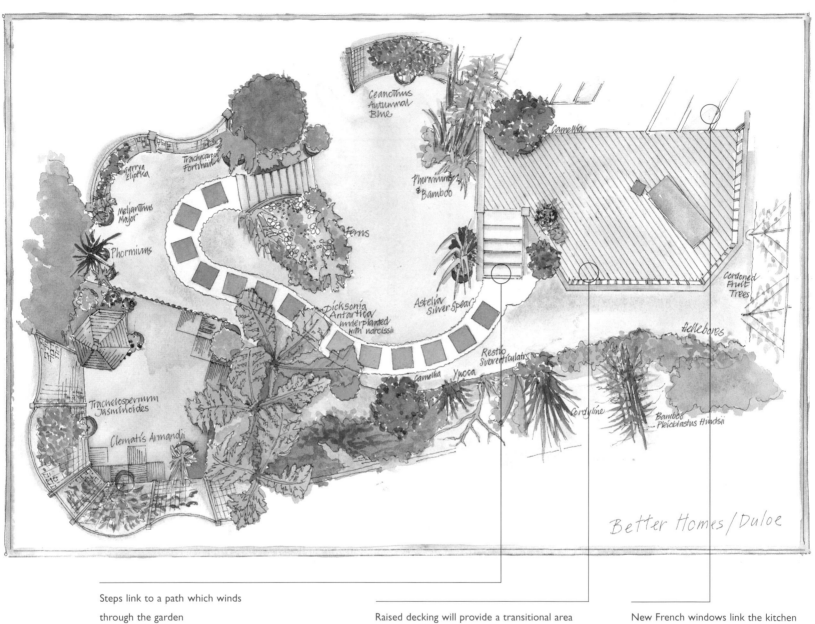

Garrya Eliptica

Trachycarpus Fortunei

Melianthus Major

Phormiums

Trachelospermum Jasminoides

Clematis Armandii

Ceanothus Autumnal Blue

Camellia

Phormiums & Bamboo

Ferns

Dicksonia Antartica underplanted with narcissii

Astelia Silver Spear

Camellia Yucca

Restio Subverticulatis

Cordyline

Helebores

Bamboo Pleioblastus Hindsii

Cordoned Fruit Trees

Better Homes / Duloe

Steps link to a path which winds through the garden

Raised decking will provide a transitional area between house and garden

New French windows link the kitchen with the new terrace

ideas... Kieran Kelly is the designer, with Ginni Gillam looking after the planting scheme, and twin Adrian providing the brawn. Having surveyed the site and talked to Sue and Phil, Kieran acknowledged that lack of easy access to the garden was the root of the problem. He decided to build a veranda and create an opening from the kitchen to give direct access to the new deck. The deck would provide a halfway house between home and garden. It would be so easy to step out for a moment to admire the view, take the air or sip a cup of coffee that the garden would feel part of the house in a way it never had before.

ADRIAN & NEIL'S

DIY TIPS

Growing azaleas

Azaleas don't like limy soils so if your garden is on chalk or limestone, keep the plant in its pot. They grow beautifully in pots and will thrive anywhere in the country

Laying decking

If you lay your decking straight onto the ground it will rot in time. Protect it by laying it on specially treated timbers which are guaranteed for about 15 years. Raising it off the ground also allows air to circulate. Place black plastic sheeting underneath to prevent weeds from growing through

Potting on

Don't transfer pot-bound plants into huge pots. Choose a pot that is a just a bit bigger, let them grow into that and pot them on to a bigger container in the next season. That way they will develop a really strong root system

the solution...

An opening is knocked through the kitchen wall for the patio doors that will open onto the deck, and link the bungalow with the garden. Kieran has commissioned a deck from specialist decking company Archadeck, so vast quantities of timber arrive and the business of construction starts. The elements of the custom-built deck have been cut and machined off site, so the structure takes shape surprisingly quickly.

A raised patio area at the end of the garden will give Sue and Phil another garden 'room'. A trellis is erected to create a windbreak and provide some privacy. Other features include wooden tiles laid chequerboard fashion, and a winding path of the same tiles embedded in white Cornish grit to create an eye-catching pattern. A stream with a wooden bridge and a fountain in a pavilion introduce water into the garden. With the hard landscaping in place, the plants arrived – and what a lot there are. Most were destined for the different areas of the main garden, but at least a third of them went on the decking. The planting list was very extensive, but among Ginni's favourites are the following: the climber *Clematis armandii* 'Snowdrift'; bamboos and grasses including *Phyllostachys nigra*, *Arundinaria vagans*, *Sasa palmata* and *Pleloblastus hindusii*, the shrubs *Restio subverticuatus*, *Melianthus major*, *Choisya ternata* 'Sundance' and *Aestelia* 'Silver spear', and the fern *Dicksonia antatartica*.

Ginni Gillam's planting scheme

Everything in this garden is evergreen – the idea is to give the garden a year-round green 'scaffolding' which can be expanded at different times of the year, with herbaceous plants and annuals. As Sue and Phil live in north Cornwall, Ginni could use some fringe-hardy plants which might not survive in Yorkshire, for example. The plants were also selected to be visually interesting when seen from above – as the deck would probably be the most frequent vantage point. The use of camellias, which were in flower when they were filming, brought colour to the garden at a time when Cornwall can be very dull and grey. They also helped to combat the rather overwhelming stone wall on the perimeter. Ginni used curved trellis to create a serpentine windbreak on the windward side of the garden – it also acted as an enclosure and made the rear garden more private. The bamboos were 6-9 feet (2-3m) tall – this was intentional because they brought foliage from the garden level up to and above the deck – joining one level to another.

1 The decking provides a transition between house and garden. The location was chosen because it was sheltered from the prevailing wind and will catch the morning sun. The garden can be viewed from the deck

2 A winding path leads the eye from one feature to another

3 The fern *Dicksonia antartica* has large graceful fronds

4 Fiona, a survivor from the original garden, has found a home by the stream

5 The patio area catches the evening sun

**Kieran Kelly's top tips
for improving your garden**

• you want to install an elevated deck, make sure
  that it will be private. You may need a high fence
• When you are considering installing a deck area,
  find out where the prevailing winds come from,
  and which direction the house faces
• Design the garden around a natural walkway
• Know your soil type. Some plants require specific
  types of soil
• If electrics need to be supplied to the garden,
  make sure you use a qualified engineer as the
  cables have to be 18 inches (46cm) below
  the ground

Decking

Wooden decking has long been a significant
feature of North American and Australian
suburban homes. These aren't the tiny porches
or narrow verandas that grace Victorian and
especially Edwardian villas in this country, but
large outdoor rooms designed for climates that
allow outdoor living for a good part of the
year or even year-round. Wooden decking
looks attractive, blends with a garden
environment and weathers to a beautiful finish.
Decking can be laid as a surface material as an
alternative to stone or brick, or it can be raised
above the ground to create a veranda or raised
terrace. On sloping sites it can be used to
provide a level area. The system used for this
project has several useful features. The timbers
are grooved to prevent you losing your footing
in wet weather, and the wood is impregnated
under pressure with wax and other
preservative which protect the timbers and
shed water.

Toby Buckland likes a challenge, which is good because **transforming a large but featureless garden** into two separate gardens with *lots of features* was quite a task.

the problem... Alison and Andrew have two children, Bethany and Chloe, and live in Northenden, Greater Manchester. They love spending time in their extensive back garden, especially in summer, and it is ideal for the children. Andrew is a key specialist and locksmith, and Alison is a child-minder. Although their garden is large, it is rather featureless. They'd like it redesigned to provide play areas for the children Alison looks after, with swings and slides and maybe a little playhouse. But they'd also like an adult area with an exotic feel – but it needs to be low maintenance because Andrew works six days a week. A properly planned garden will probably increase the value of their house.

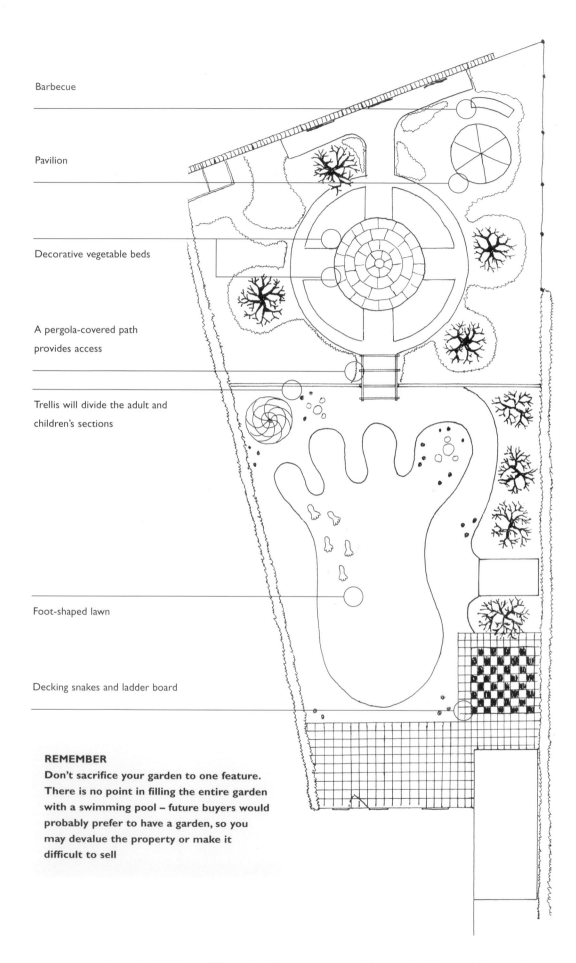

Barbecue

Pavilion

Decorative vegetable beds

A pergola-covered path
provides access

Trellis will divide the adult and
children's sections

Foot-shaped lawn

Decking snakes and ladder board

REMEMBER
Don't sacrifice your garden to one feature.
There is no point in filling the entire garden
with a swimming pool – future buyers would
probably prefer to have a garden, so you
may devalue the property or make it
difficult to sell

ideas... Toby Buckland will create two
gardens. The children's garden will be near
the back entrance of the house for easy
access and so that Alison can keep an eye
on things. The children's garden will have
lots of visual interest and activity areas.
Toby's plans include a decking snakes and
ladders board, a shed converted into a
jungle hut, a willow den, a sandpit and a
foot-shaped lawn with a running track
around it. The planting in the children's
area will be soft so that they can't hurt
themselves, and indestructible so that they
can't hurt the plants.

The adults' section will be in a
secluded area at the end of the plot. Toby
has chosen a Mediterranean theme. Key
features will be gravel paths, a stone circle
and colourful mosaics. Because the garden
will be used for entertaining, Toby intends
to provide extra seating around the existing
mature trees. He will also provide a potager
bed for growing vegetables, a barbecue and
a gazebo. The plants in this area will be
more fragile and delicate than those in the
children's garden.

the solution...

The week the team arrived in Manchester the weather was foul. The site was cleared and the design for the garden was marked out on the ground with spray paint. The garden looks like a battlefield as the various sections are set out. A heavy, and closely woven trellis is erected across the garden – this will divide the children's garden from the adult's. The small apertures mean that the children can't climb it because their hands and feet won't fit into the trelliswork.

A stone circle is set out in the adult area, with formal beds radiating out from it. Timber is used to create neat edges for the beds and paths. Gravel paths run between the beds which can be used for growing vegetables, herbs or flowers. A pavilion is constructed at the far end where it creates a dramatic focus and provides shelter – its circular plan echoes the shapes of the paved area, the potager garden and the tree-seats. Behind it a barbecue area takes shape – so that Alison and Andrew can entertain out of doors, Mediterranean-style.

Meanwhile Donna Reeves is creating some mosaic panels in Mediterranean blues and aquamarines. These will be displayed on posts, providing splashes of vibrant colour on an otherwise uninteresting expanse of brick wall. Toby constructs turf seats around the existing fruit trees.

In the children's area, the lawn is trimmed to a foot-shape and bark paths are laid for them to run around on. Donna makes a snakes and ladder board from panels of wood decking. Toby has made a marvellous den from woven willow – in time this will take root and grow.

The final stage is planting out. For the children's garden, Toby has chosen jungly, non-poisonous plants with soft leaves. These include things like bamboo, ornamental grasses and the New Zealand flax, *Phormium tenax*. He also used eucalyptus which is pretty indestructible.

For the grown-up's garden he has chosen herbs and plants with silvery foliage for a Mediterranean feel, and a medlar tree to evoke a sense of the past.

ADRIAN & NEIL'S

DIY TIPS

Plotting a circle

To lay out circles place a peg in the middle of the area, attach a length of string, mark off the radius of the circle and plot out the circle – marking it with a can of spray paint, sand or scraping a line in the soil with a stick

Bending wood

Cut slots about three quarters of the way through the plank, at intervals. This will allow the wood to make a curve. This is how the shuttering for the beds and paths was created

Making tree seats

Toby used to work at the Cambridge University Botanic Garden. While he was there they decided to recreate a Tudor garden. Gardens of the period often featured turf seats so he had to find a way of constructing one – and this is the method he devised. A circle is set out around the tree, and then hazel poles are pushed into the ground at intervals. Willow, which is very pliant, is then woven in and out of the hazel sticks to create a sturdy wickerwork structure. This is filled with soil, and turf is laid on top, to produce a permanent sitting area which blends naturally into its surroundings.

1 Tile, surrounded by stone and gravel paths, provides contrasts of colour and texture

2 A piece of living sculpture – a willow den

3 A barbecue area behind the pavillion means that Alison and Andrew can eat out with the girls or have friends round and eat alfresco

4 The brick wall is colour-washed to create a faded, Mediterranean look

5 A trellis divides the two gardens, and encourages you to explore

6 The children are bound to enjoy these quaint little mushroom seats and tables

7 Toby's childproof planting means that the children can play freely and safely

8 A turf seat provides another place to sit and view the garden

Potager gardens

A potager is an ornamental vegetable garden and takes its name from the French *potage*, meaning 'soup'. In a potager vegetables, flowers and herbs are grown together to create a garden which is useful and visually appealing. They were developed in the fifteenth and sixteenth centuries when knot gardens were all the rage. The symmetrical design of the beds may be interwoven by gravel or paved paths, and neatly edged by tiles, wood or clipped plants such as chives, parsley, chervil, yarrow, or catmint, or hedges of rosemary and lavender. The style also allows the gardener to juxtapose plants that seem to grow well together. Basil, tomatoes, marigolds, and peppers make good companions, as do the trios of sage, rosemary, and cabbage, and hollyhocks, angelica and artichokes. Often topiary or standard trees or shrubs were incorporated in the schemes. Bay is a popular culinary tree which can be clipped into shape, but shrubs like rosemary can be trained into columns and balls.

Knot gardens

Knot gardens were common in English gardens of the sixteenth and seventeen centuries. They consisted of intricate, geometric designs which were outlined in low-growing hedges of box, the spaces between filled with different coloured gravels and stones.

Toby Buckland's top tips for transforming a garden

- Consider taking down integral fences or gates to improve access
- Always start work at the furthest point of the garden away from your access so that you don't ruin what you have already done
- Your lawn doesn't have to be square and conventional – here we made a footprint
- The quickest way to make a path is to dig out four inches (10cm) of soil and hammer posts in along the edges. Nail planks to the posts and fill the area between with gravel
- Always check title deeds on boundaries to avoid disputes with neighbours

Alison said she and her boys were **'water creatures'** who like **'to hear the sound of water'.** She also mentioned *'tropical plants'.* So Toby Buckland and the *Better Homes* team turned her garden in Arnold into a **palm-fringed oasis.**

the problem... Alison and her sons, Ashley and Scott, have lived in their terraced house in Arnold in Nottingham for three and a half years. The garden is long and narrow and, as the houses in the terrace are quite cheek-by-jowl, she feels rather overlooked when she is out in the garden. The garden used to be lined with rose bushes, but they were a bit overwhelming in such a confined plot so she dug them up. After that she lost heart and the garden got more and more bare. She doesn't even bother to put pots out any more, although she did put in a small water feature and is quite pleased with that. Alison would really like more privacy, something interesting to look at and a water feature. With the *Better Homes* team on call that is easily arranged, but the result may not be quite what she expected.

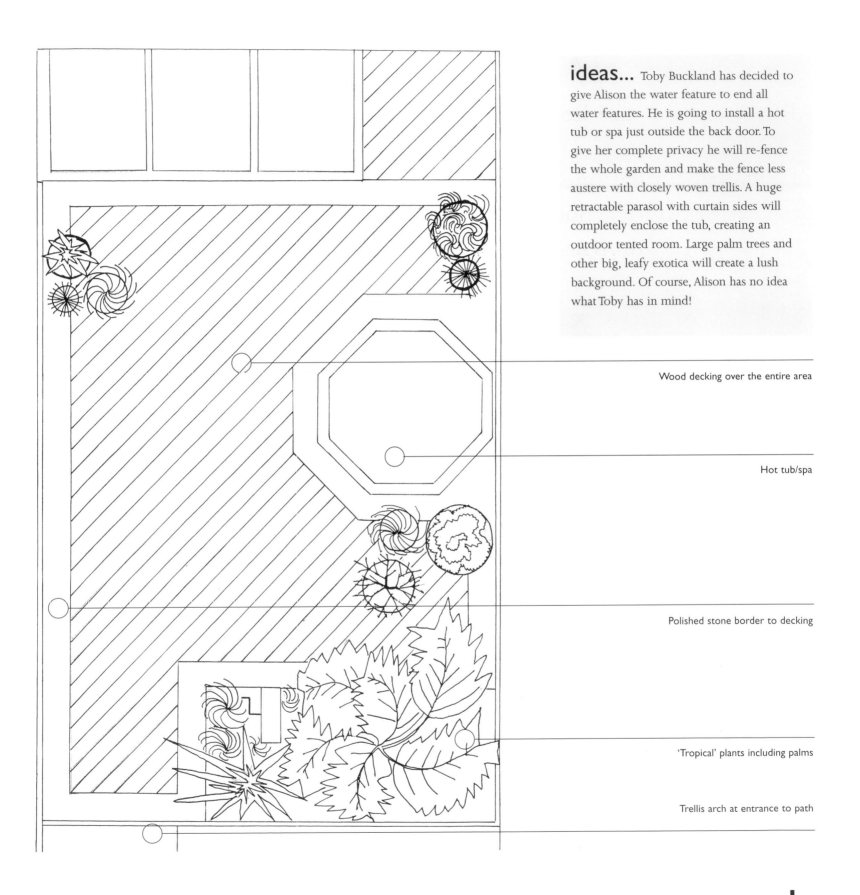

ideas... Toby Buckland has decided to give Alison the water feature to end all water features. He is going to install a hot tub or spa just outside the back door. To give her complete privacy he will re-fence the whole garden and make the fence less austere with closely woven trellis. A huge retractable parasol with curtain sides will completely enclose the tub, creating an outdoor tented room. Large palm trees and other big, leafy exotica will create a lush background. Of course, Alison has no idea what Toby has in mind!

Wood decking over the entire area

Hot tub/spa

Polished stone border to decking

'Tropical' plants including palms

Trellis arch at entrance to path

ADRIAN & NEIL'S DIY TIPS

Putting up fenceposts

The holes into which the posts go should be about one third of the height of the post, and about four inches round. Fill the hole with concrete and make sure it is compacted. Insert the first post. Cut a piece of timber or batten to the length of the panel and use that as a measuring stick to give you the location of the remaining posts

Be bold

In a small garden you can go down what Toby calls the 'doll's house route' and have lots of little features, or you can make big bold statements, with a few striking architectural elements

the solution... It's a small garden but preparing the site involved a lot of demolition and earthmoving. The existing slabs come up, the old fencing comes down, and the skip outside the house starts to fill up. A new board fence, with trellis in front, is erected on either side of the garden. The trellis is taken across the bottom of the deck area to screen the garage, with an archway to the path at the back. Panels of coloured glass inserted at intervals create splashes of vivid colour. Toby has decided to use wooden decking, which is much warmer underfoot than stone or concrete, and has the indoor-outdoor feel he is after. A polished stone edge goes in first, then gravel over the soil to suppress weeds, then the decking which has a ridged surface to make it less slippery.

Next the enormous parasol was installed. It has a winding device to raise and lower it, and curtains to screen the sides. Its waterproof canopy provides complete privacy and a dry area for bathing on rainy days. The plants Toby has chosen have a distinctly tropical look. As Carol says, 'they look like they should be in Miami' and she is concerned that they won't survive in such a northerly location. But Toby reassures her that they can 'take a few degrees of frost, particularly if they are in a sheltered garden like Alison's, and they love rain...they are not really tropical, they just look it.' With all the main structures in place and the jungle beginning to take root, it was time to bring in the hot tub. It was manoeuvred into position and connected to the water and electricity supplies – both jobs for experts. Toby had also installed subtle lighting around the tub, so that the garden can be used day and night.

But would Alison like it? That was the

Creating a 'tropical' garden

It is quite possible to create an exotic garden with big fronds and big leaves in Britain's relatively mild climate. But these gorgeous plants do need shelter – it's not the frost that does for them, it's the wind which tears them to shreds. Alison's garden was ideal, sheltered on three sides by walls and on the fourth by the walls of the house. And the brick walls have an added advantage in that they absorb heat, releasing it slowly and creating the garden's own microclimate. Toby chose evergreen specimens so that the garden looks wonderful even in wintertime. The Chusan palm (*Trachycarpus fortunei*) is very frost hardy – in fact, when it was first brought into this country it was left outside for a winter by mistake and survived. The specimen in Alison's garden is 15ft (4.5m) tall but they can grow to 20ft (6m), although they are slow growing. With its solid central truck and delicate fan-shaped leaves, it conjures up visions of palm-fringed tropical shores – although it is native to China. *Fatsia japonica* or false castor oil plant is another striking evergreen. A native of Japan, it has large, glossy, lobed leaves and will thrive in a sheltered location in sun or shade. Toby's planting also includes *Fargesia murielae*, *Cordyline australis green*, *Phormium tenax green*, *Phormium tenax red*, *Yucca gloriosa variegata* and *Trachycarpus wagnerianus*.

question on everyone's mind. Well, not only did she like it, she absolutely loved it. And when Carol and the team made a return visit almost a year later, she still loved it. She and the boys use it all the time – in fact, Ashley and Scott sometimes take a dip before they go to school in the morning. Friends are constantly dropping in for a plunge, and Alison and her twin sister, Kathy, often sit in it until they turn 'pruny'. So the gamble paid off.

Michael O'Flaherty thought the garden was 'superb' and 'outrageous', 'we have transplanted Arnold to the Florida coastline', but he issues a word of caution. Remember that 'purchasers tend to be on the conservative side, and may prefer a patio, lawn and flower borders.' But if, like Alison, you intend to stay put for a long time, you can afford to be adventurous.

Toby Buckland and Chris Maton's top tips for gardens

- Before you lay any type of wooden decking make sure you lay a 2 inch (5cm) layer of gravel to stop the growth of weeds
- A parasol with a waterproof canopy provides a dry area
- Don't be afraid of putting large features in a small garden – like Alison's spa – make it the centrepiece and work around it

1 **Coloured glass insets add a touch of luxury**

2 **The retractable parasol gives total privacy – it is like an outdoor room**

3 **Subtle lighting means the spa area can be used day and night**

4 **Architectural plants like palms add drama to a small garden, look good winter and summer and are low maintenance**

5 **Wooden decking is ideal for transitional areas**

Plant hunters

You probably never stop to wonder where the plants in your garden come from. Most are not native to these islands, but have been brought back other parts of the world, often from remote and even dangerous places. The desire to acquire the new, the exotic, the rare, and the costly goes back a long way. In 1,495 BC Queen Hatshepsut of Egypt sent an expedition to Somalia to bring back incense trees, *Commiphera myrrha*. In the seventeenth and eighteenth centuries an interest in science and a desire for trade sent botanists, travellers and collectors all over the world, in search of seeds and exotic foods for research, cultivation and profit.

Organisations such as the Horticulture Society and Kew Gardens were responsible for many plant-gathering expeditions. The most well-known plant hunters of the seventeenth century are John Tradescant (1570-1638) and his son, also John, (1608-1662). John the elder made many trips to Holland but also visited Russia. His son made three trips to Virginia – among the introductions which are credited to him are the tulip tree, *Liriodendron tulipifera*. Robert Fortune (1812-1880) was the first plant hunter to gain access to China. He collected many plants then unknown, and discovered how to cultivate chrysanthemums, tea, and dwarf conifers. Among the plants that bear his name are the Chusan palm (*Trachycarpus fortunei*) which Toby included in Alison's garden and *Rhododendron fortunei*. He also brought back many shrubs that brighten the winter months including winter flowering jasmine, *Jasminium nudiflorum* and winter flowering honeysuckle, *Lonicera fragrantissima*.

Finding more space for a family who live in a picture postcard cottage was *quite a challenge.* **But Dave Wellman and the Better Homes team** **found a** brilliant solution.

the problem... Bob and Anne and their sons, Kieran and Jonathon, live in a 120-year-old cottage in an idyllic rural location. They have lived there since 1977. Anne is a part-time teacher in the village and Bob is a systems analyst. Their cottage has spectacular views, and a stream murmurs in the background. Their only problem is lack of space – the cottage has two-foot thick walls so it is smaller inside than it looks. The age and construction of the cottage, and the fact that it is build into the rocky hillside rule out extending up, down or sideways. But they do have plenty of space in their lovely big garden. The family love parties, and they often have barbecues, pitching a fabric gazebo on the lawn to provide shelter for guests. Both boys are in bands, 'Fruit mousse' and 'Toilet', and they practise and entertain friends after gigs in the shed at the end of the garden.

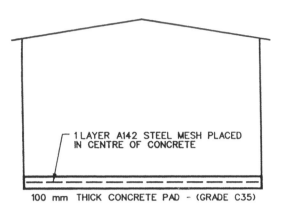

FRONT/REAR ELEVATION

1 LAYER A142 STEEL MESH PLACED IN CENTRE OF CONCRETE

100 mm THICK CONCRETE PAD - (GRADE C35)

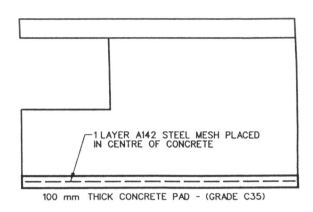

SIDE ELEVATION

1 LAYER A142 STEEL MESH PLACED IN CENTRE OF CONCRETE

100 mm THICK CONCRETE PAD - (GRADE C35)

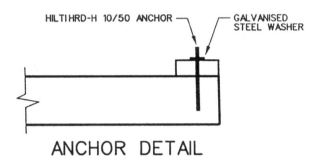

HILTI HRD-H 10/50 ANCHOR — GALVANISED STEEL WASHER

ANCHOR DETAIL

Note:
In common with all similar lightweight timber buildings, this product may overturn in very high wind conditions if it is erected in exposed or windy location. To avoid this possibility we recommend that it be erected on a 100 mm thick concrete pad as detailed on this drawing. The use of such a concrete pad will provide resistance to all normal wind conditions. The use of such a concrete pad will also provide enhanced resistance to settlement and wood decay.

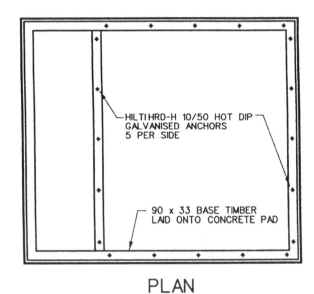

HILTI HRD-H 10/50 HOT DIP GALVANISED ANCHORS 5 PER SIDE

90 x 33 BASE TIMBER LAID ONTO CONCRETE PAD

PLAN

BALTIC SUMMERHOUSE

ROWLINSON GARDEN PRODUCT
Weston Road, Crew, Cheshire

DATE: 26/

The chalet was supplied in kit form with easy-to-follow instructions.

ideas... Dave Wellman came up with a simple but elegant solution to their problem. He decided to construct a large summer-house in the garden. It will have a veranda, and a pergola covered path will link it to the cottage and a patio area. The cabin will enable them to get more value from the garden, and will provide a retreat where they can relax, read, eat, and enjoy the view. The boys can have their band practise in comfort. For ease of construction 'Welly decided to find a summer-house in kit form.

ADRIAN & NEIL'S DIY TIPS

Constructing a pergola

Normally posts for a pergola have to be sunk into substantial holes. Welly used a different method of construction, supporting the uprights in sole plates which were bolted into the concrete base. Screws in the plates ensure the uprights are secure. Spiked sole plates were driven directly into the ground

the solution... The site is levelled for the chalet-style summer-house. When the prefabricated elements are delivered Dave sets out the floor frame, and the team make adjustments until he is convinced that the orientation gives the very best view. Meanwhile the paving for the patio area is being laid. Twin Neil constructs an 'authentic' Cornish dry stone wall using reconstituted stone – it is easy to lay and the result is very convincing.

The chalet is erected very quickly – the tongue and groove sections just slot together; 'it's like a giant jigsaw', says Welly. A large pergola is constructed along the back of the house, providing shelter for the barbecue area, and a visual link between the cottage, the patio and the summer-house.

Suzie Horton was given charge of the decoration and interior design. She wanted to give the summer-house an aged look, so that it would blend in with its surroundings and look in keeping with the lovely old stone cottage. She applied a teak wood stain, followed by a water-based wood protector which achieved the look she wanted. Inside she applied a pale wash of colour to the tongue and groove walls, which gave it a light but nicely aged look.

Choosing a barbecue

The type of barbecue you buy should depend on how often you intend to use it. It may be worth investing in a built-in barbecue if you want to do a lot of cooking outside. These are large and stable, and don't need to be cleaned or put away after use. If you're making one yourself, an asymmetrical one with rough stone or brickwork will look more natural. Built-in barbecues can dominate a small patio, so if you don't do much choose from the many foldaway barbecues, kettles (with domed lids), hibachis (portable table-top barbecues) and trolley barbecues. The most elaborate barbecues run on bottled gas or electricity, and have battery-powered spits. Keep the barbecue away from overhanging trees and wooden fences which might catch fire and choose a sheltered spot so that the wind doesn't blow the smoke everywhere. You will also need a good surface nearby for food and plates. Never leave a lighted barbecue unattended.

LISKEARD
BOB AND ANNE'S LOG CABIN

Ornamental garden buildings

Ornamental garden buildings like summer-houses, gazebos and pavilions have a long history. A summer-house is the most useful and substantial of all ornamental garden buildings. While it may be open on one or more sides, it is more usually enclosed with glazed windows and doors. The doors are often wide to let in sunshine and air. The most popular styles are square or octagonal in plan, with high-pitched, pointed roofs, but a longer, rectangular shape is more spacious. Summer-houses do not require planning permission as long as they don't exceed certain restrictions on location and size. Gazebos became popular in the eighteenth century. They provided a resting place from which to admire a beautiful or 'picturesque' view. These days they provide somewhere secluded to sit and relax. They are usually open around the sides but can be glazed and enclosed. Pavilions are decorative 'eye-catchers' designed primarily to be appreciated from the house. Arbours are sun traps with seats. Made of wood or metal, they are always open, and creepers and climbers are encouraged to clamber over them. Pergolas form arched tunnels over garden paths and paved areas, and a support for climbing plants.

**Dave Wellman's top tips
for this type of garden accommodation**

• Position the log cabin so that it gets the most sun and the best view possible

• Once the position for the log cabin has been chosen the ground must be levelled perfectly

• An electricity supply will make the summer-house more useable

• Windows make a summer-house useful all year round

• A clean pathway will keep the inside of the log cabin clean

1   **A wooden pergola defines the walkway between house and summer-house.**
    In time climbing plants will grow up and create a protective canopy

2   **Decorative trelliswork on the pergola softens the lines**

3   **The veranda with its spectacular views will be a pleasant place to sit and relax**

4   **The paved terrace provides an alternative sitting area – useful for parties.**
    Stone paving is tough and will blend with the surroundings

5   **A pale wash applied to the tongue and groove timber walls has a gently 'aged' effect**

suppliers

Paul and Joyce's conservatory, Falmouth

Aram Resources
Tel: 01326 375660
Supplied: stone and granite

Biffa Skips
Tel: 0800 307307
Supplied: skip

Ceramic Stiles
Tel: 01326 563515
Supplied: Cornish beige tiles, Cornish brown tiles, Cornish marble border and Cornish marble corners

The Chelsea Gardener
Tel: 0207 352 5656
Supplied: dolphin fountain, Adam trough and pump

Chelsea Textiles
Tel: 0207 584 0111
Supplied: cushion fabric and blue mattress ticking

Farrow & Ball
Tel: 01202 876141
Supplied: oil full gloss (no82 dix blue, no23 powder blue), oil undercoat (no22 light blue)

Hewden Hire Centres
Look in your local directory for your nearest store
Supplied: hire tools

Homebase
For details of your nearest store and opening hours please ring 0645 801800 (local call number)
Supplied: Dulux vinyl matt emulsion (magnolia), Dulux satinwood (gardenia), Dulux weathershield (magnolia), light, shade, Valencia light, light bulbs, plants, terracotta pots, table and electric wall heater

Interdesign UK Limited
Tel: 0207 376 5272
Supplied: Triesterdue armchair

Jewson
Look in your local directory for your nearest store
Supplied: all building materials

Philip Whear Windows
Tel: 01209 215759
Supplied and installed custom-made conservatory

R&J Mann
Tel: 01326 374808
Supplied: plant hire

Theobolds Tarmacadam
Tel: 01872 864667
Supplied: ground work and resurfacing

Sally and Graham's front garden, Doncaster

Banson Tool Hire
Tel: 01302 817888
Supplied: hired machinery

Bennetts Water Gardens
Tel: 01305 785150
Supplied: water plants for the pond

CED
Tel: 01708 867237
Supplied: stone paving, granite circle, granite setts, harlequin quartzite, rockery stone and granite boulders

Fitzgerald Lighting
Tel: 01208 262200
Supplied: garden spotlights, Venture II pathlighter

Granite Connections
Tel: 01773 533090
Supplied: granite cat

Hozelock Limited
Tel: 01844 292002
Supplied: pond pump, pond lining (4x25 metre roll), Autoreel hosepipe

HSS Hire Shops
0800 282828
Supplied: hired machinery

Nomas Lites Limited
Supplied: Christmas lights

Osmo/Gard
Tel: 01895 234899
Supplied: Star pergola in standard finish, Tivoli pavilion

Skillbase
Tel: 0114 268 8100
Supplied: manual labour

Tendercare Nurseries
Tel: 01895 835544
Supplied: semi-mature birch trees

Thatch International
Tel: 01256 883441
Supplied: fencing

Waddham Trading Company
Tel: 01367 850499
Supplied: wire mesh ducks

Kathy and Martin's kitchen, Nottingham

Alma Leather Ltd
Tel: 0207 375 0343
Supplied: Ottoman (made to order)

Bisque Radiators
Tel: 01225 469244
Supplied: Hot springs radiator

Danico Brass Ltd
Tel: 0207 483 4477
Supplied: chrome brackets

Handles and Fittings
Tel: 01992 505655
Supplied: set round rose levers (SST8003), pull handle

(SST5050), two-way switch (SSB4102), left-hand radius hinge (SST15105L/H) and right-hand radius hinge (SST15105R/H)

Homebase
For details of your nearest store and opening hours please ring 0645 801800 (local call rates)
Supplied: handles, Yale security door lock, standard housing units and plain door, sink mixer, chrome tap, chrome socket, kitchen/bathroom paint (crystal mint), vinyl matt emulsion (eucalyptus), Crown metallic lustre paint (moondust and silver), fluorescent strip lights (180011, 180168, 061553), stainless steel tumbler, lime vase, cream vase, blue vase, plants, Bodum frosted wine rack, Bodum translucent ice kettle, crockery and utensils

Hotpoint
Tel: 0541 506070
Supplied: The Metals Collection oven, hob, dishwasher, washing machine, under-counter larder, fridge and freezer

IKEA
Look in your local directory for your nearest store
Supplied: kitchen cabinets and Varde accessories

Inova Furniture Contracts
Tel: 0207 231 9708
Supplied: stainless steel flooring

Jewson
Look in your local directory for your nearest store
Supplied: all building materials

Kirkstone
Tel: 0207 381 0424
Supplied: Avalon glass tiles

Pure Contemporary Design
Tel: 0207 250 1116
Supplied: CD/woven stand screen

Rankins (Glass) Company Limited
Tel: 0207 729 4200
Supplied: custom-made sandblasted and toughened glass

Riches & Dean
Tel: 01689 800550
Supplied: stainless steel worktop and tabletop

Siemans
Tel: 0207 229 1947
Supplied: stainless steel microwave oven

Vink Plastics (now Amari Plastics)
Tel: 0115 942 5110
Supplied: extruded acrylic mirror (blue 2069)

Aine Marie's kitchen, Halifax

Banson Tool Hire
Tel: 01302 817888
Supplied: hire tools

The Bradley Collection
Tel: 01449 722724

Supplied: curtain rods

Comet Warehouse
Look in your local directory for your nearest store
Supplied: television

Fired Earth
Tel: 01295 814300
Supplied: Haute Provence tiles

Habitat
Tel: 0845 6010740
Supplied: blue Holst table, blue Monet chairs, pots

Handmade Frames
Tel: 01435 866778
Supplied: teapot pictures

Homebase
For details of your nearest store and opening hours please ring 0645 801800 (local call number)
Supplied: accessories, tongue-and-groove flooring, Dulux paint

Jewson
Look in your local directory for your nearest store
Supplied: all building materials

Lee Joffa
Tel: 0207 351 7760
Supplied: curtain fabric

Magnet Kitchens
Tel: 01722 325421
Supplied: Skaker-style cream kitchen units

Mr Carpet
Tel: 0207 381 1989
Supplied: vinyl wood floor

Neff UK Ltd
Tel: 0990 133090
Supplied: white electric cooker (B1420), dishwasher (S5543), white gas hob (T2113)

Phase Ltd
Tel: 0207 603 9565
Supplied: downlighters and dimmers

Richard Taylor
Tel: 0207 792 1808
Supplied: Bullrush sconces

Rivendale Kitchens
Tel: 01962 850300
Suppliers: Franke Belfast sink (VB710), Asquith swan taps, Hafele waste bin

Stephanie Dunning Interior Design
Tel: 01980 863690
Supplied: utensil hanger

Surrey Stone
Tel: 01483 300109
Supplied: granite work surface

SWSL
Tel: 01883 717551
Supplied: solid birch worktop

Claire and Colin's kitchen, Swinton
Homebase
For details of your nearest store and opening hours please ring 0645 801800 (local call rates)
Supplied: Russell Hobbs toaster, Philips kettle, Dulux silk vinyl emulsion (green walls 90YY/53/373, light green ceiling 90YY/83/214, Dulux weather shield (black for exterior door and woodwork)

IKEA
Look in your local directory for your nearest store
Supplied: Akka table (wall mounted), Dennis bar stool

John Lewis Partnership
Tel: 0207 629 7711
Supplied: stainless steel worktop savers

Optelma Lighting Ltd
Tel: 01235 553 769
Supplied: lighting system with TEC spotlights on a YUMA track, including transformer

Super Tiles Bathrooms & Kitchens
Tel: 0208 650 9730
Supplied and fitted the bulk of the kitchen including: Crown Kenton cupboards, stainless steel door fronts, Franke Papillon stainless steel sink, tri-flow tap system, childproof safety cage for poisonous cleaning products, Westinghouse oven, stainless steel hob, stainless steel splashback, Westinghouse stainless steel cooker hood, multi-function dishwasher, fridge, freezer, fine porcelain tiles, riven tiles and recycled aluminium tiles

Ashley and Julie's kitchen, Smethwick
Grinsell Skip Hire Ltd
Tel: 0121 555 6060
Supplied: skip

Homebase
For details of your nearest store and opening hours please ring 0645 801800 (local call rates)
Supplied: Boston kitchen, Creda connoisseur electric oven, Candy hob, Premier roller blinds (English blue) and café rod, Cotswold tiles (blue), small hand basin and taps, pine doors,

materials for partition – lighting, coving, skirting, architrave, Supermatt white emulsion

HSS Hire Shops
Tel: 0800 282828
Supplied: hired tools

Denise and Barry's living room, Northenden
Huw Edwards-Jones, Aqua-tech UK and Sussex Glass Bevelling Co
Tel: 0207 388 8832
Supplied: custom made fish tank table

Artisan Curtain Rails
Tel: 0207 498 3979
Supplied: wrought-iron curtain poles, cocoon galvanized steel finials and tie backs

Christopher Wray Lighting
Tel: 0207 736 8434
Supplied: Lotus floor lamp, Lotus desk lamp

Creation Baumann
Tel: 0207 388 8832
Supplied: curtain fabric and fabric leaves

Crystal Window Systems (Manchester area only)
Installed the conservatory

Fensel
Tel: 0207 388 8832
Supplied: flexible skirting

The Final Curtain Company
Tel: 0208 699 3626
Supplied: curtains and blinds

Fired Earth
Tel: 01295 814300
Supplied: blue moon matt emulsion

Habitat
Tel: 0845 6010740
Supplied: Foram wall light

Homebase
For details of your nearest store and opening hours please ring 0645 801800 (local call number)
Supplied: Crown pain (smooth velvet), Dulux matt emulsion (gardenia), star pendant light and halogen downlighters

HSS Hire Shops
Tel: 0800 282828
Supplied: tool hire

IKEA
Look in your local directory for your nearest store
Supplied: Laxne side table, Nyphus armchair and Antiman table lamp

Katy Holford
Tel: 01525 872308
Designed overmantle mirror

Monkwell Fabrics
Tel: 0207 589 4778
Supplied: Saimaro elements cushions

Newey & Eyre
Tel: 0121 455 9727
Supplied: recessed downlighter

The Pier
Tel: 01235 821088
Supplied: Firando chair, topiary pot and chenille buttoned cushions

Pods of Brazil
Tel: 01749 850466
Supplied: leather pod

Sala Design Ltd
Tel: 01935 827051
Supplied: brown candles

Shepley Windows
Tel: 07000 847243
Supplied: Visage conservatory and Visage French doors

Sofa Workshop Direct
Tel: 01443 239444
Supplied: Sonata sofa

Tarkett UK Ltd
Tel: 01905 795004
Supplied: Beech laminated floor

Wemyss Houles
Tel: 0207 388 8832
Supplied: cord

Wessex Stone
Tel: 01666 504658
Supplied: Sherborne fireplace

Woodhams
Tel: 0208 964 9818
Supplied: planters and stone ball

Jackie and Joe's kitchen/living room, The Wirral

The Blind and Curtain Store Limited
Tel: 01737 763408
Supplied: Swedish roller blinds

Donna Reeves
Tel: 0370 886764
Designed and supplied mosaics

Farrow & Ball
Tel: 01202 876141
Supplied: Farrows vinyl matt emulsion (red for the kitchen, cream for the living room)

Fireside By Design
Tel: 0151 666 1385
Supplied: Plymouth basket with a gazco fire

Flooring Supply Centre
Tel: 0151 521 5221
Supplied: quick-step universal laminate flooring

The Framing Centre
Tel: 01244 312127
Supplied: prints

Habitat
0845 6010740
Supplied: Lago low table, Toledo shelf unit, beanbag, Hampton

table and Apollo rug

Highly Sprung
Tel: 0207 924 1124
Supplied: sand-coloured Boston sofa (Romo rf500/63), sand-coloured dining room chairs (Romo rf500/63), brick-coloured dining room chairs (Romo rf500/55) and Waldorf chair (Romo rf500/79)

Homebase
For details of your nearest store and opening hours please ring 0645 801800 (local call rates)
Supplied: kitchen units, flooring, Dulux vinyl matt emulsion (30YR20/313, 30YY69/216), Dulux satinwood (gardenia BS10B/15), roller blind, standard lamp, black wall spots, light with cream shade and halogen light

Jewson
Look in your local directory for your nearest store
Supplied: all building materials

Neff UK Ltd
Tel: 0990 133090
Supplied: oven (B1420) and hob (T2113)\

Phase Limited
Tel: 0207 603 9565. Fax: 0207 602 3099
Supplied: lighting

SCR (North West) Limited
Tel: 0151 263 8921
Supplied: structural engineering and construction

Steve and Clare's loft bedroom, Smethwick

Aston Villa
Tel: 0121 327 2299
Supplied: bed linen and football merchandise

Dulux
Tel: 01753 550555
Supplied: vinyl silk emulsion (56GG64/258, 06YY49/797, 86BG43/321, 30BB11/337, 00YR08/409), eggshell (30BB11/337, 0YR08/409)

Grinsell Skip Hire Ltd
Tel: 0121 555 6060
Supplied: skip

Guild Electrical Services
Tel: 0831 217229
Supplied: lighting work

Homebase
For details of your nearest store and opening hours please ring 0645 801800 (local call number)
Supplied: green directors chairs, CD towers, swing arm clamp light, lava lamp, pine bedside tables, wardrobe system, picture frames, shelving and storage unit, roll-under storage boxes and metal shelving units

James Davidson
Tel: 07000 783873
Designed and supplied: lighting

Jewson
Look in your local directory for your nearest store

Supplied: tongue-and-groove flooring

Mainpride Lofts Limited
Tel: 0121 553 6596
Constructed the entire loft conversion

Tandy
Tel: 0990 134935
Supplied: television

Velux
Tel: 0800 003535
Supplied: window

West Bromwich Albion Football Club
Tel: 0121 525 8888
Supplied: bed linen and football merchandise

Wickes Building Supplies Limited
Tel: 08706 089001
Supplied: recessed low-voltage downlighters

Alison and Geoff's bedroom, The Wirral

Crystal Lighting
Tel: 0207 357 7244
Supplied: reproduction chandelier wall sconces

Emafyl
Tel: 0208 8543111
Supplied: antique crackle coving, antique crackle ogee skirting and antique crackle ceiling rose

Farrow & Ball
Tel: 01202 876141
Supplied: lime white estate emulsion paint

Homebase
For details of your nearest store and opening hours please ring 0645 801800 (local call rates)
Supplied: building materials

Hinc & Doubleday
Tel: 0802 443385
Supplied: Edwardian chandelier

Jewson
Look in your local directory for your nearest store
Supplied: all building materials

The London Picture Centre
Tel: 0207 371 5737
Supplied: mirror

Mostyns
Tel: 01202 398733
Supplied: custom-made curtain in flo natural fabric and custom-made bedspread in Gainsborough fabric

Myrmidon
Tel: 0207 277 2007
Supplied: custom-made wardrobes

PC World
Tel: 0541 545 580
Supplied: Patriot computer

The Pier
Tel: 01235 821088

Supplied: cream crackle vase and glass candle holders

Tracy's Florists
Tel: 0151 645 4246
Supplied flowers

Pam and Ray's bathroom, Swinton
Bella Figura
Tel: 01394 461111
Supplied: Southworld single-arm wall light, 10-inch unbleached antung silk shade

Biffa Skips
Tel: 0800 307307
Supplied: skip

CP Hart
Tel: 0207 902 1000
Supplied: Duker bath with feet, Waterloo chrome shower, Richmond toilet and high cistern, Richmond basin and pedestal, original chrome bath taps, original chrome basin taps, English chrome toilet roll holder, English chrome towel ring, Elle chrome robe hook, Hart chrome radiator towel rail and English chrome glass shelf

Handmade Frames
Tel: 01435 866778
Supplied: silver leaf mirror, Raphael A Sybil picture, Musical Putti picture

Homebase
For details of your nearest store and opening hours please ring 0645 801800 (local call rates)
Supplied: wall unit (stripped, re-painted and distressed), plumbing accessories

Hunter & Highland
Supplied: chrome shower rail

Mr Carpet
Tel: 0207 381 1989
Supplied: woodstrip floor

Titley & Marr
Tel: 02392 599585
Supplied: Provence curtain fabric (colour 04)

Simon Payle
Tel: 0207 371 0131
Supplied: voile

Skillbase
Tel: 0114 268 8100
Supplied: plumbers and electricians

Andrew and Lisa's loft, Falmouth
The loft conversion was carried out by the following companies:

Camborne Joinery Ltd
Tel: 01209 716000
Constructed and fitted staircase

Initial Deborah Services
Tel: 01872 870078
Supplied: scaffolding

Mid-Cornwall Roofing Contractors
Tel: 01326 372302

Perkins & Perry
Tel: 01209 820983

Ron Lyne Builders
Tel: 01326 290596

Other suppliers were:

Allied Carpets
Tel: 0800 192192
Supplied: Bahama sand berber carpet

Bensens Bed Centres
Tel: 01925 830111
Supplied: Stratford single bed and cathedral double bed

Homebase
For details of your nearest store and opening hours please ring 0645 801800 (local call rates)
Supplied: bathroom suite

Jewson
Look in your local directory for your nearest store
Supplied: all building materials

Jeanette and Terry's granny flat, Newbury
Alex Polkinghorne
Tel: 017687 72058
Supplied: black and white photographs

Allied Carpets
Tel: 0800 192192
Supplied: lilac carpet (705259), Soft Encounter snow carpet (705253)

Alva Lighting
Tel: 0207 482 4331
Supplied: Lan table lamp and Moo lamp

Architectural Window Systems
Tel: 0208 857 0630
Supplied and installed French doors

Authentics Ltd
Tel: 01932 859800
Supplied: metallic silver push bin

Biffa Skips
Tel: 0800 307307

Supplied: skip

Crown Wallcoverings and Home Furnishings
Tel: 0800 458 1554
Supplied: Mandara wallpaper (50910)

Currys
Tel: 01635 522558
Supplied: microwave oven (513768)

Hewden Hire Centres
Look in your local directory for your nearest store
Supplied: hired tools

Homebase
For details of your nearest store and opening hours please ring 0645 801800 (local call rates)
Supplied: Crown vinyl matt emulsion, (Georgian, lilac), glass expresso cups, cushions, bedspread, telephone, skirting, architrave, plants, wood varnish and silver paint

HSS Hire Shops
Tel: 0800 282828
Supplied: hired tools

IKEA
Look in your local directory for your nearest store
Supplied: Kajak storage unit, Kajak kitchen units, Askedal bedside table, Askedal chest of drawers, Lack shelving unit, Kvicksund coffee table, Happen female valet stand, Atlant stainless steel sink, Pronomen wooden worktop and Mockeln mixer tap

Jewson
Look in your local directory for your nearest store
Supplied: all building materials

Marks & Spencer
Look in your local directory for your nearest store
Supplied: towel rail, corner shelf, towel ring, toilet brush, soap dish and holder, tumbler and holder, toilet roll holder, Ottoman dark indigo curtain, pewter-effect rail, basket finials, storage jar and utensil rack with accessories

Neil Freeman Design
Tel: 0121 212 9273
Supplied: Birch egg wall clock, polished mirror (700mm), small glass frame, medium beech frame, Birch egg alarm clock and Dimple aluminium resin clock

Rowan Art & Editions Ltd
Fax: 0802 593 8455
Supplied: stainless steel circular mirror

Sala Design Ltd
Tel: 01935 827050
Supplied: natural laundry basket, wooden bowl, round candles, chrome tree trunk vase, slim chrome vase, small basket, medium basket and Polot stool

Spoils
Tel: 01473 603666
Supplied: napkin rings, director's chair and large candles

Sarah and Spencer's loft, Newbury
Altfield
Tel: 0207 351 5893
Supplied: wallpaper, earth fibres inlay

Biffa Skips
Tel: 0800 307307
Supplied: skip

Bisque Radiators
Tel: 01225 469244
Supplied: silver flowform radiator

Crucial Trading
Tel: 01562 825656
Supplied: seagrass flooring

suppliers

Habitat
Look in your local directory for your nearest store
Supplied: Anagram sideboard, vase, umbrella basket, dried flowers, photo frame, bathmat, hanger, nailbrush, soap dish, soap candle, salad bowl and cushion

Hewden Hire Centres
Look in your local directory for your nearest store
Supplied: hired tools

Hitchman (Newbury) Limited
Tel: 01635 254252
Constructed entire loft

The Holding Company
Tel: 0207 352 1600
Supplied: large shelf (WDF005), medium shelf (WDF004), large box (IND067), wardrobe with rail (AD0023), six shelf unit (AD0022), four shelf unit (AD0021)

Homebase
For details of your nearest store and opening hours please ring 0645 801800 (local call rates)
Supplied: Plastikote smooth silver Hammerite, cream tiles, TV wall bracket, stainless steel toothbrush tumbler, bathmat, towels, mirror, extended shaving mirror, chrome shelf, Crown Perion paint (promenade, metallic lustre, satinwood jade), glass bead lamp, lighting and building materials

HSS Hire Shops
Tel: 0800 282828
Supplied: hired tools

IKEA
Look in your local directory for your nearest store
Supplied: Kalif Harmoni mattress, Lade slatted bed base, Dunduo double duvet and Fjader pillow

Jewson
Look in your local directory for your nearest store
Supplied: all building materials

Kahrs
Tel: 01243 778747
Supplied: ash London flooring

Marks & Spencer
Look in your local directory for your nearest store
Supplied: bathroom accessories

Pure Contemporary Design
Tel: 0207 250 1116
Supplied: silk, cashmere and voile cushions

Rimex Metals
Fax: 0208 804 7275
www.rimexmetals.com
Supplied: Super mirror stainless steel sheets

Selfridges
Tel: 0207 629 1234
Supplied: blue orban throw, cushion pad and cushions

Steel Tech
Tel: 01992 505655
Supplied: round rose lever handle – sprung (SST8001-1), multi-power door closer (SS911), electrical switch (SSB410)

Tudor Flooring Co Ltd
Tel: 0208 360 4242
Installed the ash flooring

Ucosan Limited
Tel: 01625 525202
Supplied: Cayman bath (VK115LH006), Apropos basin (AQ550R), base unit with shelves, Nornina toilet, concealed cistern, standard frame support, Express chrome basin and bath/shower mixer taps, Express chrome pair heads

Velux
Tel: 0800 003535
Supplied: C/P window, roof window (V-GB), flashing

Nigel and Tracy's cellar, Halifax

Hideaway Beds
Tel: 01752 511111
Supplied: fold-away bed

Homebase
For details of your nearest store and opening hours please ring 0645 801800 (local call rates)
Supplied: tongue-and-groove panels, Moxwood solid pine panel doors, plasterboard, dining chairs, plants and planters

James Davidson
Tel: 07000 783873
Designed and supplied: lighting

Jewson
Look in your local directory for your nearest store
Supplied: all building materials

Pergo Flooring Company
Tel: 0800 374771
Supplied: flooring

Skillbase
Tel: 0114 268 8100
Supplied: carpenters and electricians

David and Janet's summer-house, Doncaster

Alpha Products Garden Furniture
Supplied: white patio furniture

Banson Tool Hire
Tel: 01302 817888
Supplied: all heavy-duty machinery

Homebase
For details of your nearest store and opening hours please ring 0645 801800 (local call rates)
Supplied: Cotswold stone tiles, wooden garden furniture, mirror, hanging baskets, plants, door furniture, Dulux paint

James Davidson
Tel: 07000 783873
Designed and supplied: lighting

Jewson
Look in your local directory for your nearest store
Supplied: all building materials

JS Supplies
Tel: 01472 355009
Supplied: fireproof lemon paint (60YY79/367)

Konstsmide UK Ltd
Tel: 01246 852140
Supplied: Christmas lights

Marbridge Productions
Tel: 01827 56655
Supplied: hanging pendant lights

Marlin Lighting
Tel: 0208 894 5522
Supplied: Aztec and Inca spotlights

Velux
Tel: 0800 003535
Supplied: window

Sue and Phil's veranda, Liskeard

Burncoose Nurseries
Tel: 01209 860 3161
Supplied: camellias and hardy shrubs

Cotswold Hardy Plants
Tel: 01984 632303
Supplied: Espalier plants and bush plants

Dandf Design
Tel: 0800 783 2909
Supplied: Archadeck American lifestyle deck and American curved bridge

Forest Fencing Limited
Tel: 01886 812451
Supplied: concave Chelsea trellis, wishing well fountain and Forest checkerboard tiles

Hardy Exotics
Tel: 01736 740660
Supplied: exotic plants

Home Products Ltd
Tel: 0113 288 8811
Supplied: rocking deckchairs

JFC Monro
Tel: 01736 755766
Supplied: Cornish grit

Ousfern Nurseries UK Ltd
Tel: 01245 421999
Supplied: tree ferns

Tendercare Nurseries
Tel: 01895 835544
Supplied: plants

Turf = Lawns
Tel: 01503 264906
Supplied and laid turf

Alison and Andrew's garden, Northenden

Atlas Stone Products
Tel: 01386 840226
Supplied: Canterbury stone circle with tile centre

Dandf Design
Tel: 0800 783 2909
Supplied: carport, pergola and Appleton gazebo

Donna Reeves
Tel: 0370 886764
Designed mosaic and mural

English Hurdle
Tel: 01823 698418
Supplied: weaving willow and hazel sticks

Grange Fencing
Tel: 01952 586460
Supplied: Baddome badminton trellis, timber decking tiles and compost bin

Homebase
For details of your nearest store and opening hours please ring 0645 801800 (local call rates)
Supplied: barbeque, Ronseal paint (rich jade, plum and mahogany), Dulux weathershield (honeytone), Dulux matt emulsion (white, zingy yellow), Dulux clear varnish, Crown emulsion (calypso, Bahama blue, Shakespeare blue, narcissus, century red), self-levelling compound silicon concrete blocks, Mediterranean terracotta floor tiles, glazed blue olive jars, terracotta pots and egg pots, deep ribbed bowls, tunis handled bowls, plants (Polyanthus, trailing ivy, grasses, Euonymus and Skimmias)

Home Products Ltd
Tel: 0113 288 8811
Supplied: mushroom table and chair set

Jewson
Look in your local directory for your nearest store
Supplied: all building materials

Melcourt
Tel: 01666 502711
Supplied: Playbark ornamental mulch bark spruce (available in bulk or from smaller stockists)

Tropical Surrounds
Tel: 01264 773009
Supplied: willow screen, bamboo poles and heather roofing

Alison's garden, Nottingham

Cedar Nursery
Supplied: Arco-baleno parasol

CED
Tel: 01708 867237
Supplied: Donegal quartzite paving, Porphyry paving, Scottish beach pebble and Scottish beach cobble

Dandf Design
Tel: 0800 783 2909
Supplied: decking system with timber supports

Glass World
Tel: 01223 511444
Supplied: stained-glass squares

Grange Fencing
Tel: 01952 586460
Supplied: badminton square trellis, close board fencing and Elite arch

Homebase
For details of your nearest store and opening hours please ring 0645 801800 (local call number)
Supplied: Ronseal garden paint (jade mist), wooden tray, galvanised tracks, washing line, horticultural fleece, blue glazed pots, compost, perspex sheet, dowel and marine plywood

Hozelock Limited
Tel: 01844 292002
Suppied: automatic micro watering kit and Autoreel hosepipe

James Davidson
Tel: 07000 783873
Designed and supplied: lighting

Jewson
Look in your local directory for your nearest store
Supplied: all building materials

Konstsmide UK
Tel: 01246 852140
Supplied: outdoor low-voltage mini lights

Lightscape Projects
Tel: 0207 231 5323
Supplied: exterior accent light

The Palm Centre
Tel: 0208 255 6191
Supplied: Trachycarpus fortunei, Fargesia murielae, Cordyline australis green, Phormium tenax green, Phormium tenax red, Yucca gloriosa variegata, Trachycarpus wagnerianus, Paurea

Spa Form
Tel: 0800 772700
Supplied: spa (175 Octagon) and spa cover

Woodlodge
(available from all good garden centres)
Supplied: terracotta glazed pots

Bob and Anne's log cabin, Liskeard

Atlas Stone Products
Tel: 01386 840226
Supplied: Autumn-blend Yorkdale paving and dry stone wall

Emafyl
Tel: 0208 301 8888
Supplied: antique crackle dado, antique crackle skirting and

antique crackle corbels

Homebase
For details of your nearest store and opening hours please ring 0645 801800 (local call number)
Supplied: Crown heritage paint (purple brown, sky blue, white), plants, 3-inch bamboo blinds, floating candles, outdoor lights, pot pourri glass nuggets, green ribbed glaze vases, sierra walnut folding chair, Cuprinol water-based wood protector and satin teak quick-drying wood stain

Louis Poulsen UK Ltd
Tel: 01372 848800
Supplied: Nimbus 1 light, Lynx light, brick light and Maxispotter light

Paperchase
Tel: 0161 839 1500
Supplied: paper

The Pier
Tel: 01235 821088
Supplied: Papasan chair, large Papasan chair cushions, blue and grey patch cushions, light-brown cushion with detail, cream chenille rug, cream/brown checked rug, tall candle light, small light blue bowl, small Kenya trunk, large Kenya trunk, bamboo chimes, table cloth, checked napkins, large dark wood bowl, bamboo picture frames and silver butterfly frames

Rowlinson Garden Products Ltd
Tel: 01270 506 900
Supplied: Leisure building, Argosy teak armchair, Argosy teak bench, Argosy deluxe teak table, drinks trolley, Toronto BBQ and custom-made pergola

The *Better Homes* team would like to thank the following companies for supplying goods and/or services during the making of the programmes:

ABC Estate Agents
Contact: Nick Bookbinder
Tel: 0161 434 2000

Allen & Harris Estate Agents
Contact: Martin Read
Tel: 01635 521050

Biffa Skips
Tel: 0800 307307 (central booking line)

Bond Wolfe Residential Estate Agents (now Paul Dubberley & Co Estate Agents)
Contact: Lee Morton
Tel: 0121 500 6006

Boococks Estate Agents
Tel: 01422 365391

C Barnsdale & Son Estate Agents
Contact: Malcolm Barnsdale
Tel: 01302 323453

Calderdale Borough Council
Tel: 01422 357257

Caradon District Council
Tel: 01579 341000

suppliers

Chubb Security Personnel
Tel: 01933 671000
with thanks to Mike Mulcahy

Chrysler
Freephone: 0800 616159
with thanks for providing vehicles for filming and transport to
locations Contact Chrysler for details on the complete
Chrysler range

Countrywide Surveyors
Tel: 01908 575000 for information on your nearest branch
Countrywide surveyed some of the properties before work
commenced

District Surveyors Association
Tel: 0207 641 8737
Fax: 0207 641 8739
e-mail:labc.services@free4all.co.uk

Doncaster Metropolitan Borough Council
Tel: 01302 734444

Dyson
Tel: 0870 527 5104 for information on your nearest stockist
www.dyson.com
The Dyson Dual Cyclone is the only vacuum cleaner to
maintain constant suction It has no bag and removes more
dust and harmful allergens from your home

Edwin Pearce Builders
Tel: 01503 262558

Entertainment Marketing
Tel: 0207 831 9000
Contact: Quentin Griffiths
e-mail: quentingriffiths@carat.co.uk
Thanks to Quentin Griffiths and all at Entertainment
Marketing for advice and assistance in sourcing products and
services used in the filming of Better Homes

Forte Hotels
Tel: 0800 404040 (reservations)
with thanks to Debbie Hills

Green Lawns Hotel, Falmouth
Tel: 01326 312734

Hewden Hire Centres
Look in your local telephone directory for your
nearest store

Homebase
For your nearest store and opening hours please ring 0645
801800 (local call rates)
Better Homes is sponsored by Homebase

HSS Hire Shops
Tel: 0800 282828

Hunters Independent Estate Agents
Contact: Steve Smith
Tel: 01326 212833

Imperial Crown Hotel, Halifax
Tel: 01422 342342

LDV
Tel: 0800 400407
www.ldv.co.uk
with thanks for providing vehicles throughout the filming of
the series For details on the complete range of LDV Pilot,
Cub and Convoy vans contact LDV

Marriott Davidson Estate Agents
Contact: Richard Jones
Tel: 0115 993 1414

**Marshall & Company Estate Agents (now Bradleys Estate
Agents)**
Contact: Francis Marshall
Tel: 01503 264888

Makita UK
Tel: 01908 211678

Moat House Hotels
Tel: 0645 102030 (central booking line)
with thanks to Trisha Trowbridge

Old Rectory, Liskeard
Tel: 01579 342617

Owen Knox Estates
Tel: 0161 794 7272

Paul Chapman Garden Design
Tel: 0161 976 1032

Philips Lighting
Tel: 0208 388 4323
Philips can provide a free book on lighting your home

Royal & Sun Alliance Property Services
Tel: 0990 841236
Call for details of your local office

Royal Town Planning Institute
Tel: 0207 636 9107

Sandwell Metropolitan Borough Council
Tel: 0121 569 2200

Tandy
Tel: 0800 358 3858 for details of your nearest store

Wallfashion Bureau
High Corn Mill, Chapel Hill, Skipton, North Yorkshire
BD23 1NL e-mail: wfe@alexanderking.co.uk
www.wallpaper.org.uk
The Wallfashion Bureau represents the UK's leading
wallpaper manufacturers. For a copy of their What's New in
Wallpaper? leaflet contact the company direct

Well House Hotel, Liskeard
Tel: 01579 342001

Other Useful Addresses

Architects Registration Board
73 Hallam Street
London W1N 6EE
0207 580 5861

Association of Building Engineers
Jubilee House
Billing Brook Road
Weston Favell
Northampton NN3 8NW
01604 404121

Association of Plumbing and Heating Contractors
14-15 Ensign House
Ensign Business Centre
Westwood Way
Coventry CV4 8JA
01203 470626

Brick Development Association Limited
Woodside House
Winkfield
Windsor
Berks SL4 2DX
01344 885651

British Bathroom Council
Federation House
Station Road
Stoke-on-Trent ST4 2RT
01782 747074

British Carpet Manufacturers Assocation
PO Box, 1155
MCF Complex
60 New Road
Kidderminster DY10 1WW
01562 747351

British Cement Association
Century House

Telford Avenue
Crowthorne
Berks RG45 6YS
01344 762676

British Ceramic Tile Council
as 'British Bathroom Council' above

British Coatings Federation (paint)
James House
Bridge Street
Leatherhead KT22 7EP
01372 360660

British Decorators Association
32 Coton Road
Nuneaton CV11 5TW
01203 353776

British Wood Preserving and Damp Proofing Association
Building 6
The Office Village
4 Romford Road
London E15 4EA
0208 519 2588

British Woodworking Federation
56-64 Leonard Street
London EC2A 4JX
Tel: 0207 608 5050
Fax: 0207 608 5051

The Charleston Trust
Charleston
Firle, near Lewes
East Sussex BN8 6LL
01323 811626

Chartered Institute of Arbitrators (CIArb)
International Arbitration Centre,
24 Angel Gate
City Road
London EC1V 2RS
0207 837 4483

Conservatory Association
44-48 Borough High Street
London SE1 1XB
01480 458278

The Construction Confederation
as 'British Woodworking Confederation' above
0207 608 5000

Council for the Registration of Gas Installers (CORGI)
4 Elmwood
Chineham Business Park
Crockford Lane
Basingstoke RG24 8WG
01256 707060

Decorative Arts Society (1850 to the present)
8 Guilford Street
NADFAS House
London WC1N 1DT
0207 4300730

Design History Society
Membership Secretary
Lesley Whitworth
Design History Research Centre
University of Brighton
Pavilion Parade
Brighton BN2 1RA

Draught Proofing Advisory Association
PO Box 12
Haslemere GU27 3AH
01428 654011

Electrical Contractors Association (ECA)
ESCA House

34 Palace Court
London W2 4HY
0207 313 4800

Electrical Contractors Association of Scotland (SELECT)
Bush House
Bush Estate
Midlothian EH26 0SB
0131 445 5577
www.select.org.uk

English Heritage
Customer Services
PO Box 9019
London SW1E 5ZS
0207 973 3434

Geffrye Museum
Kingsland Road
London E2 8EA
0207 739 9893

Georgian Group
6 Fitzroy Square
London W1P 6DX
0207 387 1720

Insulated Render and Cladding Association Limited
See Draught Proofing Advisory Association

Federation of Master Builders
Gordon Fisher House
14-15 Great James Street
London WC1N 3DP
0207 242 7583

Glass and Glazing Federation
44-48 Borough High Street
London SE1 1XB
0207 403 7177

Guarantee Protection Trust
27 London Road
High Wycombe
HP11 1BW
01494 447049

Guild of Master Craftsmen
166 High Street
Lewes BN7 1XU
01273 478449

Heating and Ventilating Contractors Association
Esca House
34 Palace Court
London W2 4JG
0207 313 4900

Independent Warranty Association
21 Albion Place
Northampton NN1 1UD
01604 604511

Institute of Plumbing
64 Station Lane
Hornchurch RM12 6NB
01708 472791

Institute of Structural Engineers
11 Upper Belgrave Street
London SW1X 8BH
0207 235 4535

Institution of Electrical Engineers (IEE Wiring Regulations)
Savoy Place
London WC2R 0BL
0207 240 1871

Interior Decorators and Designers Association (IDDA)
1-4 Chelsea Harbour Design Centre
Lotts Road
London SW10 0XE

0207 349 0800

Kitchen Specialists Association
PO Box 311
Worcester WR1 1DR
01905 726066

Master Locksmiths Association
Units 4-5
Woodford Halse Business Park
Great Central Way
Woodford Halse NN11 3PZ
01327 262255

Museum of Domestic Design and Architecture (formerly the Silver Studio Collection)
Middlesex University
Bounds Green Road
London N11 2NQ
0208 362 5244

National Federation of Roofing Contractors
24 Weymouth Street,
London W1N 4LX
0207 4360387

National Inspection Council for Electrical Installation (NICEIC)
Vintage House
37 Albert Embankment
London SE1 7UJ
0207 582 7746

National Association of Chimney Sweeps (NACS)
St Marys Chambers
Station Road
Stone ST15 8JP
01785 811732

The National Trust
PO Box 39
Bromley
Kent BR1 3XL
0181 315 1111

Royal Incorporation of Architects in Scotland (RIAS)
15 Rutland Square
Edinburgh EH1 2BE
0131 229 7205

Royal Institute of British Architects (RIBA)
66 Portland Place
London W1N 4AD
0207 580 5533

Royal Institution of Chartered Surveyors
12 Great George Street
Parliament Square
London SW1P 3AD
0207 222 7000

Royal Society of Architects in Wales
Bute Building
King Edward VII Avenue
Cathays
Cardiff CF10 3NB
02222 874753 or 874754

Scottish Decorators Federation
Federation House
222 Queensferry Road
Edinburgh EH4 2BN
0131 343 3300

The Society for the Protection of Ancient Buildings (SPAB)
37 Spital Square
London E1 6DY
0207 377 1644

The Twentieth Century Society
70 Cowcross Street
London EC1M 6BP
0207 250 3857

The Victoria & Albert Museum
South Kensington
London SW7 2RL
0207 589 4040

Water Research Centre
Fern Close
Peny-y-fan Industrial Estate
Oakdale NP1 4EH
01495 248454

The William Morris Society
Kelmscott House
26 Upper Mall
Hammersmith
London W6 9TA
0208 741 3735

The *Better Homes* team can be contacted at:

Toby Buckland
Tel: 01223 413189

John Cregg
25 Silverton Crescent, Moseley, Birmingham B13 9NH
Mobile: 09736 68704

Stephanie Dunning,
Stephanie Dunning Interior Design, The Beeches, The Plantation, Middle Winterslow, Salisbury, Wiltshire SP5 1RR
Tel: 01980 863690 Fax: 01980 863680

Kitty Edwards-Jones
Kitty-Lynne Jones Interior Design, 6 Cleveland Court, 88 Cleveland Street, London W1P 5DR Tel: 0207 387 3719

Orianna Fielding Banks,
Pure Living, Ground Floor, 1-3 Leonard Street, London EC2A 4AQ Tel: 0207 250 1116 Fax: 0207 250 0616
e-mail: mail@puredesignuk.com

Ginni Gillam
Mobile: 07714 517249

Zoë Gingell
Think 1 Design, 61 Rivington Street, London EC2A 3QQ
Tel: 0207 613 5510 Mobile: 07713 651895
e-mail thinkrich@easynet.co.uk

Eugenie Van Harinxma
Van Harinxma Design and Antiques, 102 Fulham Road, Chelsea, London SW3 6HS Tel: 0207 584 5209
e-mail: interior-design@vanharinxma.freeserve.co.uk

Suzie Horton
'House', 667 Wilmslow Road, Didsbury, Manchester M20 2FU
Tel: 0161 445 6196 e-mail: suzie@global.co.uk

Genevieve Hurley
Mobile: 07957 271127

Kieran Kelly
369 The Custard Factory, Gibb Street, Digbeth, Birmingham B9 4AA Tel: 0121 604 7777 Fax: 0121 604 8888
Mobile: 0961 993321

Chris Maton
c/o *Better Homes*, Dominican Court, 17 Hatfields, London SE1 8DJ Mobile: 07957 555840

Michael O'Flaherty
Roger Platt & Co, 24 Queen Street, Maidenhead, Berks SL6 1HZ Tel: 01628 773333 Fax: 01628 770 781
e-mail: oflah2370@aol.com

Dave Wellman
c/o *Better Homes*, Dominican Court, 17 Hatfields, London SE1 8DJ email: wellyman@btinternet.com

suppliers

index

index